REVISION

Information Analysis

David Badrick

Published by Certified Accountants Educational Projects Ltd

Credits for the second edition

Subject consultant
Roger Hills

Sections 1, 3, 4 and 8
Based on original drafts by Cathy Lake

Commissioning editor
Jane Elliot

Copy editor
Rick Bouwman

Managing editor
Eileen Cadman

Proofreader
Geoffrey Matthews

Production
Frances Follin, Petra Green

DTP
M Rules

Text Design
Carla Turchini

Cover design
Fielding Rowinski, Phoenix Graphics

Acknowledgements
Past exam questions and articles from the *Students' Newsletter* are reproduced with the kind permission of the Chartered Association of Certified Accountants.

First edition published March 1994
Reprinted 1994
Second edition published January 1995

Certified Accountants Educational Projects Limited
29 Lincoln's Inn Fields
London WC2A 3EE

ISBN 1 85908 039 1

Further information on Certified Accountants Educational Projects Limited products and services may be obtained from Certified Accountants Educational Projects Limited, 29 Lincoln's Inn Fields, London WC2A 3EE.

British Library Cataloguing in Publication data.
A catalogue record for this book is available from the British Library.

Printed in the UK by Page Bros Limited

INAL-RG-95A

CONTENTS

INTRODUCTION

How to use this revision text

The aim of this book is to help you maximise the effect of the work you do in the few vital weeks before the examination. It brings together information about the syllabus and the examination paper, general advice on revision and examination techniques, a bank of examination style questions and two mock examination papers.

This is a revision text, not a course book. It should be used in conjunction with the textbook or workbooks with which you have studied the full content of the syllabus.

There are many ways of using this book. It has been designed to be as versatile as possible. You may choose to go through it from cover to cover, or to select only those elements which are of particular use to you in your revision. This is what the various sections of the book have to offer:

Section 1 Introduction

This is primarily a reference section. It contains the full syllabus, notes on examinable material for the June 1995 diet and a description of the format of the examination paper.

The information contained in this section is correct at 31 December 1994. The Students' Newsletter *will contain any subsequent changes to the exam or the syllabus.*

Section 2 Reference table

This section links the examination style questions in Section 9 with the syllabus. You can use it to plan the order in which to revise syllabus topics, or to select the questions which you will work through. The section also contains a table which you can use to locate coverage of syllabus topics in the textbooks and open learning workbooks published by ACCA.

Section 3 General revision guidance

This section offers suggestions on how you can plan your general revision strategy. You may find it useful to read it before you embark on detailed revision.

Section 4 Examination techniques

Practical advice about the examination is accompanied by some suggestions on how to tackle the kinds of questions you are likely to meet in this paper.

Section 5 Key revision topics

This is the author's checklist of key information. You may use it to provide the structure of your revision plan, or as a quick reminder of the topics you should have covered.

Section 6 Analysis of past papers

The Examiner's comments are given on the June 1994 exam.

Section 7 *Students' Newsletter* articles

This brings together relevant articles which have appeared in the *Students' Newsletter* or elsewhere.

Section 8 Updates

This section includes detailed guidance from the Examiner on the syllabus. It is based on the annual meetings held for teachers at ACCA.

The information contained in this section is correct at 31 December 1994. The Students' Newsletter *will contain any subsequent changes to the exam or the syllabus.*

Section 9 Exam style questions

This selection of questions is designed to give representative coverage of the syllabus. This section is perhaps the most important part of the book and we suggest that you work through as many of the questions as possible.

Section 10 Mock examination 1

We suggest that you work through this paper under exam conditions. You will probably get most out of it if you attempt it at a fairly late stage in your revision.

Section 11 Mock examination 2

Another complete exam to work through under full exam conditions.

Section 12 Answers to exam style questions

These answers are annotated to indicate where marks can be gained or lost. You should not refer to them until you have attempted the questions in Section 9.

Section 13 Answers to mock examination 1

Once again, you should not refer to these answers until you have worked through the questions.

Section 14 Answers to mock examination 2

These answers will enable you to judge how well you fared in the mock examination.

Format of the examination paper

Three hours are allowed for the examination.

	Number of marks
Section A Case study (compulsory)	55
Section B 3 questions (out of 5 of 15 marks each)	45
	100

Section A
The number of questions may vary from year to year, but usually there will be 4 or 5.

1 The syllabus for Paper 5

This Paper introduces the different types of information systems and how they can contribute to the management decision-making process. It includes coverage of the development, introduction and use of computer-based information systems and the advice that might be given regarding the control, privacy and security procedures. Students' appreciation of the role of IT in the organisation will be reinforced in Paper 12, where the strategic implications of IT are examined. Students are assumed to be familiar with the basic components of computer systems - hardware and software - and the ability to relate to business the basic structure of a computer, computer peripherals and communications devices.

1 Systems to handle and process information

a Systems theory, classification of systems and the nature of feedback and control.
The emphasis here will be on the use of these concepts in a business context and in relation to financial information systems
- i) an outline of general systems theory
- ii) definition of a system
- iii) types of system
- iv) basic elements of systems control
- v) positive and negative feedback
- vi) delays in systems.

b The nature of systems needed for transaction processing
- i) data capture
- ii) batch systems
- iii) on line systems
- iv) data storage.

2 Forms of financial and related information systems

This section covers the different types of organisational structures and the different types of information systems.

a Organisational structures.

b Structures of information systems and their appropriateness to different organisational structures
- i) development of different types of system
- ii) independence of data structures from the organisational structure
- iii) formal and informal information systems.

c Types and nature of information systems for operational, tactical and strategic planning and control
- i) management information systems
- ii) internal reporting systems
- iii) decision support systems
- iv) executive information systems
- v) strategic information systems
- vi) expert systems.

3 Systems analysis and design

This section covers the design and use of human computer interfaces and the legal requirements of data protection legislation.

a Basics of human computer interface design
- i) means of interacting with a computer
- ii) prototyping
- iii) implications of poor design
- iv) preferences for type of interface from novice and experienced users
- v) validation and verification of data
- vi) security measures depending on the type of system.

b The requirements of data protection legislation
- i) principles of the Data Protection Act 1984
- ii) privacy of information
- iii) accuracy of information
- iv) accessibility of information
- v) purpose for which the data is to be used
- vi) ability of individuals to correct data held about them
- vii) organisations distributing information should ensure the reliability of the information
- viii) effect of EC legislation.

c Use of feasibility studies
- i) assessment of the feasibility/desirability of potential computer projects from the viewpoints of technical, social, operational and economic feasibility including the use of cost-benefit analysis
- ii) the production of a feasibility report and project plan.

d Requirement analysis
Use of appropriate fact-finding techniques in order to establish client's system requirements in terms of
- processes to be carried out
- outputs to be produced
- functional areas to be covered.

e Determination of systems design criteria
To consider aspects such as
- client requirements
- need for internal controls
- client competence
- cost, budget and timescale constraints
- compatibility.

f Systems analysis and design tools
Identification and application of appropriate systems analysis and design tools and techniques such as
- data analysis
- database management systems
- structured methodology
- prototyping
- CASE tools

to enable production of program specifications, database structures, network specifications, document/screen layouts, dialogue design etc.

4 Systems evaluation

This section provides the criteria for evaluating potential and actual systems against performance criteria.

a Identifying, agreeing and documenting criteria for evaluating potential suitable systems
- i) systems proposals
- ii) software design and documentation tools
- iii) bench marking
- iv) conversion plans.

b Evaluating potential suitable systems and packages against agreed criteria
- i) needs analysis
- ii) systems development life cycle
- iii) upgrade paths for hardware and software
- iv) switching costs and costs of locking into manufacturers.

c Designing and implementing procedures for systems operation and control

- *i) the application of administrative controls to the acquisition, development, use and maintenance of data processing resources*
- *ii) the application of operational controls built into individual computer applications*
- *iii) the issues raised by the concepts of privacy, data protection and computer misuse*
- *iv) the use by internal or external auditors of computer-based audit techniques.*

d Drawing conclusions from the evaluation and proposing an optimal system
- *i) the possiblity of creating an optimum system*
- *ii) judging whether an optimum system has been achieved*
- *iii) costing of different systems options*
- *iv) prioritising needs*
- *v) political considerations*
- *vi) trade-off between strategic needs and impact on IT strategy*
- *vii) cost of information and cost of lack of information.*

e Explaining, negotiating, agreeing and documenting systems modifications.

5 *Implementation of systems*

This section covers the life cycle of a system and the backup systems needed for a system and also considers the role of the system developer in giving and seeking advice.

a Negotiating and agreeing procedures and plans for the implementation, monitoring and maintenance of a new system
- *i) need for project management*
- *ii) the tools of project management*
- *iii) project team concepts*
- *iv) monitoring criteria*
- *v) organisation control*
- *vi) systems changeover.*

b Informing and advising on relevant aspects of the nature/purpose/functions/operation of the system to appropriate personnel
- *i) software upgrades*
- *ii) role of database administrator*
- *iii) system/network manager*
- *iv) external impacts on IT system*
- *v) advise on the appropriateness and completeness of user, administrator, software and hardware documentation.*

c Minimising the possibility of system failures
- *i) backup systems*
- *ii) log file systems.*

d Obtaining and analysing information on the operation of the system
- *i) the need for measures of performance*
- *ii) error detection and correction*
- *iii) meeting new user requirements*
- *iv) flexibility and adaptability*
- *v) integrity*
- *vi) effect of increasing volumes of transactions and users.*

e Systems modifications
- *i) creating criteria for the changing and upgrading of systems*
- *ii) effort expended in relation to the upgrading and improvement of systems*
- *iii) fault rectification*
- *iv) systems records*
- *v) alignment with manufacturers' upgrades*
- *vi) training and retraining*
- *vii) help lines*
- *viii) user groups*
- *ix) advantages and disadvantages of experts/contractors.*

SECTION 2

REFERENCE TABLE

This Section contains a table which shows the links between the syllabus for this Paper and this revision text as well as the relevant chapters from the second edition of the ACCA textbook and the workbooks in the Open Learning programme.

You can use the table to plan the order in which you revise syllabus topics, or to select the questions you will work through.

Syllabus Paper 5	Textbook chapters	Open learning sections	Revision topics	Mock exam 1						Mock exam 2					
				Case	6	7	8	9	10	Case	5	6	7	8	9
1a	1, 4, 5, 7	W1 S1–4	1		■										
b	1, 5, 7	W1 S10–13	2, 5	■	■										■
2a	2, 3, 5, 6	W1 S5	3	■											
b	2, 3, 5, 6	W1 S6–8	3	■				■	■				■		
c	2, 3, 5, 6	W1 S9	2, 4										■		
3a	9	W2 S9–12	11	■						■					
b	14,16	W3 S1–3	17							■					
c	8	W2 S3–4	7			■			■	■					
d	9	W2 S5–6	8								■				
e	9	W2 S7	10												
f	10	W2 S14–19	13	■		■	■								
4a	10, 11	W3 S4	7							■	■				
b	8, 9, 11	W3 S5	6, 9			■					■				
c	13,14,15,18,19	W3 S6, 10–14	12, 17					■		■					■
d	13, 18, 19	W3 S7	7, 10						■	■					
e	11	W4 S12–13	15												■
5a	12	W4 S1–6	6, 14, 16									■			
b	12	W4 S6–7	16	■											
c	15, 16, 17	W4 S8	18					■							
d	16, 17	W4 S10–12	8												
e	11	W4 S13–16	15									■		■	

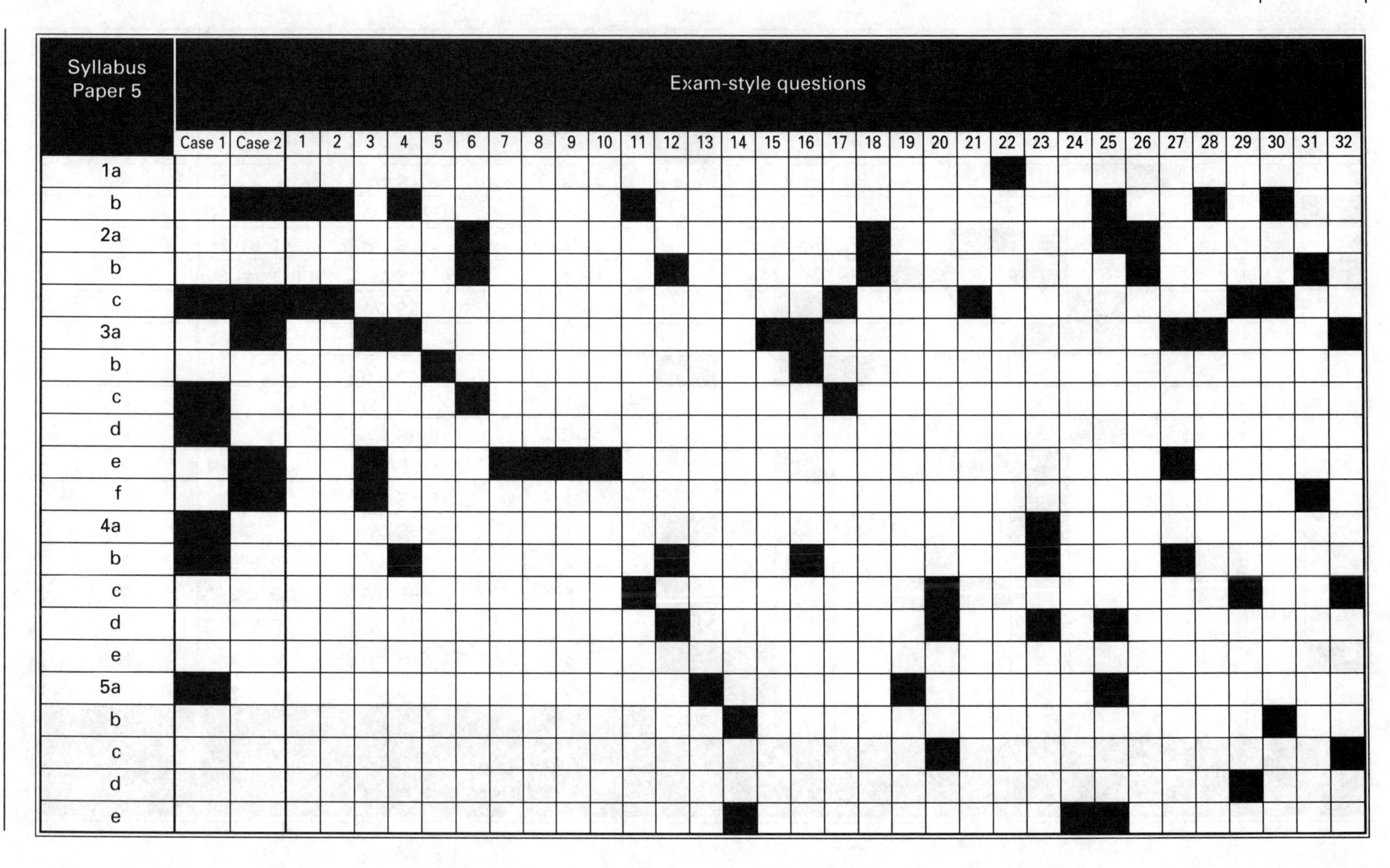

Syllabus Paper 5	Case 1	Case 2	1	2	3	4	5	6	7	8	9	10	11	12	13	14	15	16	17	18	19	20	21	22	23	24	25	26	27	28	29	30	31	32
	Exam-style questions																																	
1a																								■										
b		■	■	■		■							■														■			■		■		
2a								■												■							■	■						
b								■						■						■								■					■	
c	■	■	■	■															■				■								■	■		
3a		■			■	■											■	■											■	■				■
b							■											■																
c	■							■											■															
d	■																																	
e		■			■				■	■	■	■																	■					
f		■			■																												■	
4a	■																								■									
b	■					■								■				■							■				■					
c													■									■									■			■
d														■								■			■		■							
e																																		
5a	■														■						■						■							
b																■																■		
c																						■												■
d																															■			
e																■										■	■							

SECTION

3

GENERAL REVISION GUIDANCE

Planning your revision

What is revision?

Revision is the process by which you remind yourself of the material you have studied during your course, clarify any problem areas and bring your knowledge to a state where you can retrieve it and present it in a way that will satisfy the Examiners.

Revision is not a substitute for hard work earlier in the course. The syllabus for this paper is too large to be hastily 'crammed' a week or so before the examination. You should think of your revision as the final stage in your study of any topic. It can only be effective if you have already completed earlier stages.

Ideally, you should begin your revision shortly after you begin an examination course. At the end of every week and at the end of every month, you should review the topics you have covered. If you constantly consolidate your work and integrate revision into your normal pattern of study, you should find that the final period of revision – and the examination itself – are much less daunting.

If you are reading this revision text while you are still working through your course, we strongly suggest that you begin now to review the earlier work you did for this paper. Remember, the more times you return to a topic, the more confident you will become with it.

The main purpose of this book, however, is to help you to make the best use of the last few weeks before the examination. In this section we offer some suggestions for effective planning of your final revision and discuss some revision techniques which you may find helpful.

Planning your time

Most candidates find themselves in the position where they have less time than they would like to revise, particularly if they are taking several papers at one diet. The majority of people must balance their study with conflicting demands from work, family or other commitments.

It is impossible to give hard and fast rules about the amount of revision you should do. You should aim to start your final revision at least four weeks before your examination. If you finish your course work earlier than this, you would be well advised to take full advantage of the extra time available to you. The number of hours you spend revising each week will depend on many factors, including the number of papers you are sitting. You should probably aim to do a minimum of about six to eight hours a week for each paper.

In order to make best use of the revision time that you have, it is worth spending a little of it at the planning stage. We suggest that you begin by asking yourself two questions:

- ▶ How much time do I have available for revision?
- ▶ What do I need to cover during my revision?

Once you have answered these questions, you should be able to draw up a detailed timetable. We will now consider these questions in more detail.

How much time do I have available for revision?

Many people find it helpful to work out a regular weekly pattern for their revision. We suggest you use the time planning chart provided to do this. Your aim should be to construct a timetable that is sustainable over a period of several weeks.

Time planning chart

	Monday	Tuesday	Wednesday	Thursday	Friday	Saturday	Sunday
00.00							
01.00							
02.00							
03.00							
04.00							
05.00							
06.00							
07.00							
08.00							
09.00							
10.00							
11.00							
12.00							
13.00							
14.00							
15.00							
16.00							
17.00							
18.00							
19.00							
20.00							
21.00							
22.00							
23.00							

1 First, block out all the time that is **definitely unavailable** for revision. This will include the hours when you normally sleep, the time you are at work and any other regular and clear commitments.

2 Think about **other people's claims on your time**. If you have a family, or friends whom you see regularly, you may want to discuss your plans with them. People are likely to be flexible in the demands they make on you in the run-up to your examinations, especially if they are aware that you have considered their needs as well as your own. If you consult the individuals who are affected by your plans, you may find that they are surprisingly supportive, instead of being resentful of the extra time you are spending studying.

3 Next, give some thought to the times of day when you **work most effectively**. This differs very much from individual to individual. Some people can concentrate first thing in the morning. Others work best in the early evening, or last thing at night. Some people find their day-to-day work so demanding that they are unable to do anything extra during the week, but must concentrate their study time at weekends. Mark the times when you feel you could do your best work on the timetable. It is extremely important to acknowledge your personal preferences here. If you ignore them, you may devise a timetable that is completely unrealistic and which you will not be able to adhere to.

4 Consider your **other commitments**. Everybody has certain tasks, from doing the washing to walking the dog, that must be performed on a regular basis. These tasks may not have to done at a particular time, but you should take them into consideration when planning your schedule. You may be able to find more convenient times to get these jobs done, or be able to persuade other people to help you with them.

5 Now mark some time for **relaxation**. If your timetable is to be sustainable, it must include some time for you to build up your reserves. If your normal week does not include any regular physical activity, make sure that you include some in your revision timetable. A couple of hours spent in a sports centre or swimming pool each week will probably enhance your ability to concentrate.

6 Your timetable should now be taking shape. You can probably see obvious study sessions emerging. It is not advisable to work for too long at any one session. Most people find that they can only really concentrate for one or two hours at a time. If your study sessions are longer than this, you should split them up.

What do I need to cover during my revision?

Most candidates are more confident about some parts of the syllabus than others. Before you begin your revision, it is important to have an overview of where your strengths and weaknesses lie.

One way to do this is to take a sheet of paper and divide it into three columns. Mark the columns:

OK	**Marginal**	**Not OK**

or use similar headings to indicate how confident you are with a topic. Then go through the syllabus (reprinted in Section 1) and list the topics under the appropriate headings. Alternatively, you could use the list of key topics in Section 5 of this book to compile your overview. You might also find it useful to skim through the introductions or summaries to the textbook or workbooks you have used in your course. These should remind you of parts of the course that you found particularly easy or difficult at the time. You could also use some of the exercises and questions in the workbooks or textbooks, or some of the questions in this book, as a diagnostic aid to discover the areas where you need to work hardest.

It is also important to be aware which areas of the syllabus are so central to the subject that they are likely to be examined in every diet, and which are more obscure and not likely to come up so frequently. Your textbooks, workbooks and lecture notes will help you here. (You may also find it useful to read the guidance notes on the syllabus provided in Section 8.) Remember, the Examiner will be looking for broad coverage of the syllabus. There is no point in knowing one or two topics in exhaustive detail if you do so at the expense of the rest of the course.

3

Writing your revision timetable

You now have the information you need to write your timetable. You know how many weeks you have available, and the approximate amount of time that is available in each week.

You should stop all serious revision 48 hours before your examination. After this point, you may want to look back at your notes to refresh your memory, but you should not attempt to revise any new topics. A clear and rested brain is worth more than any extra facts you could memorise in this period.

Make one copy of this chart for each week you have available for revision.

Using your time planning chart, write in the times of your various study sessions during the week.

In the lower part of the chart, write in the topics that you will cover in each of these sessions.

Example of a revision timetable

Revision timetable Week beginning:							
	Monday	Tuesday	Wednesday	Thursday	Friday	Saturday	Sunday
Study sessions							
Topics							

Some revision techniques

There should be two elements in your revision. You must **look back** to the work you have covered in the course and **look forward** to the examination. The techniques you use should reflect these two aspects of revision.

Revision should not be boring. It is useful to try a variety of techniques. You probably already have some revision techniques of your own and you may also like to try some of the techniques suggested here, if they are new to you. However, don't waste time with methods of revision which are not effective for you.

- Go through your lecture notes, textbook or workbooks and use a highlighter pen to mark important points.
- Produce a new set of summarised notes. This can be a useful way of re-absorbing information, but you must be careful to keep your notes concise, or you may find that you are simply reproducing work you have done before. It is helpful to use a different format for your notes.
- Make a collection of key words which remind you of the essential concepts of a topic.
- Reduce your notes to a set of key facts and definitions which you must memorise. Write them on cards which you can keep with you all the time.
- When you come across areas which you were unsure about first time around, rework relevant questions in your course materials, then study the answers in great detail.
- If there are isolated topics which you feel are completely beyond you, identify exactly what it is that you cannot understand and find someone (such as a lecturer or recent graduate) who can explain these points to you.
- Practise as many exam standard questions as you can. The best way to do this is to work to time, under exam conditions. You should always resist looking at the answer until you have finished.
- If you have come to rely on a word processor in your day-to-day work, you may have got out of the habit of writing at speed. It is well worth reviving this skill before you sit down in the examination hall. It is something you will need.
- If you have a plentiful supply of relevant questions, you could use them to practise planning answers, and then compare your notes with the answers provided. This is not a substitute for writing full answers, but can be helpful additional practice.
- Go back to questions you have already worked on during the course. This time, complete them under exam conditions, paying special attention to the layout and organisation of your answers. Then compare them in detail with the suggested answers and think about the ways in which your answer differs. This is a useful way of 'fine tuning' your technique.
- During your revision period, do make a conscious effort to identify situations which illustrate concepts and ideas that may arise in the examination. These situations could come from your own work, or from reading the business pages of the quality press. This technique will give you a new perspective on your studies and could also provide material which you can use in the examination.

SECTION

4

EXAMINATION TECHNIQUES

The examination

This section is divided into two parts. The first part considers the practicalities of sitting the examination. If you have taken other ACCA examinations recently, you may find that everything here is familiar to you. The second part discusses some examination techniques which you may find useful.

The practicalities

What to take with you

You should make sure that you have:

- your ACCA registration card
- your ACCA registration docket.

You may also take to your desk:

- pens and pencils
- a ruler and slide rule
- a calculator
- charting template and geometrical instruments
- eraser and correction fluid.

You are not allowed to take rough paper into the examination.

If you take any last-minute notes with you to the examination hall, make sure these are not on your person. You should keep notes or books in your bag or briefcase, which you will be asked to leave at the side of the examination hall.

Although most examination halls will have have a clock, it is advisable to wear a watch, just in case your view is obscured.

If your calculator is solar-powered, make sure it works in artificial light. Some examination halls are not particularly well-lit. If you use a battery-powered calculator, take some spare batteries with you. For obvious reasons, you may not use a calculator which has a graphic/word display memory. Calculators with printout facilities are not allowed because they could disturb other candidates.

Getting there

You should arrange to arrive at the examination hall at least half an hour before the examination is due to start. If the hall is a large one, the invigilator will start filling the hall half an hour before the starting time.

Make absolutely sure that you know how to get to the examination hall and how long it will take you. Check on parking or public transport. Leave yourself enough time so that you will not be anxious if the journey takes a little longer than you anticipated. Many people like to make a practice trip the day before their first examination.

At the examination hall

Examination halls differ greatly in size. Some only hold about ten candidates. Others can sit many hundreds of people. You may find that more than one examination is being taken at the hall at the same time, so don't panic if you hear people discussing a completely different subject from the one you have revised.

While you are waiting to go in, don't be put off by other people talking about how well, or badly, they have prepared for the examination.

You will be told when to come in to the examination hall. The desks are numbered. (Your number will be on your examination docket.) You will be asked to leave any bags at the side of the hall.

Inside the hall, the atmosphere will be extremely formal. The invigilator has certain things which he or she must tell candidates, often using a particular form of words. Listen carefully, in case there are any unexpected changes to the arrangements.

On your desk you will see a question paper and an answer booklet in which to write your answers. You will be told when to turn over the paper.

During the examination

You will have to leave your examination paper and answer booklet in the hall at the end of the examination. It is quite acceptable to write on your examination paper if it helps you to think about the questions. However, all workings should be in your answers. You may write any plans and notes in your answer booklet, as long as you cross them out afterwards.

If your paper contains multiple choice questions, these will be on a separate paper which will be collected before the end of the examination.

If you require a new answer booklet, put your hand up and a supervisor will come and bring you one.

At various times during the examination, you will be told how much time you have left.

You should not need to leave the examination hall until the examination is finished. Put up your hand if you need to go to the toilet, and a supervisor will accompany you. If you feel unwell, put up your hand, and someone will come to your assistance. If you simply get up and walk out of the hall, you will not be allowed to re-enter.

Before you finish, you must fill in the required information on the front of your anwer booklet.

Examination techniques

Tackling Paper 5

The paper consists of two sections. Section A contains a case study, followed by questions referring to it. All questions in Section A *must* be answered. The number of questions may vary from year to year but you can expect about four or five. The number of marks obtainable will also vary from question to question, but the total number of marks obtainable from Section A will always be 55. Study the case study carefully before attempting the questions. You will be expected to demonstrate that you can apply your knowledge to the situation portrayed in the case study, not simply to repeat everything you know about a particular topic.

Section B consists of five questions. Each is worth 15 marks. You are required to answer any *three* questions from this section. Again, where appropriate, you should apply your knowledge to a given situation.

4

In both sections, questions may take the form of essays or problems, and many will contain more than one part.

Your general strategy

You should spend the first ten minutes of the examination reading the paper. If you have a choice of question, decide which questions you will do. You must divide the time you spend on questions in proportion to the marks on offer. Don't be tempted to spend more time on a question you know a lot about, or one which you find particularly difficult. If a question has more than one part, you must complete each part.

On every question, the first marks are the easiest to gain. Even if things go wrong with your timing and you don't have time to complete a question properly, you will probably gain some marks by making a start.

Spend the last five minutes reading through your answers and making any additions or corrections.

You may answer written questions in any order you like. Some people start with their best question, to help them relax. Another strategy is to begin with your second best question, so that you are working even more effectively when you reach the question you are most confident about.

Once you have embarked on a question, you should try to stay with it, and not let your mind stray to other questions on the paper. You can only concentrate on one thing at once. However, if you get completely stuck with a question, leave space in your answer book and return to it later.

Answering the question

All Examiners say that the most frequent reason for failure in examinations, apart from basic lack of knowledge, is candidates' unwillingness to answer the question that the Examiner has asked. A great many people include every scrap of knowledge they have on a topic, just in case it is relevant. Stick to the question and tailor your answer to what you are asked. Pay particular attention to the verbs in the question.

You should be particularly wary if you come across a question which appears to be almost identical to one which you have practised during your revision. It probably isn't! Wishful thinking makes many people see the question they would like to see on the paper, not the one that is actually there.

Read a question at least twice before you begin your answer. Underline key words on the question paper, if it helps focus your mind on what is required.

If you don't understand what a question is asking, state your assumptions. Even if you do not answer in precisely the way the Examiner hoped, you may be given some credit, if your assumptions are reasonable.

Presentation

You should do everything you can to make things easy for the marker. Although you will not be marked on your handwriting, the marker will find it easier to identify the points you have made if your answers are legible. The same applies to spelling and grammar. Use blue or black ink. The marker will be using red or green.

Use the margin to clearly identify which question, or part of a question you are answering.

Start each answer on a new page. The order in which you answer the questions does not matter, but if a question has several parts, these parts should appear in the correct order in your answer book.

If there is the slightest doubt when an answer continues on another page, indicate to the marker that he or she must turn over. It is irritating for a marker to think he or she has reached the end of an answer, only to turn the page and find that the answer continues.

Use columnar layouts for computations. This will help you to avoid mistakes, and is easier to follow.

Use headings and numbered sentences if they help to show the structure of your answer. However, don't write your answers in one-word note form.

If your answers include diagrams, don't waste time making them great works of art. Keep them clear, neat and simple. Use your rule and any templates or geometric instruments you have with you. Remember to label the axes of graphs properly. Make reference to any diagrams in the body of your text so that they form an integral part of your answer.

It is a good idea to make a rough plan of an answer before you begin to write. Do this in your answer booklet, but make sure you cross it out neatly afterwards. The marker needs to be clear whether he or she is looking at your rough notes, or the answer itself.

Computations

Before you begin a computation, you may find it helpful to jot down the stages you will go through. Cross out these notes afterwards.

It is essential to include all your workings and to indicate where they fit in to your answer. It is important that the marker can see where you got the figures in your answer from. Even if you make mistakes in your computations, you will be given credit for using a principle correctly, if it is clear from your workings and the structure of your answer.

If you spot an arithmetical error which has implications for figures later in your answer, it may not be worth spending a lot of time reworking your computation.

If you are asked to comment or make recommendations on a computation, you must do so. There are important marks to be gained here. Even if your computation contains mistakes, you may still gain marks if your reasoning is correct.

Use the layouts which you see in the answers given in this booklet and in model answers. A clear layout will help you avoid errors and will impress the marker.

Essay questions

You must plan an essay before you start writing. One technique is to quickly jot down any ideas which you think are relevant. Re-read the question and cross out any points in your notes which are not relevant. Then number your points. Remember to cross out your plan afterwards.

Your essay should have a clear structure. It should contain a brief introduction, a main section and a conclusion. Don't waste time by restating the question at the start of your essay.

Break your essay up into paragraphs. Use sub-headings and numbered sentences if they help show the structure of your answer.

Be concise. It is better to write a little about a lot of different points than a great deal about one or two points.

The Examiner will be looking for evidence that you have understood the syllabus and can apply your knowledge in new situations. You will also be expected to give opinions and make judgements. These should be based on reasoned and logical arguments.

Case studies

A case study asks you to apply your knowledge in a particular situation. It is useful to spend up to a third of the time available for the question in planning your answer.

Start by reading the questions based on the case study. Then read the case study, trying to grasp the main points. Read the case study through again and make notes of the key points. Then analyse the case and identify the relevant issues and concepts. Before you start your answer, read the questions again and relevant parts of the case study.

If alternative answers present themselves, mention them. You may sometimes find it helpful to consider short and long term recommendations separately.

There is an article '*Tackling Case Sudies*' in Section 7 of this book.

Reports, memos and other documents

Some questions ask you to present your answer in the form of a report or a memo or other document. It is important that you use the correct format – there are easy marks to be gained here. Adopt the format used in sample questions, or use the format you are familiar with in your day-to-day work, as long as it contains all the essential elements.

You should also consider the audience for any document you are writing. How much do they know about the subject? What kind of information and recommendations are required? The Examiner will be looking for evidence that you can present your ideas in an appropriate form.

SECTION

5

KEY REVISION TOPICS

The aim of this section is to provide you with a checklist of key information relating to this Paper. You should use it as a reminder of topics to be revised rather than as a summary of all you need to know. Aim to revise as many topics as possible because many of the questions in the exam draw on material from more than one section of the syllabus. You will get more out of this section if you read through Section 3, *General Revision Guidance* first.

1 General systems theory and its applications to organisations

The main elements of any system are: inputs, processes, outputs, and the environment surrounding the system's boundary. A system that is isolated and has no interaction with its environment is called **closed** and one that has varied and unpredictable interactions is called **open**.

A system will usually have some objectives and control mechanisms to help it achieve those objectives. An important feature of control mechanisms is feedback – information gathered from the system's outputs and environment which is used to compare the system's performance with its objectives so that control action can be taken if necessary. Closed loop control systems use only feedback from the system, whereas feedback in an open loop control system can come from both the system and its environment.

Two particularly useful categories of system are: **deterministic**, where the systems behaviour or reaction to a given input is predictable and predetermined, and **stochastic** (or **probabilistic**), where the outputs are not predetermined but depend on probabilities.

Many systems, such as organisations, are complex and composed of sub-systems. These sub-systems will have their own objectives, which should be co-ordinated and aimed at the system's overall objectives but which, if not carefully managed, may lead to conflicts between sub-systems and result in sub-optimal performance.

2 Data and information, properties of information

Data is the raw material which can be processed and put into context. It is turned into information that is more meaningful. Information is a vital resource for an organisation and it can be categorised, according to its use and purpose, into levels within the organisation.

At the highest level (strategic), organisations need information in order to make important decisions about their long-term overall strategies and objectives. In the middle term, middle-management (tactical) decisions must be made as to how best to manage resources and run the organisation in order to achieve the overall objectives. At the lowest level (operational), an organisation's routine transactions provide the basic data which is input to the organisation's operational level processes and used to make short-term decisions. At the operational level, transaction processing requires systems for data capture, batch and/or demand and online processing, storage and output.

The level at which information is used within an organisation will determine what qualities it should have. Typical qualities which should be considered are clarity, completeness and degree of detail. There are costs associated with gathering and using information and these should be weighed against the information's value. Both the value and cost of information can be difficult to determine.

3 Activities and organisational structures

The activities within an organisation can be viewed as either primary activities, if they contribute directly to the organisation's main outputs, or support activities, which do not contribute directly to the main outputs but which facilitate and assist the primary activities. Since an information system provides a support service for all activities within the organisation, it is important that the system and its data structures are not constrained by any one particular structure or narrow purpose.

Organisations can be structured in different ways. Two commonly used structures are:

- a functional structure, where the organisation's activities and personnel are grouped according to the main function they provide, such as manufacturing or finance, usually with a hierarchy of sub-functions within main functional areas
- a matrix structure, where personnel are grouped according to their function but also into teams to provide a particular product or service.

In order to maximise the benefits of information, organisations should establish an overall information strategy with high-level staff, such as an information director, responsible for implementing it. This is often managed by setting up a steering committee responsible for advising the high-level management, setting up feasibility studies, recommending projects and then monitoring their progress.

A modern trend is to move away from specialised information systems departments towards end-user computing. This means that users take more responsibility for purchasing and operating computer equipment and for specifying and designing applications often using 4GLs (fourth generation languages). The triggers for this trend include the availability of powerful, low cost, office-based computers which are easy to use and the development of LAN (Local Area Network) technology.

To counter the risks of uninformed and uncontrolled development and use of information technology, organisations have introduced information centres staffed by skilled information systems staff. They liaise with and advise users, creating an element of consistency and exercising a central control over their systems.

4 Types of information systems

Information systems can be categorised according to the level and purpose of the information they provide. Categories include:

- EIS (executive information systems): high-level decision making and presentation of information.
- DSS (decision support systems): to provide information in a flexible way to aid decision makers.

- ▶ Expert systems: to provide a database of information about a specific area and make decisions related to that area.
- ▶ MIS (management information systems): to provide management information about the organisation's operational performance in a routine and easily understood format.
- ▶ TP or DP (transaction or data processing systems) which routinely capture, process, store and output the low-level, transaction data.

5 Hardware and software

You are very unlikely to be asked an examination question specifically about information technology – that is, the hardware and software used in information systems. However, you may need to consider and refer to particular aspects of hardware and software that have an impact on the way information systems perform and can be used.

Information technology can be considered according to the stage of data processing that it is used for:

- ▶ data capture and input equipment, such as terminals, visual display units (VDUs), electronic point of sale systems (EPOS), document scanners
- ▶ processing equipment such as the central processing unit (CPU)
- ▶ storage equipment like magnetic disks and tape, optical disks
- ▶ output equipment like printers and plotters
- ▶ communications equipment such as modems.

In addition, recent technological developments affect the way systems are used. These include things like:

- ▶ miniaturisation of powerful systems
- ▶ artificial intelligence and natural language interfaces
- ▶ EDI (electronic data interchange)
- ▶ ISDN (integrated systems digital networks)
- ▶ local area and wide area networks (LANs and WANs).

6 Systems development lifecycle and methodologies

Projects to develop information systems are difficult to manage because of their complexity and the uncertainty involved in estimating and monitoring them. The difficulty is usually compounded because users may not fully understand how best to use or develop a system and employ specialist developers who may not appreciate the users' needs or sphere of operation. This often leads to systems which are over-budget, overdue and unable to satisfy the users' requirements.

The systems development lifecycle (SDLC) provides a useful model upon which to base the study of the activities involved in systems development. The SDLC presents the development as a series of distinct phases:

5

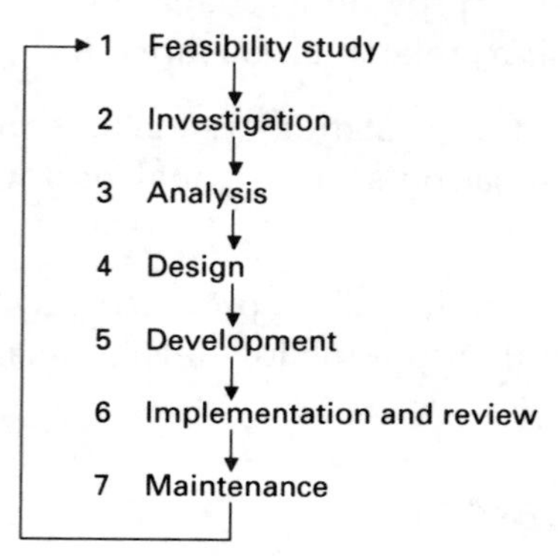

Figure 5.1 The traditional model of the systems development lifecycle

Different methodologies emphasise different aspects of development. Three methodologies or approaches are:

- process-driven – often called structured systems analysis and design methodologies – which emphasise the functions or activities which the system must carry out.
- data driven, which concentrate on analysing the data and its uses and then providing a flexible system which can be easily modified for different purposes
- user-driven, which highlight the key role that user involvement must play in developing a system that suits their needs and different viewpoints in complex situations.

7 Feasibility studies

The purpose of a feasibility study is to gather information about the users' requirements and to establish and/or assess proposals for systems options. This information should be presented in a report to help decision makers. The activities and techniques used during the study are likely to be similar to those used during detailed systems investigation and analysis.

The main areas that should be covered in a feasibility study report are, for each proposed system:

- technical feasibility: matching things like response times, the numbers of users supported, storage capacity, etc., with the user's requirements
- operational, social and organisational feasibility: looking at things like departmental structures and responsibilities, staffing issues, the organisation's image and so on
- economic feasibility: analysing and estimating costs and benefits which may be direct or indirect, tangible or intangible.

Accountants play a major part in preparing the report as the cost and benefits have to be quantified and compiled into a cost-benefit analysis using techniques such as:

- volume/cost/profit analysis
- breakeven point and payback period
- discounted cashflow (DCF), net present value (NPV) and internal rate of return (IRR).

8 Systems investigation and analysis

The main methods of gathering information about users' requirements are:

- analysing and collecting documents
- interviews
- surveys and questionnaires
- observations.

The areas which should be analysed include:

- current methods and working practices
- alternative methods of achieving the required results
- constraints and restrictions on the current system and any that may affect proposed systems
- numbers of users, required volumes of transactions, response times, and so on
- likely expansion and changes to requirements
- access and security requirements
- backup procedures and requirements.

The users' needs should be compiled into a detailed specification of requirements.

9 Systems developers and suppliers

Information systems development often requires specialised techniques and equipment. If an organisation does not have the required expertise or does not feel there will be a long-term need for it, then external specialists can be used. These may be systems consultants, analysts, designers, programmers, technical authors and systems installers.

Systems development can be difficult to plan and manage and systems require maintenance to ensure they continue to satisfy users' requirements. Organisations may try to reduce some of the costs and uncertainties of developing and maintaining a tailor-made system by purchasing some or all of their system off-the-shelf (providing they are satisfied that the off-the-shelf system will meet their requirements satisfactorily).

There has been a move towards 'open systems' to avoid users becoming locked into a particular supplier because of incompatibilities between competing suppliers. The use of industry standards for hardware, software and communications has been encouraged by the International Standards Organisation (ISO), who produced a model of how systems should be produced according to publicly available protocols. The model is known as OSI (open systems interconnection).

10 Design aspects

The aims of systems design should be to:

- produce a logical design of the system showing its data structure and what it should do
- produce a physical design of how to make the system operational – a detailed specification of hardware and software.

Some of the common major design issues are:

- Which processing options are required? For example:
  - batch processing
  - online demand processing
  - real-time processing
  - a combination of the above.
- Should processing be centralised, with a multi-user operating system (which will allow system managers to control access and use of data and resources), or distributed (which provides flexibility and reduces reliance on central hardware)?
- Should data be stored in a shared central database used by all applications, or should there be an integrated system allowing automatic communication of data between applications, or should data be stored and accessed separately by each application?

11 The human computer interface

The human computer interface (HCI), or user interface, is the means by which the users interact with the system. Its design is critical to the efficiency and effectiveness of a system since a poor design leads to increased error rates, low productivity and user disenchantment with the system.

The main factors involved in the HCI are the equipment used – such as keyboard, VDU, mouse, bar code readers and keypads – and the style of interaction. The HCI should be designed to be appropriate to the purpose of the system, its physical location, and its users' levels of expertise (which may be anything from novice user through to experienced user and expert). Typical styles of HCI include:

- easy-to-use menus
- command languages, such as query languages
- input/output screens often designed in a format similar to paper documents
- natural language interfaces using modern speech and text recognition techniques
- graphical user interfaces (GUI) of which the WIMP style is commonly used (they require, however, equipment that has relatively powerful processing capabilities).

12 Controls and audit

Some of the major methods used to control systems and maximise data and systems integrity are:

- access controls such as

- physical security on computer terminals and equipment
- log-in procedures and user authorisation incorporating passwords
- several levels of access permissions on files and applications

▶ data controls such as:

- verification to check the accuracy of input data
- validation to check the reasonableness, completeness and consistency of data
- file identification checks on transaction and master files
- checks on the results of processing operations
- encryption of data using DES or other encoding/decoding systems

▶ personnel controls like:

- job sensitivity analysis and screening of job applicants
- appropriate training
- division of responsibility and well-defined staff roles

▶ logs to record and monitor systems access and usage

▶ computer-based audit techniques such as:

- internal audit trails built into applications
- external audit trails linking computer processes with appropriate paper documents
- CAAT (computer-assisted audit techniques).

Risk analysis can be used to identify the potential dangers of fraud.

13 Systems analysis and design tools

There are a variety of specialised tools and techniques used by analysts and designers. Some of them are used in several methodologies and others are specific to one particular methodology. For any particular technique there may be different conventions for the symbols used, but within a project one convention should be used consistently.

The tools can be categorised according to whether they are primarily concerned with a system's data or its processes. You should be able to explain the use and construction of tools such as:

▶ Analysis of processes

- data flow diagrams (DFD) which can be constructed as a levelled set by decomposing processes to show progressively more detail
- entity life histories (ELH) to show the processes that act upon an entity.

▶ Analysis of data

- data dictionaries
- entity relationship diagrams to show the relationships which may be: one-to-one (1:1), many-to-one (M:1), one-to-many (1:M), many-to-many (M:M).

▶ Design of processes:

- structured English, using the English language in a narrow, formalised manner approaching the way it is used in traditional programming languages
- decision trees to graphically emphasise the logic of a process
- decision tables to show what actions should be taken in a given set of conditions.

▶ Design of data structures:

- the three main logical database models: **hierarchical**, which is an intuitive but inflexible model; **network**, which provides flexibility but can become unwieldy; **relational**, using the technique of normalisation to remove data redundancy and improve flexibility and data independence
- database management systems (DBMS) can be used to design a database structure and provide for facilities operational use, such as sorting and searching.

Most methodologies emphasise the need for a structured, modular approach to software design. This is where a program is split into progressively smaller modules, which makes software easier to code, test and maintain.

Use of these tools and techniques can be computerised using CASE (computer-aided software engineering) tools. Like other applications software, an integrated set of tools can increase its users' productivity and improve the presentation, completeness and consistency of their work.

Prototyping can be used to produce a working version of some or all of a system to allow users to comment on its features and contribute to its refinement. However, indiscriminate or mismanaged use of prototypes can lead to wasted resources and inefficient systems.

14 Implementation and changeover

Installing and testing a system should be carried out in a controlled manner to ensure a smooth changeover. Changeover methods include:

▶ Direct changeover, where there is no overlap period between the use of the old and new systems. This can be a risky but, if all goes well, a relatively cheap method.

▶ Parallel running, where both old and new systems are run together allowing a period for testing and familiarisation. This is safer but more expensive than direct changeover and may not be practicable.

A compromise between the risk of direct changeover and the cost of parallel running can be achieved by some form of partial changeover, based on changing over one function or part of the system at a time or gradually increasing the number of transactions processed by the new system.

File conversion from the old to the new system can often be phased by dealing with fixed/static data first and then converting the variable/volatile data quickly to ensure it is up to date.

15 Maintenance

Maintenance involves servicing or modifying a system to ensure it continues to satisfy users' requirements. Maintenance activity can be classified according to the reason, or trigger, for it:

- preventive: regular, routine servicing to keep equipment in good working order
- corrective: to cure problems such as design faults or software 'bugs'
- perfective: to take advantage of new equipment or techniques
- adaptive: to keep it in line with things like changing organisational procedures or external legislation.

Maintenance activities should be carefully controlled and documented; piecemeal changes can have unexpected side-effects and lead to an inefficient system that is progressively more difficult to maintain.

16 Project management

Systems development projects require careful planning and constant monitoring. The staff involved in a project are usually broken down into teams whose size and composition should be appropriate to the nature of work involved. Techniques used in project management are:

- Network charts and critical path analysis (CPA), where a project is broken down into its smaller component activities and tasks. The relationships between tasks can be shown graphically and the durations and resources associated with the tasks can be estimated and analysed.
- Gantt charts, where tasks and their progress are represented to scale graphically.
- Resource allocation charts, which allow the resources required for tasks to be shown graphically and help to identify where shortages of resources occur.
- Structured walkthroughs, where staff meet to analyse and discuss designs.

Training activities which are appropriate to the users' requirements should be incorporated into the schedule.

The documentation associated with the development, use and operation of a system can be classified according to its intended audience:

- user documents providing end-users with information
- systems documents which form part of the systems design and provide technical details which should be referred to and kept up to date during systems maintenance.

17 Legislation

Many countries have introduced data protection legislation to safeguard the rights of individuals and ease the administration of cross-border information transfers. Typical of this sort of legislation is the UK Data Protection Act 1984, which requires data users to register the automatic processing of information referring to living individuals. It sets out data protection principles and gives individuals rights of access to personal data.

Unauthorised access and modification of data is covered in the UK Computer Misuse Act 1990. It is aimed at tightening the law on computer fraud and criminalising activities such as 'hacking' and infecting a system with a computer virus.

Use of computer software usually requires that a licence is purchased restricting its use. Copyright laws apply to computer software and the UK has tried to deal with it by introducing the Copyright (Computer Programs) Regulations 1992.

18 Backup systems

Many organisations are partially or totally dependent on their information systems and it is vital to their survival that they employ appropriate security, backup and recovery systems. Backup copies of software should be taken at frequent and regular intervals and stored safely, preferably off-site. Backup systems provide necessary but expensive insurance against the threats of systems failure caused by events like equipment failure, floods, fire, sabotage and terrorism.

A centralised information system is vulnerable to failure of its central computer equipment and backup can be provided by a duplicate (or standby) system. The standby may be established by the organisation or facilities may be provided by an external supplier. Where appropriate, a backup system may be maintained in a state of constant readiness (a 'hot standby').

Distributed systems offer a greater degree of flexibility and are less dependent on a central component. If one part of the system fails, such as a file-server, it may be possible to provide the missing facilities and functions in another part of the system.

SECTION 6

ANALYSIS OF PAST PAPERS

The June 1994 examination was the first based on the new ACCA syllabus. Certain topics are similar to those in the old syllabus, however, and an analysis of past papers is always helpful in providing an idea of the type of question asked. You should be careful not to 'question spot', though, i.e. guess which topics will be included in the examination. Only a thorough understanding of all topics in the syllabus will ensure your success.

When you are looking through previous (old syllabus) exam papers it would be particularly beneficial to examine any practical or problem-solving and scenario questions rather than just discussion questions.

The following, reprinted from the *Students' Newsletter*, summarises the Examiner's comments on the June 1994 examination, question by question.

ANALYSIS OF THE JUNE 1994 EXAM PAPER

Summary of Examiner's comments, June 1994 Examinations
Certificate Stage

It is intended that questions in this Paper will become increasingly practical in nature. In this first examination session under the new syllabus, some steps have been taken in this direction. The results indicate that descriptive questions have been satisfactorily answered by all candidates. However, it has been noticed that some candidates have experienced problems with the practical questions. These candidates are reminded that as practical questions are becoming increasingly significant in future diets, they should work on this important area.

Question 1 was a relatively straightforward scenario-type question which required candidates to demonstrate knowledge of the following: in part (a), the systems development lifecycle; in part (b), the project control tools such as CASE, PERT, Gantt Charts, spreadsheets; and in part (c), why user participation is important and how tools/techniques such as 4GLs and prototyping might be made use of.

Part (a) was generally well answered. In part (b) very few candidates read the question carefully enough to realise that a discussion of project control tools was required, not how the use of computers might benefit the entire organisation. In part (c) the 'why' was often adequately answered, but not the 'how'!

Question 2 required candidates: in part (a), to explain the relationships of the various types of information systems to both levels of management and types of decision; and in part (b), to relate each system type to sales and marketing, and to finance.

The majority of candidates attempted this question and the standard of their answers for what is essentially a descriptive question was very high; in many cases the marks gained here compensated for the lower scores on the more practical questions.

6

Question 3 required candidates to identify and explain ten system characteristics against which managers can evaluate the success of the information system.

This question was neither popular nor well answered. Many of those who attempted it restricted their response to a discussion of the qualities of good information (as opposed to an information system), which is only one aspect of the topic. A good answer should additionally have covered areas such as cost, efficiency, effectiveness, reliability, acceptability, compatibility, etc. However, there were many answers of ten lines, each containing a few words, which were not an adequate response.

Question 4: part (a) required candidates to apply their knowledge of a common computer application (order processing), and an equally common systems development tool (dataflow diagrams) to a simple situation. Part (b) required candidates to refer to process specification tools; decision tables, decision trees and structured English.

This was the least popular question on the Paper, and was generally poorly answered. In part (a), most candidates had knowledge of either order processing or how to produce a dataflow diagram, but not both. Similarly, many could not apply their knowledge. In part (b), the well prepared candidates produced good answers. It was very apparent that some candidates only attempted the question because they could cope well with part (b).

Question 5: part (a) required candidates to discuss the need for and the nature of various types of maintenance. Part (b) required candidates to explain both the documentation and the nature of that documentation.

This produced a mediocre performance. In part (a) candidates failed to gain marks due to not discussing all aspects of maintenance such as hardware, software, adaptive, corrective and perfective. Instead, candidates concentrated on hardware. There were many good answers to part (a) (ii), which asked for an analysis of why this particular system might require excessive maintenance; relevant points included insufficient user contact, inadequate testing, hardware problems, systems management, user training and change in environment. In part (b) many candidates explained either the need for documentation or the nature of that documentation, but not both. Some answers restricted their responses to a (relevant) discussion of audit trail requirements, but failed to cover also the systems documentation aspects.

Question 6: part (a)(i) asked how the project might be assessed, and looked for a discussion, in the scenario context, of the operational, technical and economic aspects. In part (a)(ii), candidates were required to outline the contents of a feasiblility study report. Part (b) required the application to the specific scenario of techniques such as interviewing, questionnaires, observation and document perusal.

In part (a) many answers covered one or two of the three required aspects (operational, technical and economic); fewer covered all three. In part (a) (ii) many good marks were gained, but a surprising number of candidates simply repeated the material already written down in answer to part (a)(i). Part (b) was generally well answered.

Question 7 required candidates to analyse assertions of interest to both company management and the computer community, such as production of information for management, computers and unemployment, and privacy.

6

Candidates who answered this popular discursive question generally gained up to half marks. However, it was disappointing to note the very low number of answers which achieved marks in excess of 60%. Few candidates were able to analyse each statement from more than one angle, and although it was not expected that they could cover all aspects, this obviously restricted the marks that could be awarded.

SECTION 7

STUDENTS' NEWSLETTER ARTICLES

The *Students' Newsletter* regularly carries articles on accountancy, law and taxation and it is in your own interests to read these thoroughly as the contents may be relevant to a question in the examination. Also the *Certified Accountant, The Journal of the Chartered Association of Certified Accountants* has regular articles which may be of interest to you (published for the Chartered Association of Certified Accountants, Cork Publishing Ltd, Granary House, 19 Rutland Street, Cork, Ireland). Besides this there are several computer magazines, such as *Computer Weekly*, which contain useful information.

AN INTRODUCTION TO SYSTEMS THEORY

A SYSTEMATIC APPROACH TO INFORMATION ANALYSIS [PART 1]

By Adrian Bolton

The object of this paper is to investigate the subject matter of part 1(a) – (Systems to handle and process information) – of the new syllabus of Module C – Paper 5, Information Analysis, which is designed 'to ensure students' appreciation of information systems to meet the goals and needs of business and understand ing of procedures for the development, introduction and use of computer-based systems.'

Even before computers found their way into virtually every limited company, auditors were obliged to understand the concept of a system. Today, computer-based auditing techniques make it even more important to come to terms with this basic, but slightly enigmatic, concept.

To be able to put this into perspective the accountancy student must have a firm grasp of what is meant by 'a system' and how the concept of systems theory fits into the business world. By understanding how systems operate within the firm, the student will be better equipped to tackle the concept of a systems audit. (A systems audit is: 'The procedure by which the auditor reviews, records and tests the accounting system in order to assess its strengths and weaknesses as a basis for further reviewing and testing of the transactions flowing through it'.)[1]

Systems defined

Few days pass by without the word 'system' being used – political systems, the postal system, the economic system and so on. But just what is a system?

Professor Brian Underdown of Sheffield University defines a system simply as: 'A set of elements which operate together in order to attain a goal.' [2] George Reynolds of the University of Cincinatti gives us another definition of a system: 'A system is a group of interrelated elements organised to achieve a common purpose. All elements of the system have a logical relationship; they all work toward the system goal rather than their own separate goals. If a system is one of the components of a larger system, it is called a sub-system.' [3] We can apply these definitions to organisations which are familiar to us and observe that they form a conceptual model of a firm – people working together in groups and subgroups, in an organised way, each in their own division of labour as envisaged by Adam Smith, contributing to the common goal of the agreed output.

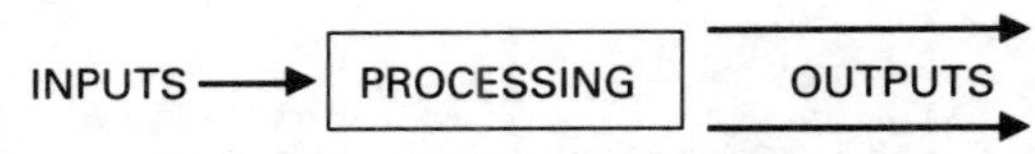

Figure 7.1 System input/output model

General systems theory (GST)

GST is a philosophy which grew out of the organismic views of the biologist Ludwig von Bertanlanffy and thus the concepts can be readily related to the living organism. This makes sense as the modern company is nothing else if not a living organism! GST looks at the constituent parts of the whole system (the reductionist approach) and assesses them in isolation from their surrounding systems. GST also views a system in its entirety (the holistic approach) and takes into account the fact that the resultant product from that system is synergistic – that is to say, the resultant output of the system is greater than the sum of the individual inputs.

To be able to define a given system we must be able to identify the boundaries of the system under consideration. These boundaries are not physical ones but logical ones as seen by the viewer. This perspective can be highly subjective and suffer from confiicting views; the system boundary set by one person can include or exclude areas set by another, depending on the objectives and viewpoint of the analyst.

Once the system and sub-system boundaries have been set, the relationships between the sub-systems within the system, (and, indeed between the system and its operating environment) have to be established. Let us now look at the system map below which illustrates the concepts of a system as a whole, including some of its environment and the constituent parts of the system (the sub-systems and sub-sub-systems).

Types of system

We have so far looked at what is meant by a system and we have described the possible extent of a system. Now let us examine the types of system which are relevant to this analysis of systems concepts.

If we accept that a system is a theoretical model of a real world business, it follows that we should specify different types of system to accommodate different representations of reality. Thus I shall outline three widely accepted system models:

1. *Mechanistic systems.* The outputs from these systems can be determined, accurately forecast and are directly attributable to a given input; hence their alternative name, 'deterministic' systems.
2. *Probabilistic systems.* The outputs of these systems are less predictable than mechanistic systems and it is this type of system that the accountant is more likely to encounter in business. In this type of system we know (or seek to determine) the input and environmental factors that affect the output and, given these variables, we can assess the likely outputs within a certain degree of probability. Because this type of system is encountered more frequently in business and due to its inherent uncertainty, the greatest attempts are made to install control processes to reduce the uncertainty.
3. *Self-organising or cybernetic systems.* These are the most complicated of the three types of system discussed here. These types of system usually involve living things such as people, who continually adapt to the changing environment to keep pace with the changes. Organisations can be regarded as cybernetic systems and it is management's function to plan to accommodate change and ensure that a firm's systems adapt to change.

An open and closed case!

Systems encountered in a firm can be further classified as being an open system, a closed system or, more likely, somewhere on a continuum between the two. An open system can exchange information, energy or material with its environrnent; it interacts with its environment to receive various inputs, transforms the inputs in some way, and exports outputs. A closed system, on the other hand, is self-contained and has no interaction with or influence on its surrounding environment. Biological and social systems are inherently open systems; mechanical systems may be open or closed.

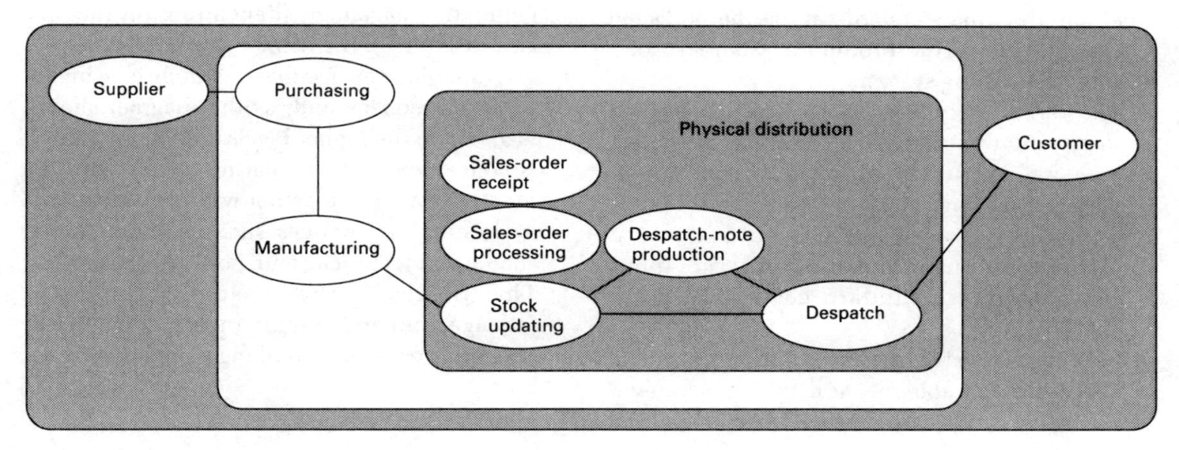

Figure 7.2 System map

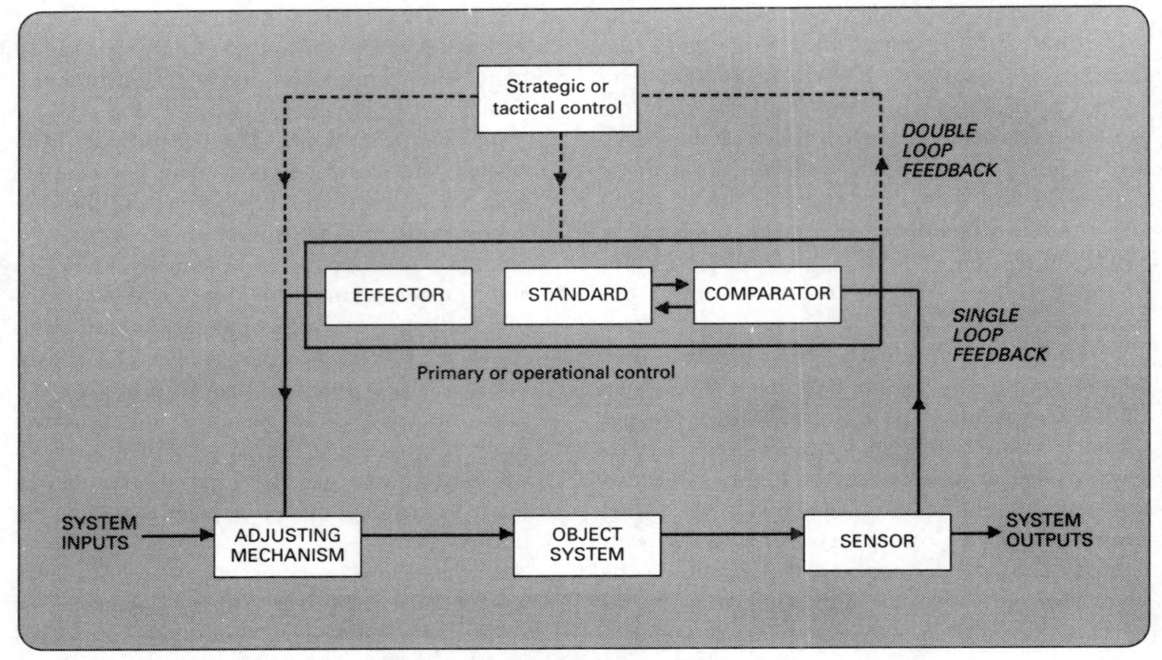

Figure 7.3 Diagrammatic representation of control and feedback

Systems controls

A control is the function that attempts to achieve the closest possible output of a system compared to the original planned output.

A readily understandable (and often quoted) example of this is a room thermostat: where the room is sensed to be too cold compared to the desired (given standard) of heat, the heating control (thermostat) will switch on a heater until such time that it is sensed that the room has achieved the desired temperature, when it will then switch the heater off.

Let us now examine this concept of control a little further to ascertain what elements go into making up the control of a system.

Certain conditions must exist for a control or set of controls to be effective

In order for a control or set of controls to be effective, the following conditions must exist:

1. The standard or expected performance must be specified. In the context of management accounting, the standard can be the budgeted expenditure or the production standard of a standard costing system.
2. The performance is to be objectively measured in commonly acceptable units (e.g. monetary measure or units of production) at an appropriate time.
3. Comparison of the actual output to the planned output in meaningful terms (once again, think of standard costing/variance analysis).
4. Feedback – using the information output of Processes 1-3 above – and taking whatever corrective action is necessary where a material deviation is seen to exist.

This is an appropriate time to remind ourselves of the basic qualities of information which should be – Brief, Accurate, Timely, Complete, Appropriate and Relevant – (mnemonic BATCAR!).

The system sensor measures the performance of the system. Once this information has been sensed, the information produced should be fed back and compared to the desired standard, either by trained staff looking for deviations or by computer exception reports.

This information feedback can then be used by the manager with appropriate responsibility, who should then take the appropriate action to remedy any material deviations from the planned standard. This manager can be said to be the 'effector'.

Feedback can take two basic forms:

- A single loop feedback, which is concerned with the routine correction of deviations from a given plan. This will usually be ascribed to operational management or less usually tactical management (depending on the size and structure of the firm)
- The double loop feedback, which is a higher level of feedback and, as the diagram shows, feeds up to the higher levels of management. It is concerned with comparing results with the longer-term plans together with considerations of strategic influences such as sociological, economic, technical and political variations. The feedback that reaches high-level management will result in the adjustment, alteration or total rethinking of organisational plans.

Positive and negative feedback

I have described the basic concept of feedback, but if we are to consider the aspects of this area of the syllabus more fully we need to go a little further down the road and examine the concepts of positive and negative feedback and what systems theory has to say about delays in feedback.

Increasing incentives can improve demand beyond that anticipated

Positive feedback is the effect of a control system being used to increase the deviation from the standard or norm. An example of this would be the increase of salespersons' incentives where it is found that such an increase improves demand beyond that anticipated at the outset.

It follows then that negative feedback has the opposite effect – i.e. it is used to decrease or dampen the deviation from the norm. This type of feedback is more likely to be encountered as its aim is to smooth out fluctuations to bring them in line with the planned level of performance. An example of this would be the monitoring and resultant correction, where necessary, of excessive departmental expenditure levels with a view to reducing the deviation back to the planned levels.

For an example of the effect of positive and negative feedback, see the diagram above.

Delays in systems

We have already seen that one of the essential qualities of information, if it is to be useful, is that it must be timely. If feedback is delayed it can have a sub-optimal effect on the eventual output of the system. By delaying the corrective action of the information feedback process, rather than bringing a deviation from the norm back in line, the resulting effect can be to amplify the oscillation in the opposite direction.

For example, feedback could be in the form of monthly exception reports produced in the normal course of a budgetary control sub-system; delays in providing the information fed back to managers may result in consequent corrective action having an adverse rather than a beneficial effect. Put more simply, the managers may be applying the brakes when they should be hitting the accelerator, or vice versa!

Conclusion

Accounting is a social science and relies on systems for the collation of meaningful information in order to both monitor and control performance, as well as providing a cost-effective means of obtaining audited financial information for users of that information.

Managers can control the performance of their firm by arming themselves with high-quality information provided by an information system and take appropriate and timely action.

Certified accountants are involved as auditors, managers and in a stewardship role and need to know how business systems interact within themselves and within their surrounding environments.

This article is a concise outline of systems theory in the context of an accounting environment. Readers preparing themselves for Paper 5 should use this discussion as an introduction to the fundamental concepts of systems and as background knowledge upon which the principles and details of management information systems can be built.

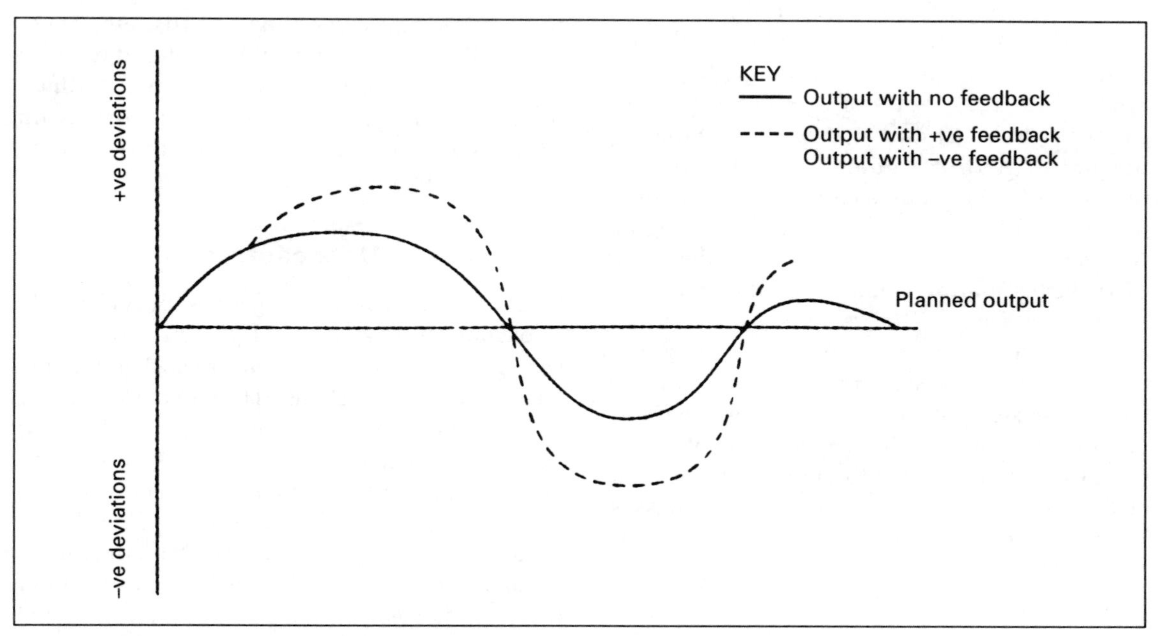

Figure 7.4 Effects of positive and negative feedback

7

Further Reading

R.G. Anderson, *Data Processing: Vol 1, Information Systems and Technology*, Pitman.

T. Lucey, *Management Information Systems* (6th edition), DP Publications Ltd.

References

1. Lee, *Company Auditing*, 1986.
2. Glautier and Underdown, *Accounting Theory and Practice*, 1991.
3. G.W. Reynolds, *Information Systems for Managers*, 1992.

An Outline of Systems Needed for Transactions Processing

A SYSTEMATIC APPROACH TO
INFORMATION ANALYSIS [PART 2]

By Adrian Bolton

The object of the second part of this article is to investigate the subject matter of part 1(b) ('The nature of systems needed for transaction processing') of the new syllabus of Module C – Paper 5 – Information Analysis which is designed 'to ensure students' appreciation of information systems to meet the goals and needs of business and understanding of procedures for the development, introduction and use of computer-based systems.'

Last month the first of part of this article investigated some of the concepts of a system in the light of an organisation and introduced the idea that a business system is heavily dependent on information. Indeed, a primary function of an accountant is that of a catalyst in the provision of information for interested business information user groups (for a definitive list of these user groups, see 'The Corporate Report' (Accounting Standards Committee – 1975)). As technology advances, information systems become ever more entwined with computer information technology.

It is also important to grasp at this stage that there are links between Certificate Paper 5 and Professional Paper 12 (Management and Strategy). In 1985 Professor M E Porter (Harvard Business School) and V E Millar (Managing partner of Arthur Andersen) postulated the theory that 'information technology is permeating the value chain at every point, transforming the way value activities are performed and the nature of linkages among them. It is also affecting competitive scope . . .'[1]

It is therefore important for business managers, strategists and, especially in this context, accountants to understand the relevance of how information technology relates not only to business systems and information analysis, but also to the strategy of competitive businesses. Within the second part of this article I shall be looking at the nature of:

- data capture
- batch systems
- online systems and
- data storage

and how these aspects of an information system fit into the information analysis 'jigsaw'. It is important for the student to understand that the chosen method of processing information can not only enhance the controls of a system but also give a firm competitive advantage in the market place. This is equally relevant in the heat of competition of commerce and industry as well as in the budget-oriented and efficiency-conscious public sector.

Before we investigate methods of data capture, let us take a moment to remind ourselves of the meaning of data and the difference between data and information. Data are (note the fact that we shall use the word data as a plural form) 'the basic facts about the activities of a business', whereas 'information is obtained by assembling items of data into a meaningful form'.[2]

Data are generated in the normal course of business activities, e.g. invoices and credit notes, retail sales, employee time records, etc. These different forms of data must be captured on to an information processing system. Moreover, these data must be presented to the information processing system in a form that can be understood by the system.

Data capture

Office automation has grown dramatically throughout this century and paper-based systems have given way to, at first, electromechanical and, later, electronic systems. The human/computer interface is achieved through 'input and output devices' (of which we shall be looking at input devices). Until relatively recently, data entry was achieved by clerks punching holes into an 80-column card which was later transferred to magnetic disk or tape for subsequent computer input. This system of capturing data involved transferring the data on source documents, sending the data documents to a data preparation centre, (possibly by post or courier), preparing and verifying the data and converting it into machine-sensible form. The data, prepared in a form understood by the computer, could be validated by computer program and then processed.

However, technology has now moved on from this method and data collection can be achieved by several more direct methods, referred to as data capture. A major advantage of modern data capture is that whereas skilled keypunchers make about one error in 1,000 keystrokes, bar code scanners make less than one error in 10,000 transactions.

Data capture devices can be broadly divided into two categories:

- ► document readers
- ► data capture at point of sale (DACAPOS).

DOCUMENT READERS

Character readers consist of:

(i) *Optical Character Recognition (OCR)* – This is used extensively in billing (e.g. gas, water and electric bills); bills are prepared by the issuing firm's computer in OCR, sent to the customer who remits with the counterfoil. The counterfoil is then used to capture the remittance data variables and re-enter the computer through the OCR reader as evidence of payment (the turnaround technique).

614 3534 0729 4

614 3534 0729 X V

Figure 7.5 An example of OCR

A recent development of the OCR technique is the bar code which is being increasingly used to identify data. Examples of this are the Royal Mail Priority services (Registered and Recorded Post and Special Delivery), where a bar code is affixed to a letter or packet and used to 'track and trace' it throughout its journey to its destination. The bar code is read by a miniature laser beam and the source data is immediately transferred to the computer. Bar code data could include (for example) time, date and location.

(ii) *Magnetic Ink Character Recognition (MICR)* is extensively used in banking and also by local government authorities for collection of local taxes by instalments. The cheques, which should be regarded in this context as source data documents, are encoded before being sent to clients/taxpayers and when the cheques are presented after encashment, the bottom line is encoded with the value of encashment. An advantage of this medium is that source documents can be read at approximately 2,000 documents per hour.

(Hint – have a look at a gas or electric bill and compare it with a cheque to verifiy the difference between OCR and MICR.)

40⑈0596⑆51315513⑈

Figure 7.6 An example of MICR

(iii) *Optical Mark Readers (OMR)*. The use of OMR typically includes applications such as surveys, questionnaires and multi-choice exam papers. The style of an OMR document is that of a series of boxes which can be read as either blank or marked. The marked or filled-in box could be interpreted, for example, as 'Yes' (filled in box) or 'No' (blank box). The documents are read by beams of light emitted and sensed in an OMR, which will typically sort documents into 'successfully read' and 'rejected' at the rate of 10,000 A4 documents per hour.

Pen-based input. At the leading edge of input technologies are pen based input devices which consist of a flat screen display (similar to a notebook computer) and a pen-like writing device which emits a small signal to the electronic pad/'notebook'. These input devices transform the letters and numbers created by writing with the 'pen' onto the electronic notepad into digital input into the computer. A leading American firm to use this technology is United Parcel Service (UPS), whose van drivers request parcel recipients to sign for their packet onto the driver's 'DIAD' (Delivery Information Acquisition Device). The relevant information can then be immediately relayed to UPS's computer via satellite link and forwarded on to the customer either on hard copy or electronically. You can see that UPS is using this leading-edge technology to differentiate its product and tie its customers into its near-unique service.

DATA CAPTURE AT POINT OF SALE (DACAPOS)

Retail organisations require up-to-date information of formations on inventory movement. Modern technology enables retailers to capture that data at the moment the goods pass through the checkout. Methods of DACAPOS include:

(i) *Laser-scanned bar codes*. These are now in common use at most major supermarkets and the rapidly reducing costs of technology mean that the corner shop is now reaching out to afford this DACAPOS method.

Once scanned at the point of sale, the laser converts the data held on the bar code into machine-sensible form, thus avoiding transcription.

The information can then be used to generate a till receipt and update stock and accounting records for subsequent analysis.

Current standards of bar codes are UPC (Universal Product Code), used in the USA, and EAN (European Article Number), used in Europe. These codes can be up to 1 l digits long and carry information such as the country of origin and a product code of up to 99,999 (five characters long).

Figure 7.7 A retail product bar code

(ii) *Tags* are used to collect data extensively in the clothing industry, e.g. Marks and Spencer. These tags, often referred to as Kimball tags (after the manufacturer), were originally punch-holed cards but these have been largely superseded by tags carrying magnetic strips. The tag can also contain printed data for visual recognition. 'Kimball' tags are fixed to garments before sale and subsequently detached at the point of sale. Once removed, the tags are then sent to a data processing centre for conversion to computer input.

(iii) *Magnetic strip.* One further method used extensively by the John Lewis Partnership was the magnetic strip. Peel-off retail product price tags, as well as containing visually recognisable information such as price and product code, also carried a small magnetic strip (similar to a small thin section of audio cassette tape) which contained the necessary product data. This magnetic strip can be read by a magnetic reading wand at the point of sale which captures the data and transfers it to the computer for subsequent information processing.

Batch systems

Batch processing (BP) is so called because transactions are collected together over a period of time and then processed together in a suitably sized batch. Until the 1960s this was the only method of processing data on to computers and it is still used today on older systems.

BP is also encountered where the system would otherwise be slowed up by having to wait for operator input. BP is also used to good effect where machine time is booked for batch processing at periods of low demand on computer time, thereby freeing the computer for peak time running.

Jobs are transferred from source documents to magnetic media, giving the control opportunity to verify the inputs to a batch control total. The inputs are then stored in a 'batch queue' and run singly or in multiple batches under the control of the computer operating system.

A major drawback with this type of transaction processing is that it does not easily permit the correction of errors once the run has started and can thus further delay information output on an already (arguably) cumbersome system.

Online systems (or interactive systems)

An *interactive system* is a data processing system which processes data immediately without the delays inherent in batch processing. This is achieved by the computer and the data input operator each communicating with the other at the time of data input.

An often quoted example of an online system is the seat booking system of airlines. Prior to the introduction of online systems seat reservation agents did not know exactly how many seats had been sold on a given flight. This resulted in seat bookings being taken for fully booked flights, with an obvious resultant loss of goodwill. Other flights were under-booked, resulting in a loss of vital revenue.

The introduction of on-line systems to ticket booking agents meant that every vacant seat could be monitored 'live' at the time the customer wished to make a booking.

Another example of an on-line system is the 'Hole in the wall' or Automated Teller Machine (ATM) cash dispenser found at banks and building societies; this example will probably be familiar to you and will serve as a practical example of an online system. Once the user has been granted access to his or her account, he (she) is presented with the up-to-the-minute balance and can make a decision to withdraw an appropriate amount of money. Previously the customer had to rely on out-of-date bank statements.

Batch or interactive?

The choice of system depends on the demands of the business. If the organisation needs periodic reports such as account statements or payroll, batch processing will probably be the most appropriate choice. If the organisation needs immediate information, an online system will probably be the most suitable method.

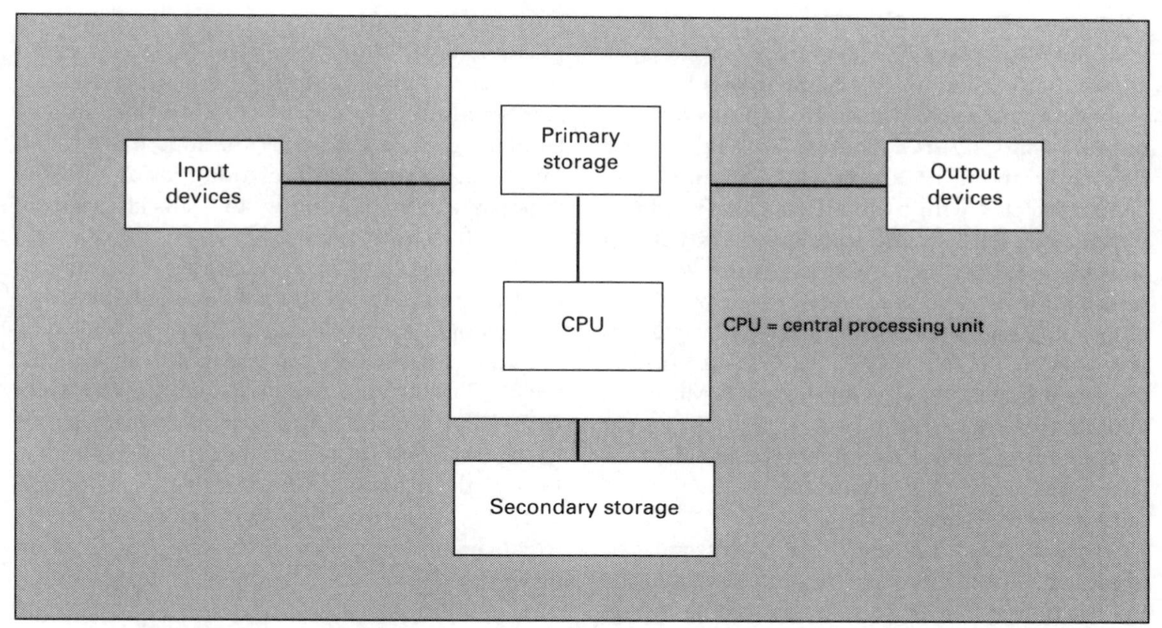

Figure 7.8 A computer's central processor

Data storage

The computer's information storage facility can be broadly divided into two types. These are the primary store (or main memory) and the secondary storage (or backing storage).

PRIMARY STORE

Those of you who have worked on a computer application such as a spreadsheet for (say) 30 minutes, without saving the work to disk or tape and experienced a power cut for some reason will be painfully aware that your work will have been lost. Data input in the manner described above is stored in the primary store, which is called immediate access storage. The semi-conductor most commonly used for main storage is called 'RAM' (random access memory) and as I have described above, RAM loses all data when power ceases to be supplied to the computer (and consequently called volatile memory). RAM is so called because it can directly access any random memory location to retrieve or store data and programs in current operational use within the same amount of time.

Primary memory represents data electronically in memory cells in binary form. Each memory cell will store eight 'Bits' (BInary digiTS) which will represent a digit, letter or symbol (e.g. the œ or the # signs). The computer will keep a record of where all the digits are recorded in RAM by means of a specific address.

Recent technological developments have pushed up the handling capacity of information from 8 bits up to 32 bits by transferring 4 × 8 bits of information in each single operation and this technology is still advancing. 8 bits are measured as a byte and 1,048,576 × 8 bits = 1 megabyte (Mb). Many current software demands have pushed up the minimum required size of the RAM and applications such as Microsoft Windows™ operating environment require at least 4 Mb of RAM.

Whilst we can write information to the RAM, the computer has another area of the primary storage, called the read only memory (ROM). This is a semi-conductor microchip which has been permanently programmed at the time of manufacture and contains crucial operating instructions which need to be retained within the computer at all times.This memory is non-volatile and thus does not lose its information when power is disconected.

The central processing unit (CPU) referred to in the diagram above is the area of the computer that manipulates numbers, letters and symbols. The CPU contains an arithmetic logic unit and a control unit for controlling other parts of the computer.

SECONDARY STORE

Once the data has been processed in the primary storage area, it will need to be written to a more permanent medium at regular intervals to avoid loss of data/information when the power ceases. This can, of course, be done by printing out on to hard copy (paper) but it will also need to be 'saved' on to more technologically advanced information storage methods called secondary or backing storage, for future recall. The devices in most common use for this purpose are as follows:

(i) magnetic disk ('hard disk')
(ii) magnetic diskette ('floppy disk')
(iii) magnetic tapes
(iv) optical disks
(v) mass storage devices.

(i) *A magnetic disk (hard disk)* is now fitted to virtually all modern PCs (personal computers) as standard. It consists of several rotating disks coated in iron oxide, mounted on a common central shaft which rotates at high speed (typically about 3,500rpm), the whole of this being protected within an airtight case. Read and write heads fly over the spinning disks without touching them but reading and writing information in a similar electronic manner to a domestic audio recorder on tracks and sectors of the disks. Hard disks mounted inside microcomputers usually store from 30Mb up to 200Mb, but can now store over 500Mb. Larger magnetic disks found in commercial installations can store up to 7.5 gigabytes (1 gigabyte = 1,000,000,000 bytes).

Because fixed hard disks are an integral part of most PCs, it is important to remember that the information stored thereon is vulnerable to loss or theft and should be remotely stored (e.g. tape streamer). It should be noted that hard disks can be obtained in stand-alone versions as well as those integral to the computer. These work on exactly the same principle and are often referred to as Winchester drives.

(ii) *Magnetic diskettes (floppy disks)* are single disks which are activated by inserting them into a disk drive unit, usually in the front of a PC (free-standing or external floppy disk drives are also available). The disk itself is made of a thin floppy plastic material coated with magnetic media. The disk(ette), which is now mainly 3.5 inches in diameter, is protected by a plastic case with a sliding protective shield over a read/write opening in the case. Older types of floppy disk were 8 and 5.25 inches in diameter with lower storage capacity and less robust protection features than the later 3.5-inch disk.

These disks work on a very similar principle to the hard disk: they rotate at about 360rpm when in operation and usually hold either 720k (kilobytes) or 1.4Mb of information. The benefits of mass production mean that the cost of a disk is now measured in pence rather than pounds. Disadvantages include the relatively low storage capacity and slower speed of operation than hard disks.

(iii) *Magnetic tapes* of the reel-to-reel type have been used for many years on mainframe computers and are still in common use for storing large amounts of data and information. The reels are usually 14 inches in diameter and contain about 2,400 feet of 1/2-inch magnetic tape. The main advantage of this type of storage is that it can contain large volumes of information.

A significant disadvantage is that information is stored sequentially and thus it can be relatively slow to access individual records. A further disadvantage is that its operating environment must be carefully controlled, including features like vacuum columns to cushion the force of sudden stops and starts of the tape drive. Such tapes hold about 40Mb of information and the tape passes the read and write heads at speeds of up to 200 feet per second.

A development of magnetic tape is the tape streamer, which typically holds up to 250Mb and records on 1/4-inch magnetic tape. Another type of tape streamer, closely resembling a small version of an 8mm camcorder and using 4mm DAT (Digital Audio Tape), can store up to 1.3 gigabytes. The purpose of both these versions is to copy the contents of the hard disk to safeguard against data loss (e.g. in the event of an irrecoverable disk crash or inadvertent deletion of files).

(iv) *Optical disks,* which are also referred to as Compact Discs (CDs) or laser optical disks, are used with microcomputers as well as larger machines. These hold information in binary form usually on a 4.75-inch disk that can hold hundreds of megabytes of information. The major difference between these disks and secondary storage devices mentioned above is that they are read-only devices. The data held on them cannot be changed once written. Suitable applications include directories, databases, catalogues and they can even hold visual images such as organisation members' photographs and signatures.

A further form of optical disk is the WORM disk (write once read many) which allows a computer user to record data onto the disk once only; thereafter the data cannot be erased and forms a permanent copy.

The last form of optical disk to be mentioned here is the magneto-optical disk, which has the storage power of a CD but can be written to by the user. This is achieved by a high-powered laser heating the disk to form binary magnetic patterns on one of the magnetic layers of the disk. Subsequent reading of the information is data by a lower-powered laser. These disks can be written to hundreds of thousands of times and thus form a high-storage alternative to floppy disks and magnetic tape. The main drawback at present is that the time taken to write to this form of storage is slower than conventional magnetic disks and tapes; technological progress will probably alter this.

(v) *Mass storage devices* are used by organisations needing massive information storage such as major banks and financial houses, multinational corporations and national governments. The principle of this storage method is rather like the juke box, in which an electronic retrieval arm withdraws the required disk or tape and loads it in the same automated manner. As one would expect, the storage capacity of these information giants is measured in hundreds of gigabytes.

Conclusion

It must be borne in mind that the computer features discussed above are part of a technological information system designed to give organisations the optimum amount of information at the right time and at the greatest cost-benefit. Computer systems are not an end in themselves but rather a processing device forming part of an organisation's information strategy.

It is important that the input and storage devices must be carefully chosen, not only to match the complementary hardware and software but also the overall strategy of the organisation. Indeed, the available information technology can significantly influence the strategy of a firm. As you digest the information contained in this article, remember it in the context of Porter and Millar's comment that 'IT should transform the way activities are performed and affect an organisation's competitive scope.'

Further reading

Information Analysis (1994), Eardley, Marshall and Ritchie, CAET ISBN 1-85908-005-7.

A Glossary of Computing Terms (1991), British Computer Society, Pitman ISBN 0-273-03645-9.

Computer Studies (1993), C.S. French, DP Publications ISBN 1-873981-18-X.

Data Processing and Information Technology (1993), C.S. French, DP Publications ISBN 1-85805-027-8.

References

1 *Harvard Business Review* July-August 1985.

2 *Data Processing and Information Technology* (1993) C.S. French, DP Publications ISBN 1-85805-027-8.

Tackling Case Studies

You will have noted, that with the introduction of a new syllabus, the ACCA has taken the opportunity to bring in new types of questions in some of the examination papers.

This article discusses the introduction of 'case study' type questions and gives you some ideas on how to tackle these types of questions for the June 1994 examinations.

Why use case study questions?

The ACCA syllabus is a very practical one and the introduction of a new syllabus has assisted in enabling the Examiners to place an increased emphasis on examining what an accountant actually does in the workplace and assessing students' knowledge of this in a realistic manner. Case studies offer an opportunity to simulate a real-life situation in the examination room.

As with the world of business, case studies do not have one correct answer – in fact often the choice to be made is choosing the 'least worst' option. You will need to consider a number of different options before recommendations are made.

Again, as with the world of business, not everything provided in the material for the case study will be relevant. You will be required to sift through the material to decide what is extraneous to the requirements.

How to gain marks from a case study

- Spend time reading and making sense of material before writing.
- Remember this is not an essay. Work out which format you will use for your answer – usually this will be a report format, but you may be asked to structure your ideas in the form of a presentation to senior management or in a memo or in a letter.
- Adopt a simple structure with appropriate language and a clear presentation. Remember that one of the aims of case studies is to test your comunication skills.
- Make use of headings.
- Identify key issues and use them as the fundamental structure to your report.
- Outline a range of possible solutions and discuss the practical and commercial implications of each one. Then make your recommendations based on the alternatives you have considered.

Remember that there is no one correct answer. The Examiner will award marks for the development of a case and a logical answer.

7

What not do do!

- Don't repeat case study material, use it!
- Don't waffle – identify what is relevant and discard what is not.
- Don't panic if you are faced with what seems unknown. Read the material carefully and plan your time to allow time for reflection on what is being asked. Remember that the Examiner is expecting you to bring to your recommendations any experience you have of business life as well as integrating relevant material from other subject areas.
- Don't assume there is only one answer. You can gain marks from reasoned, logical recommendations.

Finally

Remember that the Examiner is trying to examine how you would tackle practical issues. He/she does not want to see how well you have remembered and can regurgitate a set of rote-learned facts.

Therefore, approach case studies with the practical aspects in mind.

You are also advised to refer to the section called 'Studying for Success' on pages 36-40 of the ACCA booklet: 'Studying and the Examinations – ACCA Syllabus'. This section gives you tips on how to prepare for the exams, how to prepare for the exams, how to present answers to computational and essay questions as well as a checklist on good exam technique. This guidance will help you in your preparation for the June 1994 exams.

UPDATES

Guidance notes

Paper 5, as the first IT paper in the new scheme, will assume prior knowledge of, for example: input and output; data capture and data storage; processors; mainframes; minis; micros; utility and applications software, batch; on-line; and real time.

Development of IT in the scheme

There is significant development of IT from Paper 5 to Paper 10 Accounting and Audit Practice, in the area of computer-assisted auditing techniques, and to Paper 12, Management and Strategy, which reinforces students' appreciation of the role of IT within the organisation and its strategic value to organisations.

Practical experience

Wherever possible, students are advised to obtain hands-on experience in the use of basic packages in, for example, spreadsheets, database, accounting, statistics and project management, because this will help them both with the questions in Section A, based on the case study, and the scenario-type questions in Section B.

Questions and Answers

Q *(i) What does the Examiner mean by 'evaluation'? Testing seems to be merged with implementation and some of the design aspects are merged with evaluations.*

(ii) In case tools, what are the major features and their names?

A (i) Evaluation, in the context of the syllabus, is used in two ways:
– the evaluation of the possibility of introducing a computer-based system; and
– evaluation of that system once installed.

(ii) Case tools: students need to be able to perceive how much of a life cycle a case tool is able to cover. They should have an appreciation of where and how in the life cycle a case tool may be of use. The students will not be required to know about specific products.

Q *Are data flow diagrams relevant to the practical accountant?*

A Yes, because the accountant is a user who needs to understand how a system is constructed and, because of the involvement of accounts in computer systems, accountants will not know what is going on unless they are familiar with the tools and techniques involved in the 'cradle to grave' approach. Data flow diagrams are also useful in a non-IT context and, while accountants in their work would probably not be asked to draw a data flow diagram, they would need to know how to interpret them.

8

Q Will students be expected to construct decision trees and tables?

A Yes.

Please remember to read the *Students' Newsletter* for information on any changes to the exam or the syllabus. Note the change to the exam format as outlined at the end of Section 1 of this revision text.

EXAM STYLE QUESTIONS

The best way to assess your progress is to practise for the examination by trying to tackle the types of question which you will meet in the examination room. This Section provides you with a selection of questions which illustrate the kind contained in the exam. They give representative coverage of the paper and are designed to help you practise answering questions in the different question formats which you will find in the exam paper itself. Try as many questions of this type as you can during your revision. You will find suggested answers in Section 12, together with advice on where marks can be gained or lost.

Section A – Case Studies

Case 1: Elite Gifts Direct Limited

Elite Gifts Direct Limited sell high-quality products such as decorative plates, ornaments and prints. The products are marketed through high-profile advertising in the colour supplements of national newspapers. Customers place orders by mail or telephone. Elite hold high volumes of stock of the products that are currently being marketed but the range of goods at any one time is limited. The products are purchased prepackaged from the suppliers so that shipments can be prepared simply by attaching the customer's name and address to the packaging. Some of the goods form a series which customers can subscribe to. Each item in a series is shipped monthly with customers being given a week's approval period before payment becomes due.

In 1993, Elite shipped 168,000 items of which 9,000 were returned under the approval offer. Turnover in 1993 was £4.6 million.

The Marketing Department, managed by Stella Smith, has a total of seven staff who select new products and design the marketing material.

The Sales Department, managed by Sam Winter, employs 18 sales order clerks who take orders made by telephone. When not busy on the telephones, they process the orders which have arrived by post. A further three staff handle returned goods and try to respond to customer complaints.

The Accounts Department, managed by Laura Jones, has five payments clerks who handle payments made by customers and three credit control clerks who contact customers with outstanding accounts.

Elite employs six staff including the manager, Keith Banes, in its Warehouse and Despatch Department. Each morning they receive a list of shipments from the Sales Department. Each item on the list has a self-adhesive address label. They pick out the required products, attach the address label and load the packages onto vans ready for shipping to the customers.

In 1985, Elite purchased a mini-computer running a multi-user operating system. In 1992 the original computer was replaced by a more powerful mini-computer from a different manufacturer. Tony Thorp was appointed computer manager in May 1994 and has eight programming staff who make modifications to the software packages and maintain the mini-computer. Tony has heard stories about the problems experienced by Elite in 1992 when the new system was installed. Apparently, the initial changeover to the new system failed and

Elite had neither the old nor the new system available for two weeks while problems with the new system were sorted out. The mini-computer is specified to be able to support 30 simultaneous users. It now runs three main applications – a word processing package, a spreadsheet, and a tailor-made transaction processing system – which handle the basic sales and accounting functions.

Tony Thorp has tried to encourage the use of information systems within Elite but the Managing Director, Tim Clancy, is reluctant to invest heavily in more information technology and has warned Tony that the company must not encounter problems with its systems as it did in 1992. However, Tony has managed to ensure that all managers and all the staff in the Sales and Accounts Departments have access to a terminal attached to the mini-computer. The Marketing Department have two powerful workstations on which they prepare advertising material.

The Managing Director, Tim Clancy, holds a meeting with all the departmental managers at the start of each month to discuss performance and set targets. At the October 1994 meeting the issue of the computer systems is raised.

Tim has asked Stella Smith, the Marketing Manager, to present figures about the costs and responses of the various advertising campaigns run by Elite recently. At the meeting Stella says that it is very difficult to find accurate information since the transaction processing system does not have facilities for recording information about where individual customers have seen Elite's goods advertised. Tony Thorp reports that he has looked at the possibility of adapting the software to include this information and provide suitable reports but he knows that the programmers already have a full workload, mainly because the transaction processing system is poorly documented and the conversion of the program in 1992 was poorly implemented.

Both the Sales and the Accounts managers say that they would be unhappy if the transaction processing system were to be more heavily utilised. They are already dissatisfied with the response time provided by the system at peak periods of activity. This has led to backlogs of work and difficulties in Sales, because the system sometimes shows a customer has overdue payments when in fact the payments have been received in Accounts several days earlier. Accounts have problems with an increasing number of customers being sent goods when their credit limits have been exceeded but up-to-date information is not available to the Sales clerks.

Keith Banes, Warehouse and Dispatch Manager, adds that about once a week there are problems getting the shipping lists to the warehouse in the morning; his staff have been idle for several hours and then have to rush to complete the work, which leads to to more mistakes being made.

At this point Tony realises that the management team may have provided enough evidence to force Tim into considering a major change to the computer systems. Tony offers to look at possible solutions to the various problems.

Tony Thorp's initial idea is that the mini-computer could be used purely for transaction processing. The mini-computer could be attached to a local area network with some or all of the users having low-cost personal computers. Word-processing and spreadsheet applications could be done on the personal computers and users could access the transaction processing system via the network. Tony also has doubts about the transaction processing software since it has proved difficult to adapt and maintain. He has heard from a friend of his that a software package for some mail-order applications is available off the shelf.

Required

1) Tony Thorp decides to carry out an investigation into the current performance and future requirements of Elite's computer systems. Briefly describe the data collection methods available in this situation and outline a plan for the investigation. [10 marks]

2) Discuss how information and activity within Elite can be categorised according to different levels within the organisation and explain how computerised information systems can be used to process low-level transaction data to provide useful information at the higher levels. [10 marks]

3) Write down a brief description of the likely costs and benefits of Tony Thorp's ideas and explain how they may be quantified. [15 marks]

4) What factors should Tony Thorp consider when trying to decide whether to purchase a new mail order information processing system that is available off-the-shelf, compared with modifying and maintaining Elite's existing software? [10 marks]

5) Describe the factors involved in converting data and changing over to a new system and suggest how to reduce the risk of problems such as Elite experienced in 1992. [10 marks]

[Total 55 marks]

Case 2: International Investment Services Limited (IIS)

International Investment Services Limited (IIS) employ a total of 600 staff, including 300 at their headquarters in London and the rest at 12 offices around the world. IIS specialises in providing advice and management of funds for investors, either individuals or organisations, who wish to take advantage of special conditions within the financial markets, such as areas which have beneficial tax laws, and occasions when there are major fluctuations in the currency markets.

Since its establishment in the 1970s, the management of IIS have always viewed information technology as a vital element in gaining competitive advantage in an area of business where success is dependent upon up-to-date information and fast, reliable communication. At the London headquarters there are about 140 specialist information systems staff, of whom about two-thirds are involved in systems development and the remainder maintain and operate the existing systems and provide technical support for users.

A large mainframe computer at the London headquarters provides a centralised database, which includes a real-time processing system that is fed with data directly from the major financial institutions around the world, such as the London Stock Exchange. High-speed telecommunications networks are designed to allow all IIS's personnel to access the information on the central mainframe and there is intensive use of these networks for electronic mail (e-mail) and other forms of electronic data interchange (EDI).

Dan Bates is the chief executive of IIS. Dan has become increasingly concerned that some of the organisations who are competing with IIS seem to be able to take better advantage of the changing conditions within the world's financial markets than IIS. Dan has discussed this issue with John Kline, the Information Systems Director. John assures Dan that IIS's hardware and communications systems are at least as well advanced as any of their competitors. The software performs well as a transaction processing system to handle clients' accounts and it processes the basic financial information that the investment staff require.

Dan discusses his concerns with Marie Sims, the Personnel Director, who has overall responsibility for staff and recruitment around the world. Marie assures Dan that IIS's investment appraisal staff are the best available in terms of both qualifications and experience and their salaries and conditions are considered generous within the industry. Dan next speaks to Frank Heinman, the Senior Investment Executive deputising for the Investments Director, who has taken a period of extended leave due to illness. Frank is relatively new to IIS and he mentions that one of his previous employers had been developing a sophisticated computerised investments analysis system. In 95% of instances this system is able to provide investment advice which is proving to be at least as effective as top-class human consultants, but it provides the advice much more quickly than a person could. The company concerned is naturally keen to take maximum advantage of its system and is therefore unlikely to make it available to the competition. When Frank left that employer, he had only seen a prototype of the system which produced printed reports, but he understood that the aim was to use a graphical user interface to the system.

Dan asks John Kline to discuss the situation with Frank Heinman and then report back to Dan in two days with some ideas on how IIS should react.

For the past several years IIS have developed their own software. When John Kline joined the company, IIS had standardised on the use of SSADM (Structured Systems Analysis and Development Methodology) in all development projects. John is aware that the Information Systems Department and its staff are regarded as elitist by other staff and that recent surveys of the users of the information systems have shown a decline in user satisfaction with the systems and the support they get from the Information Systems staff. John is considering whether IIS can usefully adopt a 'soft systems' approach to new systems development projects.

Marie Sims has asked John Kline about the use of data flow diagrams (DFDs) in systems analysis and design. Marie has identified the following files within the personnel department which may be used during recruitment procedures:

- a job specification file holding a job description of every job type in IIS
- an establishment file, holding, for each department, the maximum number of staff permitted for each job type
- a personnel file, holding details of each employee, one record per employee
- a vacancy file, holding details of unfilled vacancies
- an applicants file, holding details of all job applicants
- an interview file, holding a diary of all forthcoming interviews.

Required

1) Explain the features of a real-time system and why IIS has chosen one to handle the basic data fed from the financial institutions. [10 marks]

2) Explain what an expert system is and describe some of the features of an expert system which could help IIS with its investment analysis and appraisal. [10 marks]

3) Describe the main features of Structured Systems Analysis and Design Methodology (SSADM) and discuss features of soft systems methodologies which could be adopted by IIS. [15 marks]

4) Using as many of the files mentioned in the case study as you consider necessary, draw a data flow diagram of likely recruitment procedures at IIS. [10 marks]

5) Describe the use of prototypes and graphical user interfaces and discuss their appropriateness for applications such as the investment analysis application that IIS is considering. [10 marks]

[Total 55 marks]

Section B

1 (*Note:* This question is included for revision purposes. An understanding of information technology will aid your ability to understand many of the issues that are related to computerised information systems. You are unlikely to be asked a question like this specifically about hardware details in the examination.)

Office-based transaction processing systems require facilities for:

- inputting data
- data processing
- data storage
- outputting data and information.

Required

a) For each of these, briefly describe two examples of the sort of hardware used to provide them. [8 marks]

b) The terms 'batch', 'demand', 'interactive' and 'real-time' are used to describe different modes of transaction processing using computers. Briefly explain these terms, with the aid of examples, and discuss how the mode of processing will affect the choice of computer equipment. [7 marks]

2 A retailer with several sales outlets and a central warehouse is considering the use of a transaction processing system based upon electronic point of sale (EPOS) and electronic funds transfer (EFT) equipment linked to a central computerised accounts and stock control system.

Required

a) Describe the types of equipment which would be required for such a system and explain how it operates. [8 marks]

b) Three categories of information systems are:

- Management Information System
- Executive Information System
- Expert System.

Describe each of these systems and briefly explain how the information from the retailer's transaction processing system can be used by them. [7 marks]

3 An insurance company has purchased a database management system which is to be used to set up a database to hold all details of their clients' insurance policies and personal details. Users will have a computer workstation on their desks. Although not an information systems specialist, the Administration Manager has been chosen to represent the system's users in assisting with the design of the system's user interface. Knowing that your studies include information systems, the Administration Manager has asked you to prepare some background material.

Required

Write a report to the Administration Manager to cover the following points:

- the benefits and problems associated with involving users in systems design [8 marks]
- the use of fourth-generation languages (4GLs) and the technique of prototyping. [7 marks]

4 A mail-order retail company currently accepts orders received through the post on their standard paper order form. They also accept telephone orders, with the salesperson filling in a standard order form on the customer's behalf. During normal office hours, sales staff take orders, check them and contact customers when necessary. Each evening data-entry clerks enter the day's orders into the central computer system and the system processes them overnight as a batch. The company is considering changing the method of operating to allow orders to be taken over the telephone and entered directly onto the computer system by the sales staff; the system will then process each order immediately while the customer waits for confirmation.

Required

a) Describe and compare techniques for controlling the data on the system under both the current and proposed operating methods. [10 marks]

b) Compare the mail order company's current and proposed methods of data entry with respect to the effects on staff and customers [5 marks]

5 Many organisations operate in countries which have data protection legislation, such as the UK. On 5 March 1993 The Times reported on a court case where a court held that accountants who prepare accounts on behalf of clients must register as data users under the UK Data Protection Act 1984 if the accounts are processed by computer.

Required

With reference to a country which has data protection legislation, such as the UK:

a) i) Explain why the data protection legislation was passed, including the implications of the growth of electronic data interchange (EDI). [4 marks]

ii) Briefly describe the data protection legislation. [6 marks]

b) As well as data protection legislation, there is other legislation which relates to the use of computer programs and access to computer systems. Briefly describe the purpose and implications of such legislation. [5 marks]

6 Many organisations regard information as a valuable resource and have organisational structures which allow them to manage their information strategy and systems appropriately.

Required

a) Describe the structures and personnel that organisations use to manage their information strategy and control the development and use of their information systems. [8 marks]

b) A sales organisation is considering a proposal for establishing telecommuting for its travelling sales representatives by providing them with portable computers which can be used independently or linked to the organisation's existing central records computer

Briefly describe the contents of a report on the feasibility of this proposal. [7 marks]

7 a) Explain what is meant by the logical design and the physical design of an information system and discuss their role in the overall development of a system. [5 marks]

b) Describe and compare the three main models upon which the logical structure of a database can be designed. [10 marks]

8 Data flow diagrams (DFDs) are widely used in the analysis and design of information systems.

a) Explain the use of DFDs by:

- describing their purpose
- illustrating the symbols used
- discussing the use of levels of DFD. [5 marks]

b) The booking office manager of a small car-hire business describes the way cars and their hire are handled:

> 'We keep a file of details about all our cars which is updated whenever a car is returned from hire or serviced by our mechanics. Bookings are held in a bookings file to which we refer to check available cars. The bookings file is used to record the deposit paid in exchange for a contract when customers take a car out, and usage details (mileage, etc.) when they return it. Deposits and usage details are then prepared into an account and passed to the finance department who handle customer accounts. We produce a monthly report on car usage and servicing for our managers to study.'

Draw a DFD, including the files mentioned, to show the likely procedures that are used. [10 marks]

9 a) The personnel department of a large organisation has the following procedure for handling job applications:

> 'Applicants who have the relevant qualifications and experience are shortlisted for interview. Applicants with neither qualifications nor experience are rejected. Applicants with experience or qualifications, but not both, are put on a waiting list, with the exception that internal applicants with qualifications are always shortlisted. References are requested for all those external applicants who are put on the shortlist or waiting list.'

Construct a decision table for this procedure. [10 marks]

b) Briefly describe two other techniques that systems analysts use to describe procedures. [5 marks]

10 a) Briefly explain the features and benefits of modular design of software. [4 marks]

b) The software for an customer records system is required to provide the following functions:

- log-in and log-out procedures to limit access to specific files and applications
- data entry routines with initial verification checks followed by validation checks
- generation of standard reports
- facilities for *ad hoc* enquiries and non-routine report generation
- security routines for backup and restoration facilities
- a top-level menu to allow users to choose a function.

Outline a program structure chart for this software. [7 marks]

c) Describe structured walkthroughs and their purposes in systems development. [4 marks]

11 Write a report on the way that banks and other financial institutions have made increasing use of information technology in the processing and communication of financial transactions. The report should include:

- explanations of terms such as:
  - electronic data interchange (EDI)
  - electronic point of sale systems (EPOS)
  - electronic funds transfer (EFT)
  - automated teller machines (ATM) [10 marks]
- controls and legislation aimed at combating fraud. [5 marks]

12 The management of FastLane Tyres Limited have sent out requests for tenders for a new computerised stock control system. Two companies have tendered:

- *Company A:* to supply a centralised system and to develop stock control software that will be tailor-made specifically for FastLane
- *Company B:* to supply a network of computers providing a distributed system and using an off-the-shelf stock control software package.

Required

Write a report comparing these two systems. [15 marks]

13 The development of computerised information systems does not always prove to be successful.

a) Briefly explain why projects to develop computerised systems need careful planning and control. [4 marks]

b) A project manager has split a software development project into four tasks, then identified the order they must be carried out in, estimated their durations and the number of programmers needed for each one. There are a maximum of eight programmers available. The information is shown in the table below:

Task	*Duration*	*Preceding tasks*	*Programmers*
A	5 weeks	–	4
B	3 weeks	–	3
C	4 weeks	A	0
D	8 weeks	B	6

Apply the following project management tools to this example, and briefly describe the purpose, features and use of the tools:

- network charts and critical path analysis (CPA)
- Gantt charts
- resource allocation charts. [11 marks]

14 The development and use of information systems should be accompanied by facilities to assist the specialist systems developer and the end-user.

a) Documentation associated with information systems can be categorised as *systems* documentation and *user* documentation. Briefly explain this categorisation and, with the aid of examples, describe the features and purposes of:

- four key items of systems documentation
- two key items of user documentation. [8 marks]

b) Describe the features and benefits of:

- on-line help facilities
- software support help-lines
- user groups. [7 marks]

15 A specialist book retailing company is having a new computerised information system developed. The company's management committee have been asked to meet the system's developers to discuss 'the human-computer interface'. You have been asked to brief the managers for this meeting.

Required

a) Explain what is meant by the 'human-computer interface' (also known as the 'user interface') and briefly describe the kinds of human-computer interface found on office-based computer systems in terms of the equipment and styles of interaction used. [6 marks]

b) Discuss the main factors which systems designers should consider in the design of the human-computer interface and suggest suitable forms of human-computer interfaces for each of these activities:

- invoicing and processing sales, purchase and nominal ledger data
- sorting and searching data in a database
- logging the movements of books in and out of the warehouse. [9 marks]

16

A small retail business is changing over from a manual information system to a new computerised system. The system will process accounting, payroll, personnel and customer enquiry information and will operate on a local area network (LAN) of personal computers.

Required

Prepare a two-part memorandum for the managing director which briefly explains:

a) the legal issues and legislation relating to the new computerised system [8 marks]

b) how access to the new system can be controlled. [7 marks]

17

Many organisations use computerised systems to handle routine transactions such as sales and purchases.

Required

a) Explain how activities within an organisation, including decision making, can be considered to form three levels and describe how the information, such as sales and purchase data, handled by computerised transaction processing systems can assist the activities at all levels within the organisation. [5 marks]

b) Outline the main areas which should be included in a feasibility study report on the conversion of a manual transaction processing system to a computerised one. [10 marks]

18

Two alternative forms of organisation structure are:

- functional structure
- matrix structure.

Required

a) Outline the main objectives of an information system and discuss the effect that each of these organisation structures can have upon its information system. [7 marks]

b) Describe the trend towards 'end-user' computing and how it affects and is affected by organisational structures. [8 marks]

19

An organisation has agreed a proposal for a project to develop a new computerised accounts system. The system will use a multi-user computer running software which will have to be customised to meet the organisation's requirements.

Required

a) Outline the primary objectives of project management and explain the key factors and elements which must be managed in order to achieve these objectives for this project. [5 marks]

b) The project has been broken down into its main activities. Their estimated duration (in days) and the order in which they should be carried out are shown in the following table:

Activity	Estimated duration	Preceding activities
A	5	–
B	4	A
C	6	A
D	15	A
E	12	B
F	8	B, C
G	5	D
H	7	F, G
I	2	H, E
J	20	I

Use the techniques of critical path analysis (CPA) to:

- construct a network chart for these tasks
- indicate the critical path through the network
- calculate the total duration of the project
- calculate the amount of float associated with each activity. [10 marks]

20 An organisation which occupies a suite of offices in one building has two separate computerised systems:

System A: the legal department has a personal computer that is used as a reference library of case law and legislation which has been purchased on CD-ROM (Compact Disc Read-Only Memory).

System B: a central multi-user system is used by all staff for word processing and by the accounts department to carry out accountancy functions.

Required

a) Briefly discuss and compare Systems A and B with respect to the possible threats to the integrity of the systems and their data. [5 marks]

b) Outline suitable procedures for safeguarding the integrity of these systems and their data. [10 marks]

21 UC Clothing Limited is a company which designs and manufactures a small but expensive range of clothes. The clothes are of a traditional design and UC have established a good reputation for high quality. However, in an increasingly competitive market, UC's profits have fallen. The marketing director has been instructed to take a radical look at the situation and guide the board of directors towards a scheme for improving profits.

Required

a) Outline the general stages of the decision making process and relate this to the marketing director's task at UC Clothing. [6 marks]

b) Discuss the ways that computerised information systems could be used to assist UC Clothing in the decision making process. [9 marks]

22 UC Clothing Limited have decided to set up a subsidiary company, called UC Designwear, to design and manufacture a range of fashion clothing aimed at the mass market. The clothes will be sold in large quantities to city-centre shops and mail-order retailers.

Required

a) Use the terminology of general systems theory to describe UC Designwear as a system with suitable subsystems, including a 'design' subsystem and 'manufacturing' subsystem. [7 marks]

b) Explain what is meant by open and closed systems, using the design and manufacturing subsystems of UC Designwear as examples. [4 marks]

c) Describe the role of feedback in the control systems which would be suitable within UC Designwear. [4 marks]

23 Department X is a government department which has decided to acquire new software to run on its existing mainframe computer. Currently the department employs permanent information systems specialists to maintain its existing hardware and software. The new system is required to provide a comprehensive information system for use by all levels of staff within the department. The information systems manager has suggested that there are three options for acquiring the software:

- develop customised software in-house
- contract a specialist software house to develop the software
- purchase an off-the-shelf software package.

Required

a) Discuss and compare these three options. [9 marks]

b) Describe the activities of computer bureaux and facilities management companies and discuss their usefulness to Department X. [6 marks]

24 The chief accountant of a large retailer has looked at the outline feasibility study for a new computerised information system and has expressed concern about the costs suggested under the headings 'Prepare the systems and user documentation' and 'Systems maintenance'.

You are the representative of the accounting department on the steering committee and have been asked to respond to the following items:

Required

a) Describe the two sorts of documentation mentioned in the feasibility study report and explain their purposes. [6 marks]

b) i) What sorts of systems maintenance are there and why are they needed? [5 marks]

ii) How should systems maintenance be planned and controlled? [4 marks]

25 Reports have suggested that by the year 2000 a large percentage of the working population will be working from home and not travelling to their employer's place of work. This will be achieved by using computers and communications systems and is known as telecommuting.

Required

a) Describe the systems and technology needed to enable workers to telecommute. [6 marks]

b) Discuss which sorts of jobs would be best suited to telecommuting. [3 marks]

c) Discuss the benefits and problems associated with telecommuting from both the employer's and the employee's points of view. [6 marks]

26 MultiShop Limited is a well-established supermarket chain. Several years ago, MultiShop purchased a mainframe computer and established an information systems department (ISD) with its own specialist staff organised hierarchically. The ISD is totally responsible for information systems within MultiShop. The chief accountant has recently reviewed the costs and functions of MultiShop's departments and is concerned about the high proportion of costs attributed to the ISD. The chief accountant is interested in the possible benefits of adopting a policy of end-user computing.

Required

a) Describe the traditional organisation structure of a large information systems department. [5 marks]

b) Explain what is meant by end-user computing and outline the main reasons why is has become a major trend. [6 marks]

c) Outline the main personnel problems which could be expected if a policy of end-user computing is adopted. [4 marks]

27 SureBond Insurance is a large insurance company which is completely reorganising its information systems to make maximum use of the latest information technology. Part of this reorganisation will involve the development of a major software application. All levels of staff within the organisation will be affected.

Required

Prepare a report for the personnel manager which:

a) describes the stages that are usually involved in developing software and an outline of the activities at each stage. [5 marks]

b) discusses the human resource management factors involved in systems development and the introduction of new technology. [5 marks]

c) explains the benefits of user participation in systems development. [5 marks]

28 The Select Components Company Limited stocks a wide range of small electrical components. The management of Select consider that its warehouse operation has become extremely inefficient with high levels of stock-outs, incorrect deliveries and obsolete components. Computerisation of the warehouse administration system, with links to sales and purchasing operations, is seen as the only solution. You have been called in to advise on the design of a suitable human-computer interface (HCI) for the warehouse system.

Required

a) Outline the principles which should be applied to achieve an effective and efficient HCI. [7 marks]

b) Suggest suitable HCI for the warehouse. [4 marks]

c) Explain how recent developments in the use of electronic data interchange (EDI) could be usefully applied by Select Components. [4 marks]

29 a) Explain what is meant by centralised and distributed systems in the context of computerised systems and current trends. [7 marks]

b) Flexibility, compatibility, security and control are all important aspects of computerised information systems. Discuss these aspects in relation to centralised and distributed systems. [8 marks]

30 Briefly discuss the following assertions:

a) If they are to remain competitive, all organisations must take advantage of smaller, cheaper and more powerful computers. [5 marks]

b) The information systems specialist is on the verge of becoming extinct. [5 marks]

c) Electronic communications systems will soon eliminate the need for paper communications in business. [5 marks]

31 Organisations are becoming increasingly aware of the importance and value of information. Three general approaches to data management are:

- separate application-specific systems
- integrated systems
- a comprehensive database system.

a) Describe and compare these three approaches to data management. [7 marks]

b) Describe the sorts of database operations users require and outline the features of a database management system (DBMS). [8 marks]

32 A large multinational insurance company makes extensive use of computerised information systems and is concerned about incidents which have been reported in the press and have generated bad publicity for the insurance sector.

Required

a) Outline the basic principles of risk analysis in relation to information held on computerised systems, giving examples of typical threats. [9 marks]

b) The following incidents have been reported from other organisations:

i) Suspected unauthorised access to confidential client information by a computer programmer on a short-term contract. [2 marks]

ii) Hardware failure of a mini-computer at a rival company's head office which caused severe disruption to that company's payments procedures. [2 marks]

iii) Prosecution of an insurance company for making incorrect payments over several years due to an error in program design. [2 marks]

Suggest counter-measures that the insurance company could use to protect its system against such incidents.

Answers to Section 9 begin on page 66

SECTION

10

MOCK EXAMINATION 1

The mock examinations in this section and in Section 11 have been written by the author to give you a chance to test your understanding of much of the course material. They also provide an opportunity to attempt a full paper under exam conditions, that is, without referring to your notes, and limiting yourself to the time allowed for the exam itself. You will find advice on how you should have answered each question for this mock exam in Section 13. Remember, it is not an indication of likely topics.

Time allowed: three hours
The paper is divided into two sections.
Questions to be answered as follows:
Section A: Case study. This is compulsory and ALL the questions MUST be attempted.
Section B: There are five questions in this section, of which THREE must be attempted.

Section A – Case Study

Read the information about Better Blocks Limited and then answer *all* the questions in this section.

Better Blocks Limited

Better Blocks Limited produces and sells building materials such as bricks, blocks and cement. The company was established in the north of England in the 1960s by George Carlton. George was a bricklayer by trade who had inherited enough money to buy a local quarry and brick works which he called Better Blocks. He had identified various small quarries in the locality which were are all independently owned and either competing for the same business or selling different products to the same customers. Over the next ten years, George's company systematically bought these quarries and effectively monopolised the local market. George Carlton believed that central control and administration was the most efficient and cost-effective way of running this sort of business that operated several sites. Under George's control in the 1970s, Better Blocks continued to expand by taking over more quarries and in the 1980s, George decided to take the opportunity to broaden Better Blocks' activities by buying out small independent builders' merchants.

In 1994, the company now owns 14 quarries with associated processing plants, and 27 builders' merchants. The builders' merchants all retail to the public and use manual sales systems. They all hold high stock levels, which is considered necessary because all purchase orders have to be processed by central office before being sent to the suppliers. There is no central warehouse or stores; each builders' merchant keeps its own stock. In addition, there are six local sales offices, each run by an area sales manager and staffed by a total of 18 sales representatives who try to sell Better Blocks products to construction companies. Better Blocks' growth was mainly due to George Carlton's direction and he insisted that as many of the business activities as possible were carried out from the company's central building in Leeds; this led to the establishment of centralised services such typing, administration and information systems.

From the early 1990s Better Blocks profits started to fall. George Carlton, now in his late 60s, has expressed the view that the company could no longer continue the policy of buying out smaller businesses, as suitable businesses were now almost all owned by larger organisations such as Better Blocks and its competitors. Imported materials were also taking a larger share of the market. George advocated a period of consolidation. A customer survey at Better Blocks builders' merchants showed that the public viewed them as having a limited range of goods and slow service.

Janet Carlton, George's daughter, had studied economics and computer science at university and had worked her way up the Information Systems Department at Better Blocks. In 1983, in preparation for increased retailing activity, Better Blocks had purchased a mainframe computer to help process all payroll and accounting information. This was upgraded in 1989 to cope with increased activity. Janet Carlton was appointed Information Systems Director in 1991. Most processes carried out on the mainframe, such as processing delivery notes and issuing invoices, are operated as batch processes. All computerised data processing is carried out within the Information Systems Department so all the original data such as sales orders, purchase orders, delivery notes and reports from the builders' merchants are sent by post or delivered by hand on paper for input by the data entry staff. None of the builders' merchants, quarries or local sales offices have electronic communication facilities.

Bill Keane has recently joined Better Blocks as Financial Director. Bill has carried out an investigation and discovered that when deliveries are made to building sites, the delivery notes have to be sent to head office in Leeds to be entered onto the mainframe by the data preparation staff. As a consequence, invoicing is very slow; the company has a poor record for collection of payments and an excessive level of bad debtors. The company's 18 sales representatives travel to Leeds to attend a weekly sales meeting. At one meeting Bill told them that they would have to tighten up on credit customers but the sales representatives complain that this is not possible unless they have up-to-date information about customers' credit position.

Bill Keane is also concerned about the high cost of salaries paid to the information systems specialists in the Information Systems Department. Looking at the activities of the department's staff, he is puzzled by the amount of time that is allocated either to adapting the mainframe software or visiting local sales offices to sort out individual problems. In line with George Carlton's views on centralised services and control, Better Blocks have a policy that managers' requests for information technology should be coordinated by the Information Systems Department, and all tasks requiring computer services should be handled by them too. On visiting each of the six local sales offices, Bill Keane is puzzled by the amount of computer equipment they have and discovers that managers have been purchasing personal computers and printers but disguising the nature of the equipment under the heading 'Office equipment' on requisition forms.

Bill Keane arranges a meeting with Janet Carlton to discuss the situation. On hearing Bill's concerns, Janet says that she is aware of some of the difficulties but is surprised at the scale of the problems. Janet has tried to influence George Carlton to change the policy on centralised control and operation of the information systems but George is not inclined to support anything which involves additional direct costs or disruption to current operations. Bill and Janet agree to try to get some ideas together for a radical review of Better Blocks information systems, and to put forward their suggestions to the board of directors as a matter of urgency.

Janet is particularly interested in the decentralisation of some aspects of the information systems, such as data entry of delivery notes and also in introducing a policy of end-user computing into Better Blocks' local sales offices. Bill wants to consider how to introduce information technology into the builders' merchants.

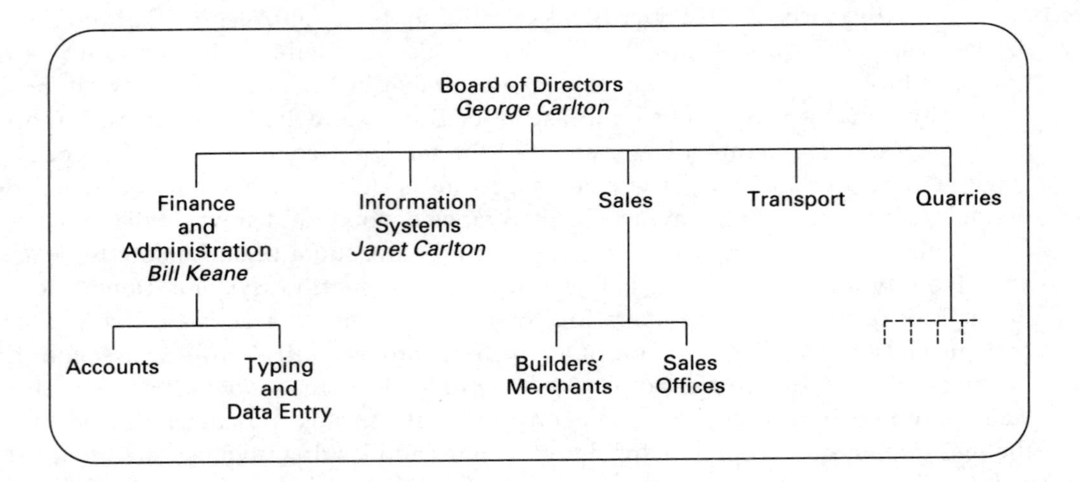

Figure. 10.1 Better Blocks Limited – organisation structure

Required

1 Explain what is meant by end-user computing and why there is a trend towards end-user computing. Discuss the advantages and disadvantages if Better Blocks adopt end-user computing in their local sales offices. [10 marks]

2 Discuss the benefits and disadvantages of decentralisation of some of Better Blocks' activites, such as the data entry of delivery notes, compared with George Carlton's preferred policy of centralisation. [10 marks]

3 Discuss the present organisation structure at Better Blocks and how it could be adapted to facilitate decentralisation and end-user computing. [10 marks]

4 Outline how information technology could be used to improve the efficiency of Better Blocks' builders' merchants. [15 marks]

5 Discuss the need to involve the users of Better Blocks' information systems in the development of new systems and how that involvement could be achieved. [10 marks]

[Total 55 marks]

Section B

Answer any THREE questions from this section.

6 Using the terms and concepts of general systems theory:

a) Explain, with the use of examples, how you would determine whether a system is open, closed or somewhere between these two extremes. [5 marks]

b) Discuss the benefits and problems associated with operating an organisation as a collection of functional sub-systems. [5 marks]

c) Outline the reasons why computerisation of accounts and payroll were among the first uses of commercially available computer systems. [5 marks]

7 In the 1960s the NCC produced what has become known as the traditional model of the system development lifecycle (SDLC).

Required

a) Outline the phases of the SDLC and discuss the reasons why this model may not reflect the way that real information systems are developed. [8 marks]

b) Information systems development methodologies can be categorised according to the different aspects that they emphasise. Three such categories are:

- process-driven
- data-driven
- user-driven.

Briefly describe the philosophy behind each of these methodologies and discuss their appropriateness for different situations. [7 marks]

8 a) An accounts clerk has described how customers' accounts are handled in the following way:

> 'When a potential customer first makes an enquiry, we open a customer record but insist on cash with the first order. After the first order we carry out a credit worthiness check and, depending on the outcome, open a credit account or it remains cash-with-order. After a long period of inactivity the record will be deleted'.

Draw an ELH of the 'customer' entity and describe the symbols used. [8 marks]

b) Explain the use of CASE tools and the benefits of an integrated set of CASE tools. [7 marks]

9 A large proportion of the organisations that experience a major physical disaster to their information systems either fail to recover from the disaster or suffer long-term harm. A bank has a central mainframe which handles all its major information processing and is reviewing its procedures for physical disaster prevention and recovery.

Required

a) Discuss the factors that should be covered in a review of the current system. [10 marks]

b) From the point of view of disaster recovery, briefly compare the current centralised system with other ways of handling the bank's information requirements. [5 marks]

10 You have been asked by a small but expanding sales organisation to carry out a cost-benefit analysis on a a proposal for a new computerised information system. The proposal suggests using a local area network (LAN) of personal computers with a central file-server.

Required

a) Outline the ways in which you could categorise the costs and benefits, giving examples of the likely items in these categories and the difficulties you may encounter when trying to quantify them. [9 marks]

b) Briefly describe and compare techniques which could be used in the economic evaluation of the proposed system. [6 marks]

Answers to Section 10 begin on page 141

SECTION

11

MOCK EXAMINATION 2

Here is a second mock exam. To gain the most benefit from it, you should attempt it under examination conditions. When you have finished, turn to Section 14 which contains advice on how you should have approached each question.

Time allowed: three hours
The paper is divided into two sections.
Questions to be answered as follows:
Section A: Case study. This is compulsory and ALL the questions MUST be attempted.

Section B: There are five questions in this section, of which THREE must be attempted.

Section A – Case Study

Read the information about Johnsons Specialist Books and then answer *all* the questions in this section.

Johnsons Specialist Books Ltd

Johnsons Specialist Books Ltd have a large bookshop with offices and warehouse in a university city. Johnsons have gained a good reputation for locating old and obscure publications and some of their clients pay Johnsons to research into the life history of particular titles and for other research services. The business was established in the early 1900s by George Johnson and has been owned and run by members of the Johnson family ever since. The business is organised in three sections:

- Shop and warehouse employing 7 warehouse staff and 12 shop assistants.
- Accounts and Administration employing five accounts clerks and ten typists/ administrators.
- Research employing 15 researchers whose work includes travel to book shops, libraries, etc.

In addition, each of these three sections has a manager and a deputy manager. The three managers and the Managing Director form the board of directors.

In 1993, James Johnson stated that he would be retiring from his position as Managing Director at the end of the year and he recommended to the board that he be replaced by his niece, Mary Johnson, who was at that time the Research Director. For several years Mary has been encouraging the other directors to carry out a review of Johnsons' use of information technology. Currently there are a few stand-alone personal computers in use at Johnsons for tasks like accounts, word-processing and for accessing booklists and catalogues stored on CD-ROM.

Soon after her appointment as Managing Director, Mary Johnson contracted a computer consultant to lead a feasibility study on options for a comprehensive computerisation of Johnsons' information systems. The feasibility study report identifies three options. The following system (Option A) is chosen on the basis of lowest costs, and the report includes an outline of the quantified costs and benefits:

The new system – Option A

A centralised multi-user system is based upon a small, powerful mini-computer that has recently come onto the market. Johnsons' researchers will have portable computers and when out of the office they will be able to communicate with the mini-computer via the telephone system. The supplier of the system is keen to get it established in the market and has offered to make small modifications to its standard software to suit Johnsons' requirements.

Initial cost in year 1: £93,000

On-going maintenance and other costs in year 2 onwards: £37,000 per annum

Benefits: Year 1 £23,000
Year 2 £89,000
Year 3 £64,000
Year 4 £52,000
Year 5 £42,000.

Note: All figures are based on present-day prices, although costs and benefits are considered as occurring at the year end.

The option recommends the appointment of a computer systems manager who will be responsible for the implementation and ongoing administration of the system. Alan Baker is appointed to the post and one of his initial tasks is to act as project manager responsible for the new system.

During the feasibility study the major activities involved in the project have been identified and listed in a table with their estimated durations and the order of tasks. The information is shown in this table:

Activity		*Duration (days)*	*Preceding activities*
A	Draw up detailed specifications	15	Start of project
B	Modify software	10	A
C	Wiring and cabling offices	4	A
D	Install new office furniture	3	C
E	Install and test hardware	5	D
F	Install and test software	4	B, E
G	Training	5	F
H	Data conversion	3	F
I	Changeover using parallel running	20	G, H
J	Acceptance testing	2	I

Alan Baker was not able to start his employment as soon as the board of directors at Johnsons would have liked. Alan is naturally very keen to make a good impression by getting the project completed smoothly and quickly. However, he is particularly concerned that activity B (modify software) is not directly under his control since it will be carried out by the system's suppliers. He is also concerned that there may not be sufficient slack time to cope with any problems that may arise.

Alan has noticed that the feasibility study has not considered any legislation relating to data protection or the need to register computerised processing of information. When asked about the existing arrangements, the administration section have replied that, as far as they know, the current payroll and accounts system is exempt.

Alan is considering how vulnerable the new system and its communications facility might be to access and use for unauthorised purposes or by unauthorised users. He has noticed that one of the benefits claimed for the new system is that it will reduce staff costs, since some of Johnsons' junior researchers and administration clerks will eventually be made redundant; the system will carry out the tasks that they currently do. Alan is considering whether this may raise security issues.

Required

1 Use investment appraisal techniques to assess the economic feasibility of the new system over five years – use the figures from the feasibility study report, given that Johnsons' cost of capital is 12%. Comment on the appropriateness of the various techniques available and of using a five-year time scale when dealing with information technology-based systems. [15 marks]

2 Draw a network chart of the project's activities as listed in the feasibility study report and identify the critical path. Comment on Alan Baker's concerns about completing the project smoothly and on time. [15 marks]

3 Briefly explain the purpose of data protection legislation, such as the UK Data Protection Act 1984, and outline its contents. In relation to Johnsons' likely uses of data and information, give examples of one use which would be exempt under the legislation and one that would require registration. [10 marks]

4 Describe the risks of unauthorised access to the new system and discuss the measures that can be taken to combat them. [15 marks]

[Total 55 marks]

Section B

Answer any THREE questions from this section.

5 A town council is concerned about the amount of paperwork that its administrative staff have to handle and the difficulty of maintaining an efficient paper record-keeping system. The council have decided to computerise their administration.

Required

a) Describe and compare the fact-finding techniques that a systems analyst could use to gather information about the council's information requirements. [7 marks]

b) As an analyst recently recruited by the council, you have been asked to prepare a **statement of the requirements** of an information system for the council's payroll section. The section prepares monthly salary cheques and bank standing orders and also handles *ad hoc* enquiries from council staff. What would your statement of requirements contain? [8 marks]

6 A small business is transferring from a manual to a computerised accounting, stock control and customer records system. Write a report to:

a) Describe the main methods of changing over to the new information system and discuss the benefits and problems associated with these methods and how to decide which to use. [9 marks]

b) Discuss the issues involved in transferring the data to the computerised system. [6 marks]

7 The chief executive of an organisation is concerned about the poor quality of financial information within the organisation and the way that it is communicated. In order to be suitable for its purpose, information should have certain characteristics or qualities. In practice, providing all the suitable characteristics is not possible and compromises have to be made.

Required

a) i) List six of the qualities which make accounting information suitable for its purpose and, for each one, give an accountancy example where that quality is particularly relevant to the information's usefulness. [6 marks]

ii) Describe two examples of situations where compromises have to be made between some of these characteristics when providing information for accountancy purposes. [4 marks]

b) Compare the use, benefits and disadvantages of informal and formal information systems in terms of the characteristics of the information they provide. [5 marks]

8 The chief accountant of an organisation has been studying a proposal for the development of a new computerised accountancy and stock-control system and has expressed surprise at the high level of ongoing costs and resources allocated to the system once it has been installed. You have been asked to discuss the activities relating to the 'Maintenance Phase' section of the proposal.

Required

a) Outline the traditional model of the systems development lifecycle and explain the importance of the maintenance phase of the model [7 marks]

b) Categorise the sorts of maintenance which are likely to be required and give examples of events that would trigger systems maintenance activities on a computerised accountancy and stock-control system. [8 marks]

9 You have been appointed as head of a newly created internal audit section within the computer department of a large wholesaler. The department has a number of operational systems, some online and some batch processing, and a central corporate database. Your first task is to review the various types of controls which exist within the department and its computer systems.

Required

a) With the use of examples, outline the areas your review should cover. [8 marks]

b) What computer-assisted audit techniques are available and where might you use them? [7 marks]

Answers to Section 11 begin on page 157

SECTION

12 ANSWERS TO EXAM STYLE QUESTIONS

Once you have attempted the questions in Section 9, you should read the advice given below on what the examiner will be looking for in a good answer. The indicative content for each answer is given in detail together with suggestions as to how the information should be presented.

Section A – Case studies

Case 1: Elite Gifts Direct Limited

1 In general there are five fact-finding methods which Tony Thorp could use to investigate the current performance and future requirements of Elite's computer systems:

Reviewing documents

Tony should review Elite's existing documents to familiarise himself with the current practice. These documents will probably fall into two categories:

- policy statements and procedure manuals
- forms and reports.

This can be done without having to refer to other staff. Tony should be aware, however, that these documents may not have been kept up to date, so actual working practices may not match with procedure statements, and not all parts of forms may now be used.

Tony should probably do this first as it will provide a good foundation for further investigation.

Interviews

Interviews are a useful way of getting in-depth information though the use of open questions. They can also allow the respondents to talk about their opinions and feelings in a way that the other methods may not. Interviews can be very time-consuming to carry out and the information gathered is often of a qualitative nature which may be difficult to analyse. It may be possible for Tony to hold group interviews, by talking to several people from a department at once, for example. There are nearly 60 staff, so even with group interviews it will not be practical to speak to everyone; Tony should therefore identify and interview the key people – all the departmental managers and then another representative from each major functional area would give good coverage of the different levels and functions within Elite.

It would probably be sensible for Tony to carry out most of the interviews before using any other methods, so that the main areas of interest and concern can be identified; this will help when formulating questionnaires. Follow-up interviews can be held later in the investigation to help to clarify or expand upon items if necessary.

Questionnaires

Questionnaires are useful in collecting information from large groups of people – it would be practical to give all Elite's staff a questionnaire to complete and fairly easy to gather all the forms back in. The low return of questionnaires can be a major difficulty in some surveys.

Care must be taken to ensure that the questions are clear and unambiguous and that major areas of relevance are not omitted. The use of closed questions, which are posed in a way which limits the number of responses available, can help to make the analysis of data much easier but the questionnaire must be properly designed to facilitate valid responses and suitable results for analysis. The questionnaire can be drafted and trialled once some of the interviews have been held, since by then the main issues should have started to emerge.

Observations

Tony may feel that the three methods described may not provide information that actually reflects the staff's true feelings or actual working practices. Interviewees' responses may be influenced by their feelings, one way or another, for the interviewer or the topic.

Having gathered some information, Tony could observe staff at work to confirm that information, or gather further information about things like the length of time taken to carry out a process, such as completing timesheets or producing an invoice. However, it is difficult for Tony to remain unobtrusive and his very presence may alter people's behaviour away from routine practices and procedures.

Prototyping

Prototyping is becoming much easier to carry out early in the development of a system because of the availability of software tools such as fourth-generation languages and screen generators. These tools would allow Tony to produce prototypes, or working models, of parts of the system such as input screens and output report layouts, whose suitability can be discussed with the staff who will be the system's users.

Tony could follow a plan for the investigation along these lines:

- Collect relevant documents and read them
- Select appropriate people for interviews
- Carry out the interviews and start to draft a questionnaire
- Complete the first round of interviews and test the questionnaire
- Distribute the questionnaire
- Gather in completed questionnaires
- Carry out an initial analysis of information gathered so far
- Decide whether there are areas where observations could be useful or further interviews are required
- Decide whether the preparation of prototypes is justified at this stage
- Carry out interviews, observations or construction of prototypes as required
- Collate information and analyse in depth.

Tony is interested in future requirements so it is important that the staff realise that they should consider potential benefits and do not have their ideas stifled by limitations in the existing system. It is also important that they are realistic when making estimates, for example, of future levels of business and transactions.

Tony should be careful not to arouse the staff's suspicions or anxieties about possible changes while he carries out the investigation. He can try to let staff know the purpose of the investigation and emphasise the positive aspects of potential changes. The success of the investigation, and possibly its subsequent development, depends heavily on how the staff perceive Tony and his role – the commitment and motivation of the users is critical to the effective and efficient development and use of a system that suits users' requirements.

Although it may be more difficult to gather, information from customers and other organisations could be useful. Questionnaires and possibly a small number of interviews would seem to be appropriate for people outside Elite's organisation.

2 A useful categorisation of information and activities, including decision making, within an organisation is into three levels with basic transaction data entering the organisation as a further sub-level:

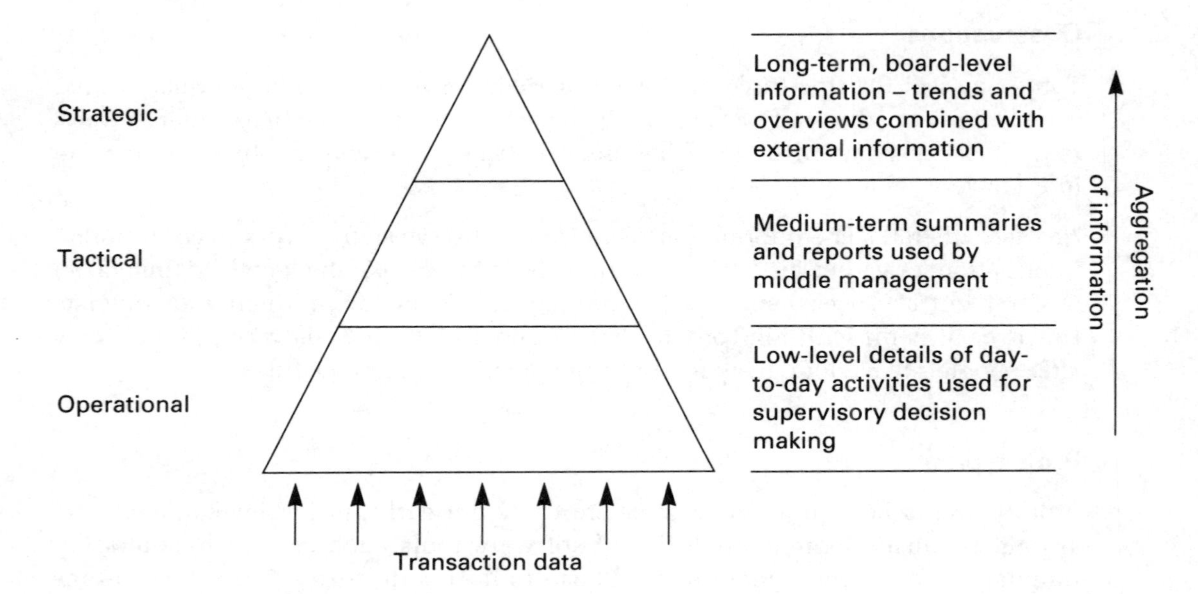

Figure 12.1 Levels of information

The low-level transaction data forms the basis for **operational-level** activities. For example, when a customer places an order, the routine, operational-level procedures will be carried out to collect basic information about the customer's name and address, etc. and the item the customer wishes to purchase.

At the **tactical level** the Sales Manager, Sam Winter, does not need to know all the details of every sale that each of the 18 sales order clerks processes. Sam has to monitor the Sales Department performance and is more interested in weekly or monthly summaries showing things like total sales in the period and sales per product in the period. So the operational-level information from all the sales clerks' activities is aggregated and summarised to provide higher-level information. Sam can then compare actual performance with planned performance and targets and, if necessary, take action to improve actual performance or revise targets.

At board level, the directors are more interested in **strategic-level** information in order to gauge the overall performance of Elite Gifts. To do this the board need summary information from all the departments so that total income and costs can be processed to show net profit and other overall performance measures. Their concern will be concentrated on longer-term growth and may be looking for summarised quarterly or annual figures from all departments. So, the information which entered Elite as detailed low-level transaction data will be further summarised and aggregated from all departments to enable strategic-level activity such as planning for new premises or new markets. The board will also want to compare Elite's performance with its competitors in the context of the economic environment and will be looking for trends to help predict long-term performance.

Many organisations now use computerised information systems to process data at the operational level – in fact, accounting and payroll systems were the first to be computerised because the processes involved consist primarily of multiple numerical calculations which are capable of being exactly specified and then automated. However, organisations are realising that these **transaction processing systems** which were designed for narrow functions, such as Elite's existing sales and accounts system, are often not flexible enough to cope with additional or changing information requirements.

Elite would benefit from a **management information system (MIS)** which could process the basic transaction data in ways that will provide tactical information suitable for middle management in all departments. For example, Stella Smith, Elite's Marketing Manager, would probably like the transaction processing system to store information about how customers decide to buy Elite's products and to be able to manipulate that information in ways that would not be of direct concern to the Accounts Department. Provided it was properly designed, a MIS would produce routine reports and summaries to assist all the departments.

At the strategic level of Elite, the MIS would be useful in providing internal information about current performance. However, at this level an **executive information system (EIS)** would be useful, since it would allow top-level management to readily view information about overall performance. Provided it was fed with the appropriate external information, the EIS would show the internal information alongside external information about competitors and the economic environment. It would enable the board to make forecasts about things like Elite's market share and view the predicted results.

3 The likely costs of Tony Thorp's ideas can be categorised as follows:

- *Development costs*, such as:
  - staff time spent on investigations
  - time spent on hardware specification and tendering
  - information systems specialists' time, which will cost substantial amounts if software is to be modified and tested.

These costs can be difficult to quantify in advance, except if an external organisation is used which provides a fixed-price contract for items such as software development. Tony could estimate the number of man-hours required and simply calculate the costs at an hourly rate appropriate to the staff involved.

- *Implementation costs*, such as:
  - purchase of hardware and equipment, such as personal computers, printers and network equipment. These can be quantified by consulting several suppliers.
  - purchase of software packages. Whether purchased off-the-shelf or specially developed, a licence has to be purchased to use most commercial software. The cost of off-the-shelf software is available from suppliers but pricing specially developed or modified software requires a process of negotiation between Elite and the supplier.

- installation and testing of the equipment and software. The personal computers and local area network (LAN) will have to installed, software configured and tested. The cost of physical installation and basic configuration can be fairly easily estimated but the cost of solving problems which show up in testing is more variable.
- changeover costs, which may involve conversion of data files and a period of parallel running. Staff time to convert the data can be estimated and costed, as can the costs of running old and new systems for a fixed period of time. However, problems experienced during the changeover are difficult to predict, so the cost of solving them is difficult to price.
- training costs, which can be estimated by analysing the staff's skills and allocating time for training, plus the cost of any external training courses which may be needed.
- redundancy costs, if staff levels can be reduced. These can be quantified provided the particular staff are known in advance.

▶ *Running costs*, such as:
- maintenance of hardware and software, which can be on a fixed cost if provided by external suppliers but is more difficult to estimate if carried out by Elite's staff.
- additional staff costs, if salaries rise due to the staff's increased skills – which will depend on Elite's attitude to the staff and the likelihood of losing staff to competitors.
- stationery and consumables, such as paper and storage media.
- insurance, security and backup facilities; the costs can be quantified by consulting suppliers if Elite use external organisations.

The benefits of a new system are usually more difficult to estimate than the costs. They can be regarded as either direct or indirect, depending on whether they have an immediate or a longer-term effect on cash flow:

▶ *Direct benefits*
- increased productivity due to the additional processing power provided by the personal computers. Tony Thorp will have to try to analyse people's work and estimate the benefit of reducing the time to carry out operations. The loading on the mini-computer system should be reduced leading to higher throughput for sales and accounts transactions. Elite will have to decide whether to capitalise on this immediately by reducing staffing levels, or allow for increased business activity to utilise the spare capacity.
- reduced staff costs, which can be estimated if there are plans to reduce staffing levels.
- reduced costs of software maintenance if updated systems are used.

▶ *Indirect benefits*, which include things like:
- better information leading to improved decision making. For example, if Stella Smith has access to information about the success of various advertising campaigns, this could lead to reduced advertising costs and/or increased sales by more effective advertising.
- greater control over operational processes which should give Elite the benefit of things like:
  - reduced errors
  - reduced stock control costs
  - better credit control.

These can be quantified if Elite can estimate what these items cost now and how much the new system will change them. For example, an error can be reckoned to have a quantifiable cost based on time spent to correct it, spoilt goods, lost business, etc. If the current error rate is reduced by, say, 50%, then the benefit can be calculated. Similar calculations can be performed for reduced stock costs and improved credit control.

- better service to customers and improved customer relations. This may be quantified by estimating the percentage increase in sales that the new system will bring.

In addition, there are *intangible items* such as:

- opportunity costs, which arise because the money and effort invested in this system are not available to be used elsewhere
- the effect on staff, who may be invigorated and enthusiastic about the new system or suffer from discontent and lower morale.

4 Tony Thorp should look carefully at the advantages and disadvantages of purchasing off-the-shelf software compared with continuing to modify and maintain the existing tailor-made software. The factors to take into account are:

- *Current requirements*
  The current system has been in use for two years and should now suit Elite's basic transaction processing requirements. However, there are areas where useful additional facilities have been identified and Tony is doubtful about the ease with which changes could be made. An off-the-shelf package is unlikely to ideally suit all Elite's requirements, although it may already have some of the additional features which Elite would find useful.

- *Maintenance and future requirements*
  The information systems staff have worked on the system and should know its internal workings, although high staff turnover may reduce the overall knowledge. With an off-the-shelf package Elite would have to relinquish control of the maintenance and upgrading of the software, but may also be able to reduce maintenance costs and the uncertainty which accompanies in-house developments. The sort of service provided by the supplier will depend on the number of packages in use, since a large user base provides an incentive to the suppliers to solve problems and provide upgrades. A reputable supplier will not want to lose its reputation by providing poor service or having its products perceived as outdated.

  A large user base also means that the users mutually benefit from the identification and solution of problems. With the current system, Elite suffer from any problems and have to provide their own solutions.

- *Costs*
  Elite may have an ongoing licence fee to pay to use their existing system. This may be lower than the initial cost of purchasing a licence for a new system. However, Tony should assess the total cost over several years and then may find that a new system is cheaper in the long term when maintenance and other factors are taken into account.

- *Availability*
  An off-the-shelf package will usually be available immediately and will provide users with facilities immediately – while changes to implement those features in an existing system can take a period of time which in some instances is not easy to predict.

- *Risks*
  The risks associated with an off-the-shelf package usually decrease in proportion to the increase in the number of sites using it, because problems should be more quickly identified and there is greater incentive to fix them.

Also, there is a greater incentive to the supplier to maintain a larger user base. Elite have modified their current package and are effectively its only user.

However, Elite do have control of the existing software and modifications can be made by Elite's staff – they are not dependent on the supplier staying in business or continuing to support the system.

- *Training*
  Elite's staff know the current system and only have to learn about the changes that Tony's staff make. A new off-the-shelf package would require staff to be trained to use it, although the supplier may offer training.
- *Competitive advantage*
  Elite may be able to implement features in their own system which are unique and would not be available immediately to their competitors – so Elite could gain competitive advantage from the control they can exert over their existing system.

Conclusions

The current system is not ideal – it requires changes to suit users' requirements and does not seem to be easy to maintain. Costs may not be an overriding factor, since it may be possible to implement features which would be unique to Elite's system and could give them a competitive advantage over their competition. Tony Thorp would need to look carefully at the features of any off-the-shelf software, the reputation of the suppliers and the size of the existing user base. If it does not suit requirements or the supplier does not provide solutions to problems then Elite could be stuck with an unsuitable system which is beyond their control.

5 *Data conversion*

Elite Gifts have a lot of customer data which will have to be converted to a format suitable for a new system. Some of the data can be classified as fixed or static if it is unlikely to change very often; an example is a customer's account number, name and address. Other data, such as a customer's account balance, will be more volatile and likely to change frequently.

The static data can be converted first over an agreed period of time. This will reduce the pressure on people needed to input the data if it can be carried out over a period of time and also allows for thorough verification and validation procedures to maintain the data's integrity. It is important that the existing data is of high integrity prior to the conversion; otherwise, errors and inaccuracies will carry through to the converted data. A useful method to help overcome this problem would be for Elite to organise a mailshot to all customers, before starting the conversion, showing them the data that Elite hold about them and asking then to check their details and notify Elite of any changes.

A problem with the volatile data is that it must be converted quickly at an agreed cut-off date. This can present difficulties of staffing the work and checking the results are accurate, particularly as this stage of the conversion is likely to be carried out under strict time constraints. Additional temporary staff could be used, but this brings its own problems, since temporary staff are unfamiliar with Elite's operations and may lack commitment to the success of the operation; this may lead to the introduction of errors in the converted data. Again, the customers can be given the details from the converted data and asked to check them.

Since much of Elite's data is already in machine-readable form, it may be possible to use a computerised process to automatically convert the bulk of the data leaving a much more manageable amount of data for manual conversion.

The changeover method

Elite experienced problems in 1992 when the initial changeover failed, leaving the staff with neither old nor new systems for two weeks. This indicates that a **direct changeover** was used where the old system is discarded at the same time that the new one comes into live operation. This is the riskiest method, since in the not unlikely event of problems on the new system the old system is not kept up to date (or may even be scrapped) and is not available to fall back on. If all goes to plan, this is the cheapest changeover method – but Tony Thorp should only use it if either the cost or the practicality of running both systems together rules out any other option.

The safest method of changeover is **parallel running**, where both old and new systems are operated live and kept up-to-date for a period of time to allow for checking of the new system and training opportunities. Problems on the new system can be dealt with without depriving Elite of up-to-date information available on the old system. When Elite's staff have sufficient confidence that the new system is operating satisfactorily then the old system can be scrapped. There is the tendency to want to keep the old system running longer than planned just in case of emergencies. Parallel running is an expensive option since both systems must be kept fully operational and inputting of data will be duplicated. It may not be practical to keep both systems running as, for example, there may not be room to physically house both sets of hardware.

There are several variations which combine aspects of both direct changeover and parallel running. It may be possible to use a **phased changeover**, where one function or department uses the new system leaving other departments using the old system. For example, Elite could use the accounting functions of the new system while keeping other aspects of customer records on the old system. Another alternative could be **gradual changeover**, where the data and loading on the new system is built up gradually. In Elite's case it may be possible to handle new customers on the new system while maintaining existing customer records on the old system.

Tony Thorp will need to emphasise that while direct changeover may be potentially the cheapest and simplest method, the other more expensive methods offer more security.

Case 2: International Investment Services Limited (IIS)

1 The term **real-time system** is used to describe a system that has to react rapidly to input as and when it occurs and then generate appropriate output. The actual time scale will vary according to the application; so, for example, a computerised system controlling a chemical process may need to react to temperature and pressure changes within fractions of a second. In IIS's circumstances, an effective system would need to capture information from the financial institutions and process it at least as quickly as its competitors so that IIS's staff have the very latest information to act upon.

Some aspects of decision making in the areas of investment and financial management can be automated so that, for example, the sale or purchase of stocks and shares is automatically triggered by specific circumstances such as a particular rise or fall in the share price or a share index. Substantial and significant changes in the financial markets often happen very quickly and are often exaggerated by these sorts of automated decisions – so it is important that IIS have a system which can react without significant delay in these circumstances.

The main features of a system designed to support IIS's real-time processing needs are:

- suitable communications links. The data from the financial institutions can be transmitted via the telephone system and, since the link will need to be permanently in place during trading hours, they should be high-speed leased lines which are solely used by IIS

- high-specification computer systems with a high-speed processor, or possibly several processors operating in parallel, and fast-access, large-capacity storage in the form of magnetic disks or some of the emerging optical-disk technology
- back-up and security facilities which can be provided by a second system on 'hot standby' or by using a distributed processing system which has sufficient spare capacity to cope if one part of it fails. Uninterruptible and backup power supply equipment should also be used
- multiple access for users, possibly with each user having a high-performance workstation which allows information to be processed quickly and shown clearly using graphical displays.

2

The purpose of an expert system is to provide specialist advice in order to emulate the analytical and choice processes undertaken by human decision makers. In order to do so, it needs to incorporate a knowledge base and choice criteria.

An expert system combines:

- a database of information about a specific topic
- a set of rules for dealing with particular sets of circumstances
- a user interface which allows the user to interrogate the system and receive the resultant output, which will usually be either a recommended course of action or the system actually taking responsibility for making the decision.

The development of expert systems draws upon the research into artificial intelligence (AI) systems which seek to simulate human activity and decision making. The increasing power of modern computer hardware has led to more rapid progress in the field of AI than has been the case in preceding years, but it is only now that AI is being harnessed in commercial applications and then in fairly narrow areas. Typical areas are:

- in the setting up and operation of credit control systems
- legal systems, such as English case law, where vast amounts of data need to be search and analysed before relevant cases can be identified
- financial markets, where Frank Heinman, IIS's Senior Investment Executive, has identified potential applications.

The main features of an expert system to handle data from the financial markets which could be of benefit to ISS are:

- the ability to actually make decisions in some situations, thus allowing IIS to reduce staffing levels or free experienced staff for less routine activities
- speed of reaction, which is improving as the power of hardware increases. Speed of reaction is important to IIS as a delay of only a few seconds can see factors like share prices change radically
- consistent reactions to situations where different humans may vary in their decisions
- the fact that they do not suffer many of the adverse reactions to pressure situations that humans experience.

However, IIS need to be aware of some drawbacks with expert systems:

- The quality of programmed decision making relies on the quality of the information fed to the system and the programming itself. A human may be aware of additional facts which have not been included in the expert system and often these facts are not directly related to the markets – for example, the effects of strife between governments can trigger a chain of events which a computerised system could not be expected to handle.

- Many successful financial decisions are made on the basis of a human's 'gut feeling' which cannot be replicated by an automated procedure.
- IIS may become totally reliant on the system, which means IIS must take great care over security and backup facilities.
- Human supervision of the decision making of an expert system is still needed but, in the long term, the availability of expertise based on years of experience will become scarce.

3 Structured Systems Analysis and Design Methodology (SSADM) is a systems development methodology which concentrates on the early stages of the life cycle of a system's development. Initial versions were developed in the 1970s and it is the preferred methodology for UK government work.

It is highly structured in that there are six main stages, each broken down into steps which are further decomposed into tasks. It requires the use of graphical representations of three aspects of the analysis and design of a system:

- Processes are modelled using data flow diagrams (DFD) which can be broken down into different levels to show more detail; this is called functional decomposition.
- Entity-relationship models (ERM) are used to show the data items that are of most interest in the system and the relationships between them.
- The events which can occur in the system are modelled by entity life histories (ELH).

Each of the stages of SSADM produces products which become the starting point for the next stage. A typical version of SSADM has the following stages:

Stage 1: analysis of current requirements and problems to enable the boundary of the system to be defined, to identify the data that will form the basis of the new system, and to allow users and developers to build up an understanding of the system and of each other's working practices

Stage 2: the requirements specification stage, where the logical requirements of the new system are defined and outlines produced of the business systems which could satisfy that design

Stage 3: production of an outline of hardware and software for a suitable system and consideration of the technical, operational and economic feasibility of various options before recommending one option to continue with

Stage 4: logical data design, concentrating on what is required rather than how it will be achieved

Stage 5: logical process design, expanding on the required processes identified at Stage 2

Stage 6: physical design, where the the outputs of Stages 4 and 5 are combined and a specification of a new computer-based system is produced.

An important aspect of SSADM is the separation of logical and physical design – so that by considering logical design first, the users and developers can establish the requirements without being constrained by preconceived ideas about the physical system.

John Kline, the Information System Director, is aware that users have expressed dissatisfaction with the information systems staff and the systems and support that

12

they provide. A common failing of many systems is that they fail to satisfy users' requirements and this is often caused by a lack of mutual understanding and communication between users and information systems specialists. This can lead to the users feeling that the specialists do not understand their business requirements and are reluctant to demystify the terminology and working practices to make them more accessible to non-specialists. In turn, the information systems specialists feel that users do not understand the complexity of computerised systems, nor do they appreciate the difficulty of modifying systems to suit the users' changing needs. Another factor to take into account is, in systems theory terms, the entropy that can arise because each functional department or sub-system has its own objectives which may conflict with those of other sub-systems and may not be fully aligned to the overall systems high-level goals.

The more traditional or 'hard' systems approach to the development of computerised information systems borrowed from the existing methodologies used for engineering projects. These projects were usually aimed at producing a physical system whose requirements and objectives could be clearly defined and stated. The development would proceed through several sequential stages and progress could be monitored against well defined criteria. Thus, once a basic requirements specification had been obtained, the systems developers could carry on through the stages and present the users with the completed system.

Advocates of 'soft' systems methodologies, such as Checkland's SSM, claim that there are many situations which are fuzzy and ill-structured, particularly human-activity systems, which need a different approach – this is not aimed specifically at information systems development but many computerised information systems are to be used in contexts where the soft systems approach could apply. The soft systems approach concentrates on getting the users fully involved in the development and accepts that different people involved with the system will have different attitudes, requirements and perceptions of the system. It is important to realise that all the people involved with the system, the stakeholders, should be included in a series of iterations to develop a rich picture of the system which can be adapted at each iteration until agreement is reached that the envisaged system is most appropriate to the situation.

John Kline can try to instil greater understanding between the systems developers and the users by involving the users more heavily in the early stages of development and encouraging them to regard the development activities as presenting shared problems which need to approached by users and technical specialists in partnership. Modern development tools are becoming more sophisticated and, in many instances, less technical in nature so the non-specialist can more readily use them and understand how they work. So, it may be possible for users to do most of the development work on small-scale systems with specialists acting as advisors; for larger systems the users can still play a major role, particularly in specifying requirements, producing test plans, etc. The information systems staff at IIS should remember that their department provides a support service for the organisation's primary activities, and that any satisfactory system must take account of the needs, views and attitudes of all staff involved with it.

IIS can continue to use SSADM as their development methodology but adopt some of the attitudes of the soft systems and build up a development team from all the people involved with the system. This may involve users in having training in development techniques and management will need to accept the importance of user involvement and make allowances for the time and effort needed to allow users to contribute effectively.

4

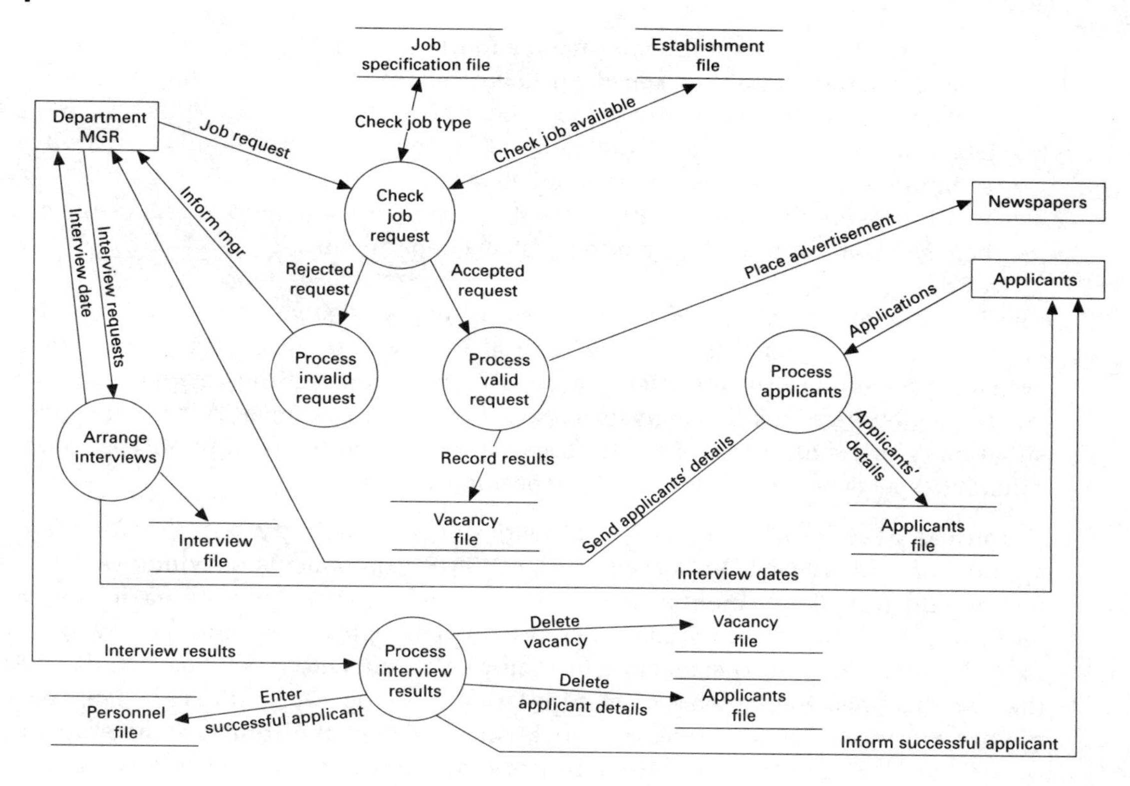

(*Note:* Different systems development methodologies may use different symbols in DFDs, but the principles remain the same.)

Figure 12.2 Data flow diagram (DFD)

5 Prototyping is the process of building a working model of part or all of the envisaged system early in the systems development lifecycle. The model provides a test of design ideas and allows users and developers to see a tangible example of what the end-results could look like. Users and developers can discuss the features of the prototype and the development becomes a dynamic process as they can discuss enhancements and developments from the evidence provided by the prototype. Compared with the completed system, it will be relatively inexpensive to make changes to the prototype, which is gradually refined until users are satisfied that it will meet their requirements.

Using a prototyping approach has other benefits in that it provides an initial focus for the development project, can give users valuable computing experience and encourage teamwork between the users and developers – although analysts and designers may be reluctant to share or relinquish their role as experts.

There are some problems associated with prototyping:

- Project planning and costing can be difficult because of the constant modification and discussion of the prototype.
- Users may get a false impression of the ease and speed with which the final system can be produced.
- Inefficiencies and shortcomings may be acceptable in a prototype but there is the risk that they will not be properly rectified, particularly if there is a lot of pressure to get the system delivered quickly or at reduced cost.
- Documentation is difficult to keep up to date if the system is constantly changing.

The use of a prototype could appeal to John Kline and ISS because, as well as the general benefits mentioned:

- User-friendly prototyping tools such as fourth generation languages (4GLs) and screen generators help to speed up development and it seems that IIS need a system quickly if they are to remain competitive.
- The final system is more likely to satisfy users' requirements – which is something the users have been dissatisfied with previously.
- It will provide the opportunity to build up teamwork and help to reduce the gap between users and the information systems department.

The investment appraisal system is a form of expert system and the prototyping approach could be used by starting with a prototype of an aspect of the expert system, such as the user interface, the report generation facilities or the 'inference engine' which performs the analysis and applies the programmed rules to the given situation. Work could proceed on all three aspects in parallel with prototypes of the different aspects being combined as they become available.

Graphical user interfaces (GUI) are becoming increasingly popular for many applications. Many GUIs are based on the 'WIMP' components of windows, icons, mouse and pull-down menus, which are claimed to offer a much easier-to-use method of interacting with a computer system. They provide an interface which is more intuitive for non-specialists and remove the reliance on keyboard skill once the user has mastered the art of manipulating the mouse or similar device. GUIs require more processing power and disk capacity than traditional command line interfaces, but the technological improvements of recent years have led to computers which are sufficiently powerful to support GUIs and sufficiently inexpensive to make them available to most commercial computer users.

For many applications, such as word processing, spreadsheets and computer-aided design, the use of GUIs is claimed to have greatly increased user productivity. However, IIS should select a style of user interface which is most appropriate to the application itself, an investment appraisal system, and to the users of the application who are likely to be experienced financial analysts.

As well as a GUI, alternative styles of user interface are:

- menus
- command line – where the user types commands at the keyboard
- screens laid out in a format similar to paper forms and documents
- query languages, which often use a subset of ordinary language but in a well defined, structured form
- screen dialogues, where the system presents the user with a series of questions to which the user responds.

It may be that two or more alternative forms of interface would be appropriate for IIS's system. For example, expert users who will spend a lot of their working hours using this application could become more efficient using a command line or a query language, since they will get to know the particular commands and will become familiar with abbreviations and short cuts using special keys. For novice users or staff who use the application less frequently, perhaps a screen dialogue style of interface will be more appropriate, since it can help to lead the user through the application by selecting the relevant questions without confusing or distracting the user with unnecessary details until they are required. A third option could be the use of a screen format reflecting the layout of IIS's existing documents, which could be an effective style of interface for staff who have a lot of routine operations to perform on the system.

Section B

12

1 a) The sorts of hardware used for transaction processing systems include the following, from which you could have chosen two in each section:

Inputting data

Keyboards which may be full 'QWERTY' key layout, possibly with additional keys such as cursor control keys, special function keys and numeric keypads. Alternatively they may be numeric keypads, or special-purpose keyboards such as are currently found on banks' ATMs (automated teller machines – cashpoints)

Pointer-based devices such as the mouse, tracker-ball, lightpen and touch-sensitive screen, which use various methods to control a pointer on a screen and draw or select items displayed on the screen. Recent developments have produced systems which enable users to enter data by writing freehand on small screens.

Bar-code readers, which use optical methods to read data coded as a series of lines of different thicknesses with variable spacing.

Magnetic-stripe or 'swipe' cards, which have data encoded on a strip of magnetic material in them.

Smart cards, which take advantage of the miniaturisation of computers by embedding a small microprocessor into a card the size of a credit-card.

Scanners, which digitise images so that they can be processed by computers.

MICR (magnetic ink character recognition) devices, which read characters that are printed with magnetic ink, such as are used on cheques

Marked cards, which read data encoded as marks on specific areas of a paper form, such as are used to process the responses on some questionnaires and multiple-choice examination papers.

Microphones, which are used as part of some 'natural-language interfaces', where the user's voice is captured by a microphone connected to a computer which analyses the sound patterns.

Data processing

Most data processing is carried out within a computer's central unit. Computers used for transaction processing can be broadly categorised into:

Mainframe systems: large, powerful systems that cost millions of pounds, require special operating environments and are usually housed in purpose-built machine rooms. They are usually multi-user systems which can support hundreds of users.

Mini-computer systems: smaller and cheaper than mainframes, 'minis' are multi-user systems supporting up to about 100 users.

Micro-computers: small, office-based systems usually consisting of a small main system unit, with a VDU and keyboard. Originally only suitable for single-user personal computers, the power of the 'micro' has increased and, with suitable operating software, they can now be used to support several users.

Portable computers: recent technical developments have led to the miniaturisation of most aspects of computer hardware and the growth of small but powerful personal computers described as 'laptops' and 'notebooks'.

The main components of the central unit of any computer are:

- the central processing unit (CPU)
- micro-chip memory in the form of RAM (random access memory) which provides temporary storage space while the computer is operating
- internal communications pathways called 'buses'
- interfaces allowing connection to external devices such as printers, keyboards, mouse, modems, etc.

Data storage

The main forms of permanent storage equipment are:

- magnetic disks, either high-capacity sealed units (called hard, fixed or Winchester disks), or lower-capacity but removable floppy disks. Disks allow random access to the data stored on them
- magnetic tapes which come in various forms, usually sealed in cartridges, and provide serial access to the large volumes of data that can be stored on them
- other devices which have recently become widely available, such as high-capacity CD-ROM (Compact Disc read-only memory), which uses optical methods, and WORM (write once, read many) systems.

Outputting data and information

Commonly used output devices include:

- screens or visual display units (VDUs)
- printers and plotters
- loudspeakers.

In addition, communications technology may be used to send and receive data. Three basic communications systems are:

- direct connections between two systems or devices using cables
- local area networks (LAN) using low cost connections to link several systems within a maximum range of a few hundred metres
- wide area networks (WAN) that usually use the public telephone system to link two or more systems. This requires the use of modems to convert between the digital signals used by computer system and the analogue signals used for speech transmission. The recent development of ISDN (integrated systems digital networks) allows systems to communicate more comprehensively without the need for modems.

b) **Batch processing** describes a method where transactions are not processed as soon as they are received but are grouped together into batches and then processed together as a batch. Examples of batch processing are:

- A bank stores all a day's transactions until after the close of normal business and then updates all customers' accounts in one overnight process.
- An organisation employing a large number of salaried staff which files all staff expense claims, pay rises, bonuses, etc. until the end of each month and then processes them altogether.

Batch processing is used where the result of any particular transaction does not need to be output as soon as it is processed. It is often not necessary to use very powerful equipment, since there may be little benefit in completing a monthly payroll very quickly if it is done overnight. The master files needed for batch processing do not need to be constantly online or stored on media with fast access times, so they can be held on removable media, such as magnetic tapes or floppy disks, which are only loaded when they are needed. A batch of data is usually prepared and possibly preprocessed and then the main batch process is executed and may be left to run for several hours or days without operator intervention.

In contrast, **demand processing** describes the method of processing each transaction on its own as soon as, or shortly after, it is received. For example, a telephone sales operation where each order is checked and confirmed while the customer waits on the telephone is using demand processing. Since there is a need to process transactions immediately, the equipment for demand processing must be powerful enough to provide a suitable response time; this will entail using a powerful CPU and any files needed should be stored on fast-access, online devices such as hard disks. Several users may want to access the system at any one time, so a multi-user system is needed, with multiple terminals capable of handling several transactions at the same time without its performance degrading to the point where the response time becomes unacceptable.

The original ATM machines (cashpoints) combine demand and batch processing: a customer's request for cash is processed when it is made, but the record of the transaction is stored in a batch, along with the rest of the day's transactions, until an overnight batch process updates all the accounts.

Interactive processing can be described as 'conversational mode', as each stage of the user's commands is checked and responded to, either by being carried out immediately or with a request for further input. A telephone sales order processing system is interactive if it checks the individual details of an order as they are entered and can respond with queries and requests for confirmation before the next detail is entered. Interactive processing usually requires equipment that is similar to, or more powerful than, that used for demand processing since it has to provide a sophisticated user interface and respond appropriately to the user at each stage of the processing of a command.

A **real-time** system is able to respond rapidly to changes in its environment. Real-time systems are used for time-critical applications such as controlling a chemical plant or power station. They must not only provide a rapid response but must have access to up-to-date information and be able to update it immediately. Airline booking systems run on real-time systems, since they depend on being able to make reservations immediately on the basis of the latest information about flights and seat reservations. Very powerful processing, storage and communications equipment is needed as they are usually multi-user systems, subject to periods of heavy usage. They often involve long distance and international networks which must provide a rapid response time and support sophisticated procedures to ensure data integrity.

The need for backup and security systems to minimise systems' downtime will depend on the importance of the availability of the system. Real-time processing, in particular, usually involves hot-standby backup systems, as the constant availability of the system is vital to the sorts of functions or services it provides.

2 a) In an electronic point of sale system (EPOS), information about individual products is read electronically. This is achieved by tagging each item for sale, with a bar code for example, and providing an electronic till at each sales point which can read the codes, with a bar code reader in this case. This information is processed by the till, which displays the information about the item on a

VDU in human-readable form and, when the sale is complete, calculates the sales total (including any discounts or special offers) and prints the customer's receipt. The till sends information about each item sold to a central computer holding stock control information which processes the information and updates stock levels. In this way, the retailer has immediate access to up-to-date information about stock levels and the demand for goods. The management can see information about individual outlets and about the overall position for all outlets. Goods can therefore be shipped to outlets to replenish their local stocks, and bulk orders can be placed with suppliers for goods to replenish the central warehouse stock.

An electronic funds transfer system (EFT) automates the process of transferring money from one bank account to another. The customer presents the shop assistant with a 'swipe' card (which is like a credit card with information coded on a magnetic stripe), or a 'smart' card which is similar, except that it contains a miniaturised microprocessor. The till reads details of the customer's bank account from the card, combines it with details of the transaction and sends the information electronically into the banking system.

In order to implement a combined EPOS-EFT system, the retailer will need suitable tills which will read both bar codes and swipe cards, or similar cards. These tills need to be linked to the central stock control and accounts system. They may be linked directly to the central computer, or each outlet may have its own local computer which is itself linked into the central system. Having computers at each outlet reduces reliance on the central system since the local computer can do some of the storing and processing if the central system is not available.

Communication between the outlets and the central system can be made using WAN (wide area network) technology which uses the telephone system to provide the communication links. The traditional telephone system uses analogue signals initially designed only to carry voice signals. Computers, and other electronic devices like telefacsimile machines, use digital signals which must be converted using modems (modulators-demodulators) to and from the analogue signals used in the telephone system. The telephone system is now being converted to ISDN (integrated systems digital network) which will carry not only voice, but also data and graphics, using digital signals. This will allow faster, more reliable electronic communication without the need for modems.

In order to process all the information as it comes in from the retail outlets, the central accounts and stock control system must have the capacity to handle several incoming communication links and be powerful enough to respond quickly even at periods of peak traffic.

b) A **management information system** is one which is intended to provide middle managers with summary and forecasting information about the organisation. They tend to use standard reports compiled from the low-level information gathered internally about operational activities. Management information systems usually operate in fairly fixed, well-structured ways and provide information upon which managers can base their decisions.

Management information systems are often an extension of the transaction processing system; they take the raw transaction data and process it into forms which are more readily understandable by middle management.

Executive information systems are used by high-level managers as a tool to aid their strategic decision making. They are often based upon an organisation's central database and often also include external information, for example, about market conditions. The main characteristics are:

- software programmed to simulate the way humans make decisions
- data manipulation facilities to allow the executive to 'navigate' around different sets of data and 'drill-down' facilities to show information about a particular area in progressively more detail. Thus an executive of a retail organisation operating several outlets with several product lines can see top-level, summary information about performance of the outlets or products, but can also get more detailed information about the performance of a particular product sold from one outlet
- sophisticated graphics displays and simple, user-friendly interfaces. Information can be displayed in a consistent format, such as a line-graph, which aids the executive when navigating or drilling down through the database.

Executive information systems build upon the low-level transaction information to provide an overall view of the organisation in a readily understandable format which can be rapidly changed with the minimum of user intervention.

An **expert system** is one which offers a consultancy service similar to that which would be provided by a highly qualified expert. They are limited to fairly narrow fields of operation within which rules can be formulated and programmed into the system. The rules may embody either the organisation's operational procedures or inferences that would typically be made by an expert in the sphere of operation. The user inputs some basic facts into the expert system whose database applies the rules and outputs the most suitable recommendation, possibly with an explanation of how the recommendation was arrived at. Typical areas where an expert system would be used by a retail organisation would be credit control, auditing, and investment appraisal.

The low-level details processed by the transaction processing system will provide useful information upon which the inference rules can be based by provided historical evidence of what has occurred either in general or relating to a particular set of circumstances. Expert systems are useful in situations which are fairly well structured. The analogy can be made with a chess-playing computer which has the basic rules of play programmed into it (plus rules about what has occurred when certain moves are made in specific situations) and is programmed to apply the rules to the current situation and make the 'best' move, depending on whether it is set to operate in an adventurous or cautious mode.

3

Report on user involvement in systems development

To: The Administration Manager

From:

Date:

Terms of reference: Background material covering:

- The need for user involvement and its benefits and problems
- Fourth-generation languages and prototyping.

The need for user involvement

User involvement in systems development can help to overcome some of the major problems that have continued to beset computerised information systems since they first became commercially viable in the 1950s. These problems are:

- overdue development projects
- over-budget development projects
- systems that fail to satisfy the users' requirements
- systems that cannot adapt to changes in the users' requirements and the users' environment
- systems that are expensive to maintain and have a shorter than expected useful lifespan.

The recognition of the key role that users play in achieving a successful development has been embodied in what can be grouped together as 'user-driven development' methodologies, such as Checkland's soft systems methodology (SSM).

The benefits of user involvement

Two major factors underlying the problems associated with developing information systems are:

- preparing realistic estimates of the costs, duration and complexity of the tasks involved in development is notoriously difficult.
- users' requirements are very difficult to specify accurately, requiring an awareness of capabilities of information technology and comprehensive knowledge of the users' organisation and its environment. The difficulty is compounded by the fact that those requirements are likely to change for a variety of reasons.

Regarding the first factor, users are rarely technical computer experts and regard a computer system as simply a tool to provide for their information needs. They do not have the technical awareness to actually make judgments or estimates about the specialised tasks involved, such as analysis, design and programming. However, being involved in the process of planning systems developments will help to make them aware of the problems and possibly reduce their expectations that things will go exactly to plan. They can then make better-informed judgments about whether or not to make contingency arrangements, or even about the desirability of the developments. As the projects progress, users will be less likely to apply unreasonable pressure when problems arise and therefore reduce the risk of the developers making hasty decisions or skimping on quality. The whole project benefits from the increased understanding and realism that cooperation brings.

The main benefit of user involvement comes from much more appropriate requirements specifications. Just as the users are unlikely to be computer experts, the developers are unlikely to be experts in the users' sphere of operation and very unlikely to know about the users' particular priorities, procedures or culture. If users and developers work together to form the requirements specification then they both get an understanding of the other's views, concerns and operations. In this way the requirements can be progressively refined, mainly before other development work starts but also as the project progresses. One of the main reasons that users' requirements change is that, as they become familiar with the system's technology and its capabilities, they realise new uses and new requirements. The sooner the users gain this familiarity then the sooner they can specify these new or changed requirements – and the sooner these can be adopted, with a resulting reduction in wasted effort, frustration and hurriedly implemented changes. For the same reasons, the completed system is more likely to have flexibility built into it, which will avoid expensive maintenance activities and extend its useful life.

Another major benefit of user involvement is that it increases the chance of the new system being accepted by users and regarded in a positive manner since they feel it is their system and not something that has been imposed upon them.

A further benefit is that it reduces the learning curve that they have to go through once the system is operational.

Problems

User involvement in systems development may lead to resentment among the developers' staff, who may feel that their expertise is being questioned if they have to justify decisions to non-experts.

There may be delays in stages of development because user involvement may lead to increased meetings and more lengthy explanations and discussions. Giving the users the opportunities to make suggestions means that they should be seriously considered and acted upon where appropriate. The delays may be real in the early stages of development but will probably lead to a shortening of the overall development – and to much less disruption and wasted effort in the later stages and during the system's operation.

Fourth-generation languages (4GLs) and prototyping

4GLs is a term used to cover a range of tools used in the development of computer applications. The term 4GL is used because these tools are a development of programming techniques used in developing computer software. Third-generation languages, also called high-level languages, allow programmers to write program code using symbols and English language words in a highly specialised and technical way. Examples of commonly used high-level languages are COBOL, C, BASIC and Pascal. 4GLs were introduced as a way of making the development of computer applications faster and less of a specialised art. Applications written in a 4GL will often be automatically converted into a 3GL, and then into assembly code and machine code languages which are the other, lower-level types of programming language.

The common characteristics of 4GLs are that:

- they use English-language statements in a much more natural way than 3GLs
- they are non-procedural, meaning that the user specifies a required result and does not have to specify the detail of the procedure and instructions needed to achieve the result. This helps to provide features that are difficult to achieve in 3GLs.

Some of the tools which come into the category of 4GLs are:

- Applications generators: these allow the development of complete applications programs by users who do not need to be programming specialists. The user specifies what the application should do and the data and files to be used. From this description of the application, the 4GL produces the program code needed to carry it out.
- Report and screen generators: the term 'report' is used in computing, particularly with reference to databases, to describe computer output, such as management reports, that is printed, or displayed on a VDU, in a particular format which is easy for users to understand. The user specifies the general contents of the report and its basic layout in simple terms. The report generator retrieves and manipulates the data and produces the report.
- Query languages: these are provided in conjunction with some database management systems to allow users to readily retrieve data using human-language statements and commands. Using them can greatly increase the

flexibility and speed of carrying out non-routine database searches and queries. *Prototyping* is a technique used in systems development which involves producing a working version of the system, or some aspects of it, early in the development. The prototype is not intended to be put into useful operation; it is used to demonstrate and test aspects of the system in a tangible rather than theoretical way. The users and developers can experiment with the prototype and refine it to suit the user's requirements. An example of the use of prototyping is when developers use 4GL screen generators to produce input and output screens to demonstrate and test their design. If it is the 'look and feel' of the screens that is being considered then the input and output routines that underlie the use of the screens need not have been fully tested and may not incorporate all the specified validation and verification procedures.

The benefits of prototyping are claimed to be the following:

- Development is speeded up because there is an immediate objective and the prototype provides tangible, early evidence of progress which helps to motivate the people involved.
- Testing can be carried out early on the prototype and corrections and refinements can be made more easily at that stage.
- It provides good opportunities to involve users in the development process.
- The final system is more likely to satisfy user requirements as a result of testing and user involvement.

Criticisms of prototyping include:

- It can be wasteful of resources and distract attention from the overall objective, which is to bring the final system into operation.
- It encourages an *ad hoc* approach to development.
- Features which have been incorporated without detailed design, proper testing or documentation in a prototype may remain in the final system.

4

a) The current system uses a **batch processing** system since each day's paper order forms are grouped together and processed together in a batch. The new system is a **demand processing** system since each customer's order is processed as soon as it is received on the telephone.

Data needs to be controlled at all stages of its life in the system – input, processing, storage and output.

Checks which can be carried out when data is input and before it is processed include:

- *Verification checks* to ensure that data is transferred accurately from the customer onto the system. This usually involves double-checking. On the batch system this can be done visually by the data entry clerk or another member of staff, or by double-keying where the data is keyed in by different staff and the system automatically checks that both inputs are identical. On the demand processing system there will not be time for a second member of staff to be involved but the order is entered directly by the data entry clerk, who has the opportunity to read back the data to the customer, who can verify it is correct. The demand processing system has the advantage that the data is only transferred once, directly from customer to data entry clerk, whereas the paper system requires two stages: the data is filled in on the order form by the customer and then transferred from the form to the system, which may increase the risk of errors. An important advantage of the demand processing system is that it provides an opportunity to immediately correct errors without the delays and inconvenience of having to refer back to the customer at a later date.

- Validation checks ensure the data is reasonable, complete and consistent. The items in each order can be checked to ensure that they are the correct format – text, dates, currency, etc. They can be checked for allowable values or to ensure that they fall within certain allowable ranges. The internal consistency of each order can be checked to make sure that there are no obvious discrepancies between items on the order. The external consistency can also be checked to ensure that the data on the order corresponds to any related, existing data on the system. On the demand processing system these checks must be carried out rapidly, because the customer awaits confirmation and the time taken to carry out validation may mean some checks cannot be fully completed during data entry, particularly if consistency checks require large amounts of existing data to be analysed. The need for rapid response is much less on the batch processing system, which allows the opportunity to carry out comprehensive checks. Because the orders are processed in a batch, some preprocessing and sorting can be carried out to make the checking processes more efficient. However, batch processing also introduces the need to check that the orders remain intact in their batches and do not get lost or misplaced.

Checks should be carried out during processing to ensure that processes are carried out fully and accurately. This is easier to control on a batch processing system, where the process starts from a known state and should be carried through to an obvious conclusion. If problems occur the batch can be rechecked and the process repeated. In the demand system the input and processing are going on continuously and it is much harder to identify a fixed state to backtrack to or to restart from. The batch processing system may only be carrying out one process at a time, but the demand processing system is probably operating as a multi-user system with several processes going on at any one time, all needing to share access to common data. This introduces problems of ensuring that data is kept up to date without becoming corrupted by processes that interfere with each.

The batch processing system offers more control over the storage of data since master computer files will only be accessed at known times; copies can be taken for backups in a controlled manner and orders can be kept in batches for future reference. Output can also be produced and included with the batches. In the demand processing system, paper records may not be made immediately and if they are then they must be handled in a controlled manner so that each order can be related to its output. Disaster and emergency recovery measures can be easier to manage on a batch processing system, since the state of the system at the start and finish of each distinct process can be recorded, whereas the batch processing system is much more volatile and harder to keep track of.

Output from the batch processing system will normally occur at the end of the batch run. While this may be easier to control in normal operation compared with the output that happens sporadically when individual orders are processed on the demand processing system, there is the possibility that a minor problem, such as a printer error, may necessitate repeating the complete and possible time-consuming process.

It should be noted that, in general, demand processing requires systems to be readily available and more powerful than batch processing systems. The need to process and check orders in a multi-user environment places varied and sometimes high demand on the system.

b) The change from the old batch processing system to the new demand processing system will have major effects on the people involved – the users (the retailer's sales and data entry staff) and the customers.

Response times and customers' expectations

The majority of customers will probably prefer the new system because:

- it is simpler to telephone their orders through than write out and post an order form
- they get immediate confirmation that the order has been received and checked
- they will be notified immediately of any problems either with the system or with their order itself
- the new system provides opportunities to start the processing and shipment of goods as soon as the orders arrive (rather than delaying them until after the batch run) so customers may receive their goods more rapidly
- existing customers may feel that the retailer is well informed because the salesperson can immediately refer to up-to-date details of the customer, including any orders that have been placed that day.

The new system raises the profile of the part that the computer plays in order processing. Some people feel uncomfortable about the increasing use of computers, particularly if they process personal details. A minor disadvantage of the new system is that as customers become accustomed to improved response times and better information they may then become more dissatisfied if there are errors or delays.

Staff

The new system will have a considerable effect on the retailer's staff. With the old system there is a group of specialist sales staff and a group of specialist data-entry staff, each group working separately at different times of day. With the new system, the roles of salesperson and data-entry clerk will be combined. Factors which need to be considered are these:

- Staff from either group will need training for the new role and may dislike new aspects of the new role.
- Working hours, payments, etc. may be altered.
- There may be redundancies as a result of more efficient procedures and reduced paperwork.
- Increased use of computers and reduction of paperwork can lead to depersonalisation, because staff have less tangible evidence of their own work, and to desocialisation of the workplace.
- The retailer's management structure may have to undergo changes.

The retailer's high-level management will have to address these factors. If they are neglected then there is the danger that the new system will cause resentment and will not be well received by staff – which is likely to reduce its effectiveness and present customers with a poor impression of the system and the retailer.

5 This answer relates to legislation in the UK, but you could have chosen similar legislation from a different country.

a) i) The UK Data Protection Act 1984 was introduced because of pressure from:

- civil liberties groups, who expressed concerns about the amount of data that computer and other electronic equipment can process, and the speed and complexity with which it can be manipulated. They were also concerned about the reduction in the amount of human intervention and judgment that might be involved in electronic data processing;

- commercial groups concerned with trade with organisations in other countries which already had data protection legislation. Much of that legislation required that data could only be communicated with organisations operating in countries with similar legislation. So the UK Data Protection Act was necessary to prevent potential trade barriers.

With the increasing use of electronic communications and data transmission facilities, EDI (electronic data interchange) is changing the ways the that organisations communicate between their departments or branches and with each other. The Act is relevant to data communications since it concerns things such as data access and disclosure and also communication across national boundaries.

ii) The Data Protection Act is concerned only with **personal data** (data that relates to a living individuals, who are called **data subjects**) that is **processed electronically**. People and organisations who control the content and use of data are termed **data users**, and people and organisations that carry out data processing or storage on behalf of others are termed **computer bureaux**.

The Act requires data users to register the with the Data Protection Registrar; detailing the sort of personal data held, its uses and the systems used to process it. The data user is required to abide by the *Data Protection Principles* which relate to:

- the way that data should be acquired
- the nature of the data and it purposes
- disclosure and security of the data.

The Registrar has the power to issue **enforcement notices** to compel data users to comply with the Act, or **transfer prohibition notices** to prevent data transfers overseas, or **deregistration notices** which prohibit the use of personal data. Data users are liable to criminal prosecution for failure to register or abide by the Act.

Data subjects are given rights under the Act to be informed of data held about them, to see the data and have inaccuracies rectified. Compensation can be claimed for damage or distress caused by inaccuracies, loss or unauthorised access to personal data.

There are various *exemptions from the Act*. These cover things like:

- data whose disclosure may endanger national security
- data that is made public by law
- data that is only held for recreational purposes or for managing personal or domestic affairs
- data held for the prevention or detection of crimes
- data held solely for research or statistical purposes
- data held for a limited number of commercial or business uses. These include payroll and pensions, accounts, mailshots and word processing.

b) As well as the Data Protection Act, the two main items of legislation that directly relate to the use of computer programs and access to computer systems are concerned with:

Copyright of computer software. The Copyright (Computer Programs) Regulations 1992 modified a patents act of 1988. This legislation makes illegal the unauthorised use and copying of software. Suppliers usually provide software for use under licence which may include:

- limits on the number of copies of the software that can be made
- limits on the number of users of the software
- limits on the purposes it is used for – educational use only, for example.

Organisations should control the use and copying of software so that they stay within the terms of the licence. Measures should include audits of all computer systems, removal of unauthorised copies, and access procedures to limit the number of users of licensed software.

Copyright laws are also aimed at preventing software developers stealing or copying the source material of other developers. This becomes a difficult issue when the ownership of the 'look and feel' of software is questioned.

Computer misuse. The Computer Misuse Act 1990 attempts to address the problems of unauthorised access ('hacking') and modifications to systems and their data or programs. Although the Act brings into force three criminal offences, it has been difficult to administer. This is due in part to the problem of tracing unauthorised access and also because of the reluctance of some organisations to expose themselves to adverse publicity if their security and controls have been breached.

Organisations should consider strict control of access to their computer systems, and the programs and data they contain, by the use of physical security measures, passwords, file access permissions and encoding techniques. However, a compromise should be achieved to avoid excessive security and costs beyond that which is appropriate to the level of risk involved.

6

a) Organisations which have recognised the value of information have an overall **information strategy** which sets out objectives aimed at making the best use of information in the pursuit of their organisational objectives. This will usually be established by board level decisions and the appointment of an **information director**.

The information strategy should cover all aspects of the organisation, since all areas of an organisation rely on information for their effective operation. In order to translate the strategy into action it will be necessary to involve appropriate staff so that all areas of the organisation are considered. This will often be done by the establishment of a **steering committee** comprising the information director and senior managers from other areas. The committee's role is to establish appropriate information systems to meet the organisation's needs in line with the information strategy. This role includes:

- advising the board on the strategic use of information systems
- to monitor the overall effectiveness and efficiency of the information system
- to set up and monitor feasibility studies and investigations
- to select development projects or recommend them for selection by the directors
- to monitor the progress of development projects
- to evaluate the completed systems developments.

Part of the steering committee's role will be to establish appropriate **feasibility study teams** to look at potential systems options. These teams should have information technology expertise and accountancy skill to carry out cost-benefit analyses, and should include representatives of the end-users of potential systems.

Once a project has been given the go-ahead to proceed, the steering committee should establish suitable *project management structures* consisting of *project managers* and *teams of development staff* to carry out the various development activities. The size and constitution of these teams should be appropriate to the tasks involved and there should be *team leaders* and clear lines of communication and responsibility. The teams may be organised so that there is one team per system or major sub-system, or functional teams who move between projects as the need for their expertise arises. People with the sorts of skills involved in systems development include:

- systems analysts and designers
- programmers
- documentation experts and technical authors
- systems installers and hardware specialists
- trainers.

In addition there are substantial benefits to be gained by involving *users, and the systems managers and database administrators*, as much as possible in the development.

A major consideration throughout should be to establish suitable structures which combine technical expertise and experience with insight and understanding of the organisation's aims, procedures and culture.

b) A feasibility study report on this proposal should include an initial investigation to establish an *outline of the users' requirements*, including any constraints that may be put upon potential projects.

Various aspects of the proposed systems feasibility should be covered in the report:

Technical feasibility

This is concerned with looking, first, at whether there is suitable information technology that can be purchased or developed and, second, the effects on existing systems. There are four main aspects to examine in this proposal:

- *The specification of the portable computers* and their performance, including things like:
  - the size of the systems – note-book or briefcase sized, for example
  - CPU (central processing unit) power
- *Suitable software* on the personal computers. This will have to allow them to be used as stand-alone systems and also linked to the central system. There may be benefits in providing software on the personal computers that is consistent with the central system. The features of existing off-the-shelf packages should be examined to see whether they would meet requirements or whether it will be necessary to take the riskier courses of developing tailor-made software or modifying existing software.
- *Communications:* hardware, such as modems, and software will be required.
- *Security and the effects on the central system.* The proposal may increase the traffic on the existing central system because there may be increased numbers of users, some of them requiring external communication links, and increased volumes of data. The likely response times should be looked at to ensure they at least meet minimum requirements, particularly as there will be variations in loading. The effects of having users accessing the system remotely should be examined to see what security arrangements should and can be provided.

12

Operational and social feasibility

The study report should include an examination of the changes that may be required to be made to the organisation's operations and the effects on the staff involved. There may be changes to management structures since the sales representatives will become more autonomous and direct face-to-face communications will be reduced. Managerial roles and lines of responsibility may need to be changed. Staff will need to be trained in the use of the new personal computers and it will be essential that they accept the new system – otherwise they will not use it fully and problems in operating the systems will be difficult to sort out 'on the road'.

Economic feasibility

The costs and benefits of the proposed system should be evaluated using headings such as:

- direct benefits, including reduced travel and time spent on administrative activities
- indirect benefits, such as better information, more flexible working hours, improved company image
- development costs, such as systems analysts' and designers' time, and software development
- implementation costs, such as the cost of personal computers, communications equipment and software, time to install the software and user training
- Ongoing costs, such as materials, telephone systems charges and maintenance.

When the items have been evaluated and quantified, a cost-benefit analysis will be carried out using techniques and factors such as

- breakeven points and margins of safety
- payback periods
- NPV (net present value) methods, using discounted cash flows to take the time value of money into account
- ARR (accounting rate of return) or return on investment.

Most or all the costs and benefits will be estimated; some of them will be relatively intangible and therefore difficult to quantify. The report should include an assessment of the likelihood of major areas where estimates should be judged cautiously.

The feasibility study report should conclude with a summary assessment of the proposal, a comparison if there is more than one variation to be considered, and, if possible, a recommendation.

7 a) Many systems design methodologies distinguish between the logical and physical design of a system, particularly in relation to the system's data structures. The logical design shows *what* the system should do while the physical design shows *how* the logical design will be implemented. The systems designer must first establish a suitable logical design that will satisfy the users' requirements. For example, if there is a requirement for an organisation's sales and warehouse staff to have up-to-date information about stock levels then a logical design decision must be made – either the staff share the same copy of the information about stock levels or they could each have their own copy of the stock information within an integrated system, where any

change in stock level on one system is reflected immediately by the corresponding change in the other system. Suppose the designer opts for a logical design showing a single copy of the stock information that is accessed by both the sales and warehouse staff. The designer then has to make the decision about whether the physical design should include a local area network of personal computers with a file server to hold the single copy of the stock information, or a multi-user mini-computer which both sales and warehouse staff can access.

When looking at detailed data structures, the designer must establish the logical relationships between data items that will allow them to be manipulated appropriately – for example, customer records may need to be accessed in different sequences for different purposes. The physical design can then be produced. It may use a random access storage method where the sequence of records on a hard disk is not related to any particular sequence.

Data flow diagrams (DFDs) can be used to show either the logical or physical data flows in a system. The designer may draw a logical DFD that shows a data flow described as 'details of customer's requirements'. This may be shown on the physical DFD as 'customer's order form', or 'fax of customer's requirements', or 'e-mail with customer's requirements'.

b) The three main models upon which the logical structure of a database can be designed are hierarchies, networks, and relational structures.

Hierarchical structures

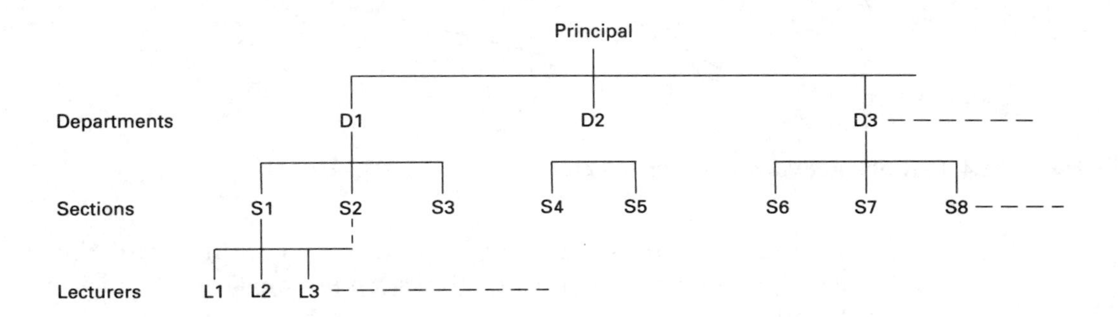

Figure 12.3 Hierarchical database structure of college academic staff

A hierarchical structure allows only 1:M (one-to-many) relationships. In our example, one section has many members of staff and each member of staff belongs to only one section. The link represents the relationship 'is a member of'. All the items on a particular level are of the same sort or entity. All the instances of the department entity are on the same level within the hierarchy.

Hierarchies are readily understandable and commonly used structures – the world is divided into continents, which are split into countries, which in turn are split into provinces or counties, and so on. However, for database designs, the structure can be too rigid for many purposes. For example, a college may not specifically offer computing courses but has computing resources that service the computing needs of several sections in different departments. A computing lecturer is responsible for all computing resources but does not naturally fit into any department or section. The options are:

- to include the computing lecturer in one section, which creates an artificial link or inappropriate link

- to link the lecturer to the principal or to a department, which creates an anomaly – the links no longer represent relationships in a consistent manner
- to link the lecturer to several sections, which creates redundancy (since the lecturer's details are held in more than one place) and obscures the fact that there is now a logical M:M (many-to-many) relationship.

In order to allow other sorts of logical relationships as well as 1:M, a network structure can be used.

Network database structures

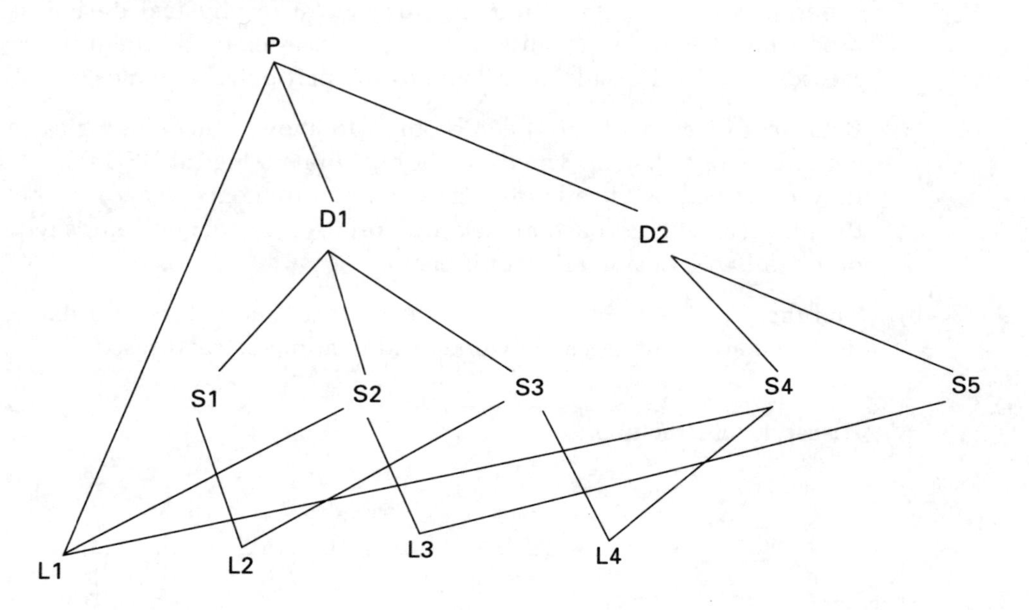

Figure 12.4 Part of a network database structure

This provides flexibility but can become very complex and the logical relationships become obscured as the links are no longer used consistently for particular relationships.

Relational database structures

Where flexibility is required in the management of large amounts of data, relational structures have been most effective. Instead of a structure that can be represented diagrammatically by links between related items, relational databases contain the data in tables which represent relations.

Lecturer details

Lecturer	*Name*	*Address*
L1	Evans	....
L2	Hammond	....
L3	Smith	....
L4	Wise	....
...		

Section–Dept

Section	*Dept*
S1	D1
S2	D1
S3	D1
S4	D2
...	

Lecturer–Section

Lecturer	*Section*
L1	S2
L1	S4
L2	S1
L2	S3
...	

The data in a relational database should be normalised to remove unnecessary redundancy, highlight dependencies and increase the manageability of the data. Normalisation is a process which derives from mathematical set theory and consists of transforming the tables into first, second and third normal form (1NF, 2NF, 3NF) using a series of rules.

A hierarchy is a useful structure if the data exhibits a natural hierarchy or tree structure of 1:M relationships but it reflects only one rigid view of the data. Network structures allow more flexibility but are suitable only for small amounts of data, since they become complex and difficult to manage and tend to obscure the relationships within the data. Relational structures require careful analysis but provide flexibility and a clear representation of the relationships.

8 a) Data flow diagrams are used in most structured systems development methodologies to show the flow of data between entities, processes and data stores in a system and between it and its environment. They form the basis from which software can be specified. There are variations on the conventions and symbols used, but consistency should be maintained within a set of DFDs. Examples of a typical set of symbols used are:

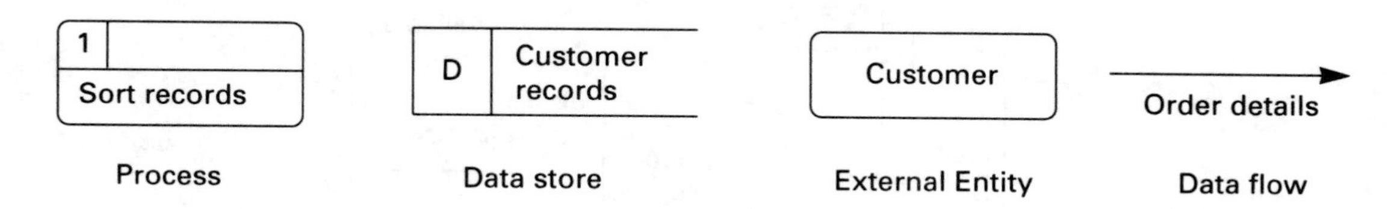

Figure 12.5 Symbols used in DFDs

DFDs are used in the description of an existing system or the design of a new system. A top-level DFD (Level 0) or context diagram shows the system's boundary and the data flows between it and external entities. A Level 1 DFD can then be drawn to show the major functional subsystems within the system and the data that flows between them. Each subsystem can then be examined in turn and Level 2 DFDs drawn for each one. This process of decomposition can be continued and will produce a levelled set of DFDs showing more details on each subsequent level. DFDs can be used to describe the physical data flows in terms of the documents and communications media (customer's order form, invoice, verbal confirmation, etc.) or the logical data flows which will describe the data itself rather than the actual media.

12

b)

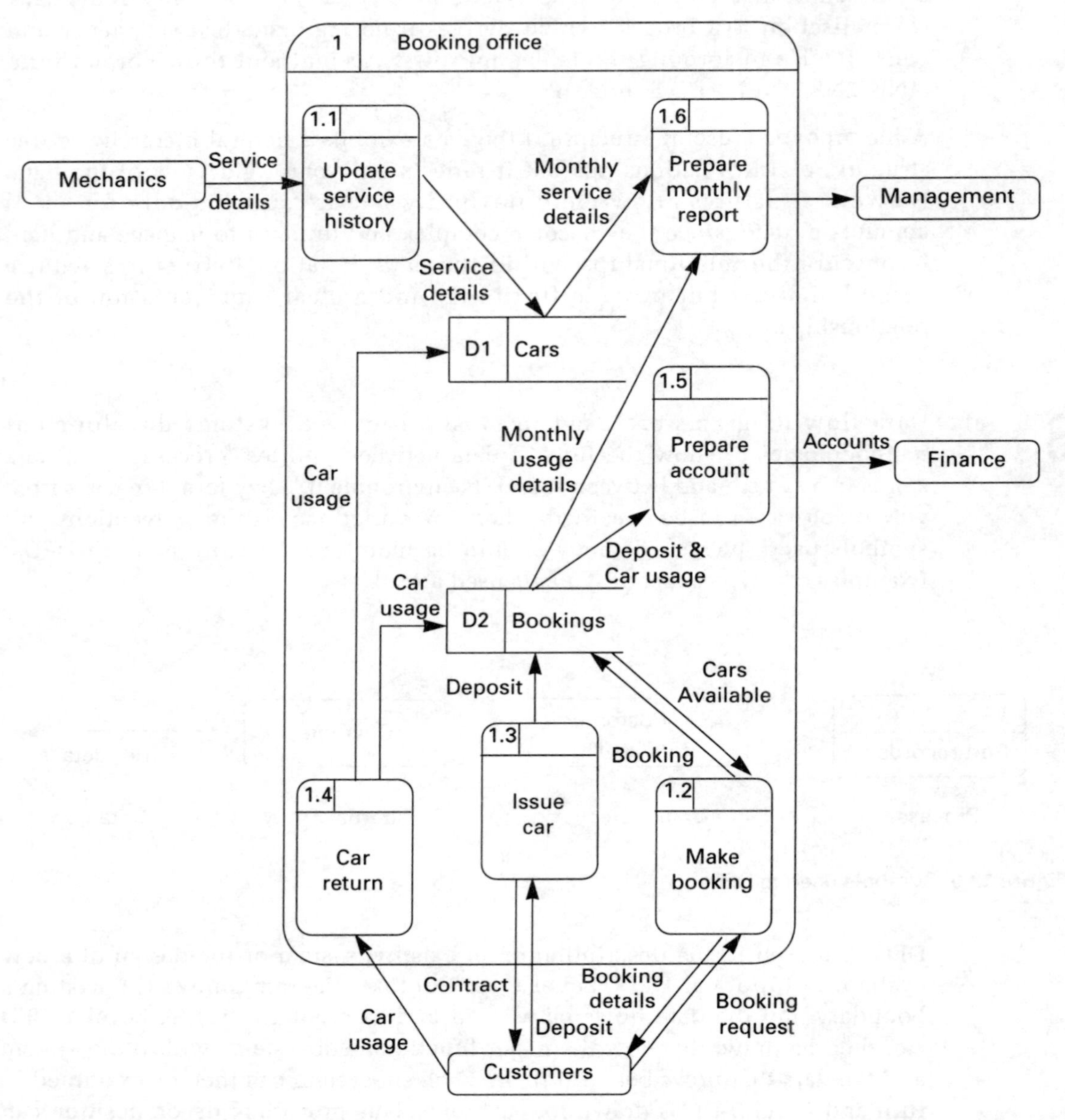

(*Note:* Different systems development methodologies may use different symbols in DFDs, but the principles remain the same.)

Figure 12.6 DFD of car hire booking office

9

a) The decision table for handling job applications is shown in Figure 12.7 opposite.

This is a limited entry decision table which could be simplified by combining rules – rules 1 and 3 can be combined as can rules 7 and 8.

b) Decision trees are useful for showing the logical design of a procedure. Wherever a point in the procedure is reached that involves a choice or where alternative actions are available, a line is drawn from that point to each of the alternatives. Part of a decision tree for handling job applications is shown in Figure 12.8 opposite.

Structured English is a technique that uses a very limited range of key English language words to describe a procedure, with the text indented to show where statements are grouped together into sub-processes, and data dictionary items underlined. A portion of a structured English description of the procedure for handling job applications is shown as follows:

```
IF candidate is qualified THEN
    IF candidate is experienced THEN
        put on short list
        IF candidate is external THEN
            request references
        ENDIF
    ELSE
        IF candidate is internal THEN
            put on short list
        ELSE
            put on waiting list
        ENDIF
    ENDIF
```

	Stubs	Entries: Rules 1	2	3	4	5	6	7	8
Conditions	Qualified?	Y	Y	Y	Y	N	N	N	N
	Experienced?	Y	Y	N	N	Y	Y	N	N
	Internal?	Y	N	Y	N	Y	N	Y	N
Actions	Reject	–	–	–	–	–	–	X	X
	Waiting list	–	–	–	X	X	X	–	–
	Short list	X	X	X	–	–	–	–	–
	Request references	–	X	–	X	–	X	–	–

Figure 12.7 Decision table for handling job applications

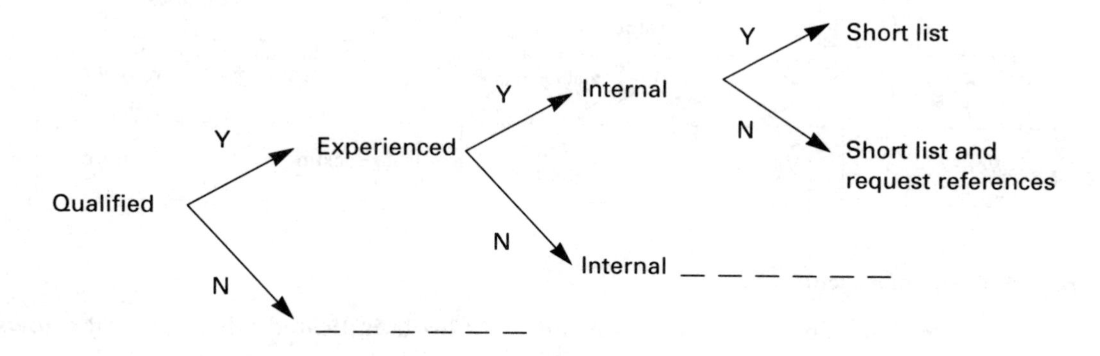

Figure 12.8 Part of a decision tree

10 a) The basis of modular design of software is to analyse the functions that the software must carry out and break them down into progressively smaller subfunctions. Each subfunction can be coded as a small, separate module. In order to do this effectively the interfaces between the modules should be well defined and as simple as possible, to avoid ambiguities. Program structure charts are used to show the modular design by:

- showing the way software is broken down into modules
- showing how modules are linked.

The benefits of modular design are as follows:

- Coding the software is quicker since each module can be coded by individual programmers working simultaneously.
- Small modules are more manageable and focus on a particular function.
- Testing can be carried out on each module, making it easier to identify where errors have been made.
- Initial test data can be prepared for each module without having to wait for all the related modules to be completed.
- Maintaining and modifying the software is easier, since changes may be limited to relevant modules which can be tested in isolation before being incorporated in the system.
- A commonly used function can be coded in a separate module and this module can be used each time the function is required. This will reduce the amount of code and the time needed to test it.

b)

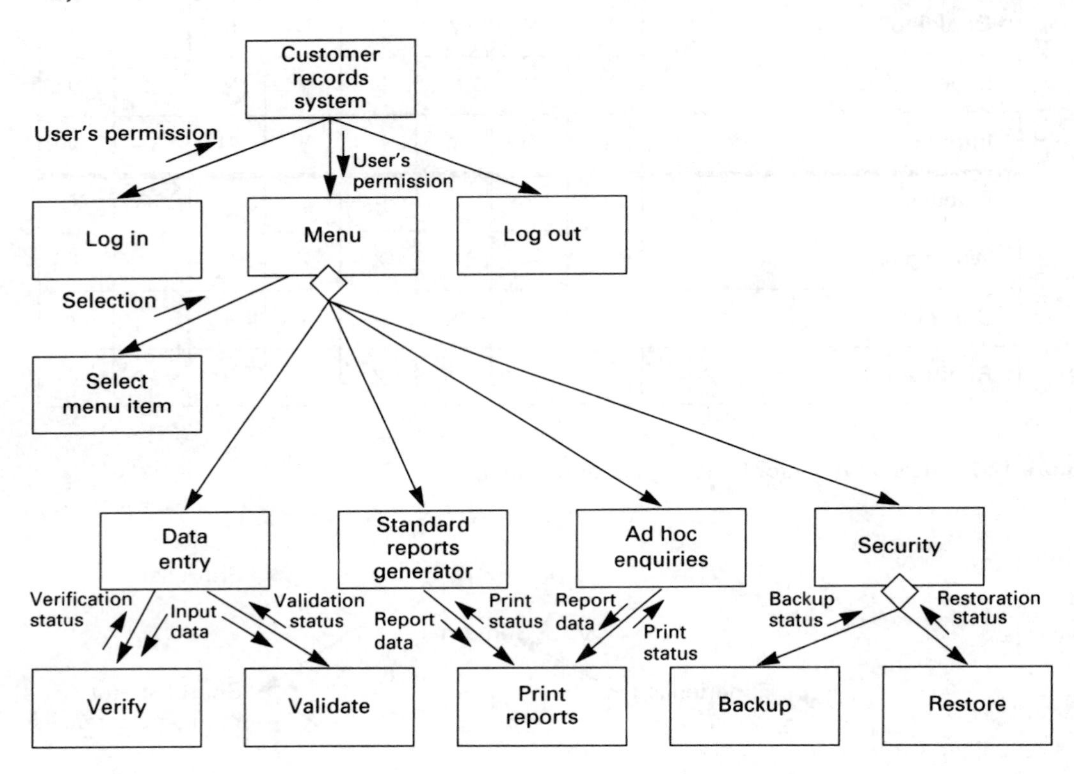

Figure 12.9 Program structure chart

Note that selection between several modules is indicated where several arrows emerge from a diamond on the edge of a module.

c) A structured walkthrough is a meeting at which the designer of an item such as a program module will describe the design by stepping through it and explaining the design decisions and problems encountered. The meeting may vary in formality from a discussion between the designer and a colleague to an organised gathering attended by the designer's peers (who have a detailed knowledge and understanding of the issues) and also staff from other areas of development, who can offer impartial assessment and advice. It may also be appropriate to have users' representatives attend as well.

The purposes of a structured walkthrough are:

- to check the results of aspects of a systems development that cannot be easily checked in other ways
- to exchange information about the concepts and decisions behind the design
- to monitor progress and identify problems.

11 The initial uses of information technology

Many banking and related applications are ideally suited to computerised information systems since they involve the capture and processing of lots of transactions made up of numerical and coded data. Banks started to use large mainframe computers. The development of multi-user systems, however, meant that enquiries could be made on demand simultaneously by many different users and batch processing could still be run for many routine transactions.

A major proportion of a bank's or building society's low-level, operational activities involves the meticulous entering and checking of transaction data such as account numbers, sort codes, cheque numbers and currency figures. The amount of manual operation was reduced by the use of magnetic ink character recognition (MICR) systems which can recognise characters pre-printed in a stylised font on cheques and other documents. This also reduced the amount of writing customers had to do and reduced the risks of customers omitting these items or entering them incorrectly. Similarly, printing devices were developed to reduce the manual effort required and the risks of errors.

Mini-computers, which are smaller and cheaper than mainframes, were installed in branch offices. The branch's mini-computers could satisfy local processing requirements and provide links to the central records computer over wide area networks (WANs), using national and international telephone systems which were developing data switching techniques such as the UK's Public Packet Switched Network.

This growing dependence on computerised systems means that expensive backup and standby facilities are used such as **hot standby systems** and uninterruptible power supplies (UPS).

The effects on the public

Most of the developments and uses mentioned provided benefits to the financial institutions but were largely unnoticed by the public. Other developments with higher public profile are:

- The use of public cash points or automated teller machines (ATMs) which automatically dispense money and process other routine transactions for customers who have to gain authorisation by using a magnetic stripe card and password or personal identification number (PIN).
- Electronic point of sale systems (EPOS) at supermarkets and other retailers, using terminals with devices such as bar code readers which read coded information from goods without the checkout assistant having to key in data.
- Electronic funds transfer (EFT), which eliminates much of the paperwork for customers paying for goods. A magnetic stripe card with the customer's name details, similar to those used in ATMs, is automatically read by a device on the retailer's till and the funds are automatically transferred over to the retailer's account by the central computer.

One of the major problems was that, despite all the technology involved, getting some transactions cleared still involved some human intervention and there was a delay in updating customers' accounts as transactions took several days passing through the banks' clearing system. This problem is being addressed by the introduction of other EFT systems such as the UK banks' BACS (Banker's Automated Clearance System), CHAPS (Clearing House Automated Payment System) and SWIFT (Society for Worldwide Interbank Financial Telecommunications).

Another application is that of credit-reference services offered by organisations which use a large database system to store and access details of companies' and individuals' creditworthiness.

Telecommunications

The use of information technology and telecommunications equipment to communicate all sorts of data is known as electronic data interchange (EDI).

A development that will accelerate the use of information technology is the development of digital telephone networks such as ISDN (Integrated Systems Digital Network) in the UK. This is replacing the analogue system, which is only really suited to voice transmissions. Using ISDN it is possible to use the same equipment, such as a personal computer attached to the telephone system, to send and receive voice, data, fax and graphics.

Benefits and problems

The main benefits of the increasing use of information technology by financial institutions can be summarised thus:

- Increased amounts of transactions can be processed and stored quickly.
- Reductions in paperwork can be made.
- Out-of-hours financial facilities do not need human tellers.
- More up-to-date information can be provided.
- Worldwide currency transactions can be processed.

There are some general problems associated with the technology:

- the depersonalisation of the workplace
- the depersonalisation of the customer-institution relationship
- dependence on information technology and the need for backup and standby systems
- the need to introduce compatibility between systems and cooperation between institutions and governments
- changing security problems.

The threats of fraud

When accounts and other records are stored centrally on computer systems there is the risk of unauthorised access and modification of data. When computer systems were initially introduced, most computer frauds were committed by in-house staff who had the necessary technical expertise and system access.

The true extent of the problem is not clear, as the institutions concerned often depend on a reputation for security and integrity and are reluctant to expose themselves to adverse publicity. Auditors have had to develop audit techniques, such as audit trails, which can be incorporated into computerised information systems – 'through-the-computer' systems are needed rather than relying on auditing the paperwork around the system.

ATMs present a risk since they are sited in unattended public places. There has been considerable concern about 'phantom withdrawals' on customers' accounts which they claim to have no recollection of. Again, the extent of the problem is not clear and there is debate over whether they are caused by systems errors or deliberate fraud.

The increasing use of telecommunications has increased the risk of unauthorised access to systems, which is known as 'hacking'. There is also the risk of the introduction of various types of computer virus, whose effect can be anything from a minor inconvenience to the complete erasure of a system's data and programs. The Computer Misuse Act 1990 has created three new offences relating to computerised systems:

- unauthorised access
- unauthorised access with intent to commit another offence
- unauthorised modification of data or programs.

However, unauthorised access can be difficult to identify and bring to court. So it is vital that organisations carry out risk analysis and take measures to prevent unauthorised access and fraud. Measures available include:

- careful screening of staff
- the use of appropriate passwords and access structures
- logs to record system's usage and access
- control of input media such as floppy disks.

12 The brief descriptions of the two proposed systems highlight two main considerations:

- benefits and disadvantage of tailor-made and off-the-shelf systems
- the difference between centralised and distributed systems and their effects on the organisation structure.

Tailor-made and off-the-shelf systems

Current requirements

A tailor-made system should satisfy the organisation's current requirements more satisfactorily than a standard, off-the-shelf system, since it is developed specifically for them. The users can cooperate with the developers and contribute to some of the phases of development. There may be competitive advantage to be gained from having a unique system.

Maintenance and future requirements

The tailor-made system can be maintained at the organisation's request without the developers having to take other users' concerns into account. This can be important, since the suppliers of a tailor-made system will be reluctant to have the administrative costs of updating all their users with an upgraded system and possibly having to support several versions of the system. On the other hand, an off-the-shelf package may be used extensively by tens or thousands of users who can mutually benefit from the identification and solution of problems. Similarly, the users of an off-the-shelf system mutually benefit from enhancements made at the suggestion of other users.

The organisation must bear all the costs of development and maintenance of a tailor-made system instead of sharing them with other users. These costs include time spent by the users' staff in contributing to things like requirements specifications.

The major proportion of the cost of producing a system, particularly software components, is incurred as salaries to the systems development staff. The marginal costs of producing a system in volume are usually relatively small, so users can benefit from lower costs as the number of systems sold increases. Similarly, it has been shown that maintenance costs form a substantial proportion of the total costs incurred by a system throughout its lifetime and much of these costs can be attributed to salaries rather than materials.

Availability

An off-the-shelf system is likely to be immediately available (although delivery and installation may take time) but there will be even more delays while the tailor-made system is being developed.

Risks

With careful consideration of its costs, features and suitability, the purchase of an off-the-shelf package should have relatively small risks associated with it. The organisation that has a system specially developed is exposed to the risks associated with systems development. These can be significant, as many of the activities involved in development are difficult to estimate and liable to unforeseen problems and delays. A lot of systems developments turn out to be unsatisfactory because they are:

- over budget
- overdue
- unsuitable for the users' requirements.

It may be possible to have a system developed on a fixed-price contract, but this will not lessen the effects of delays and may put pressure on the developer – which is likely to lead to errors and omissions.

Training opportunities and support groups

These will not be established for a tailor-made system unless the organisation sets them up and incurs their costs. Training is available for many off-the-shelf packages, either from the supplier or from specialist training organisations. Similarly, many established systems have user groups associated with them.

Conclusion

The costs and risks associated with having a system tailor-made are substantial and organisations should look very closely at available off-the-shelf systems to find out whether there are any that will meet some or all of their requirements.

Centralised and distributed systems

A centralised information system is one where all services are provided from a central point. In a large organisation this will often be a mainframe or mini-computer with a powerful central processing unit, large storage capacity and a multi-user operating system. Users can access the system using terminals either linked directly to it for local access or via the telephone system, using modems for remote access.

A distributed system is a network where some or all of the information systems services are supplied from different points. These are in effect discrete but linked sub-systems, some of whose facilities may be shared. There are many variations in the configuration of distributed systems and a useful way of examining a system is to establish how particular facilities, such as processing power or disk storage, are provided. A sub-system which supplies a particular facility is called a **server**. Two examples of distributed systems are shown below:

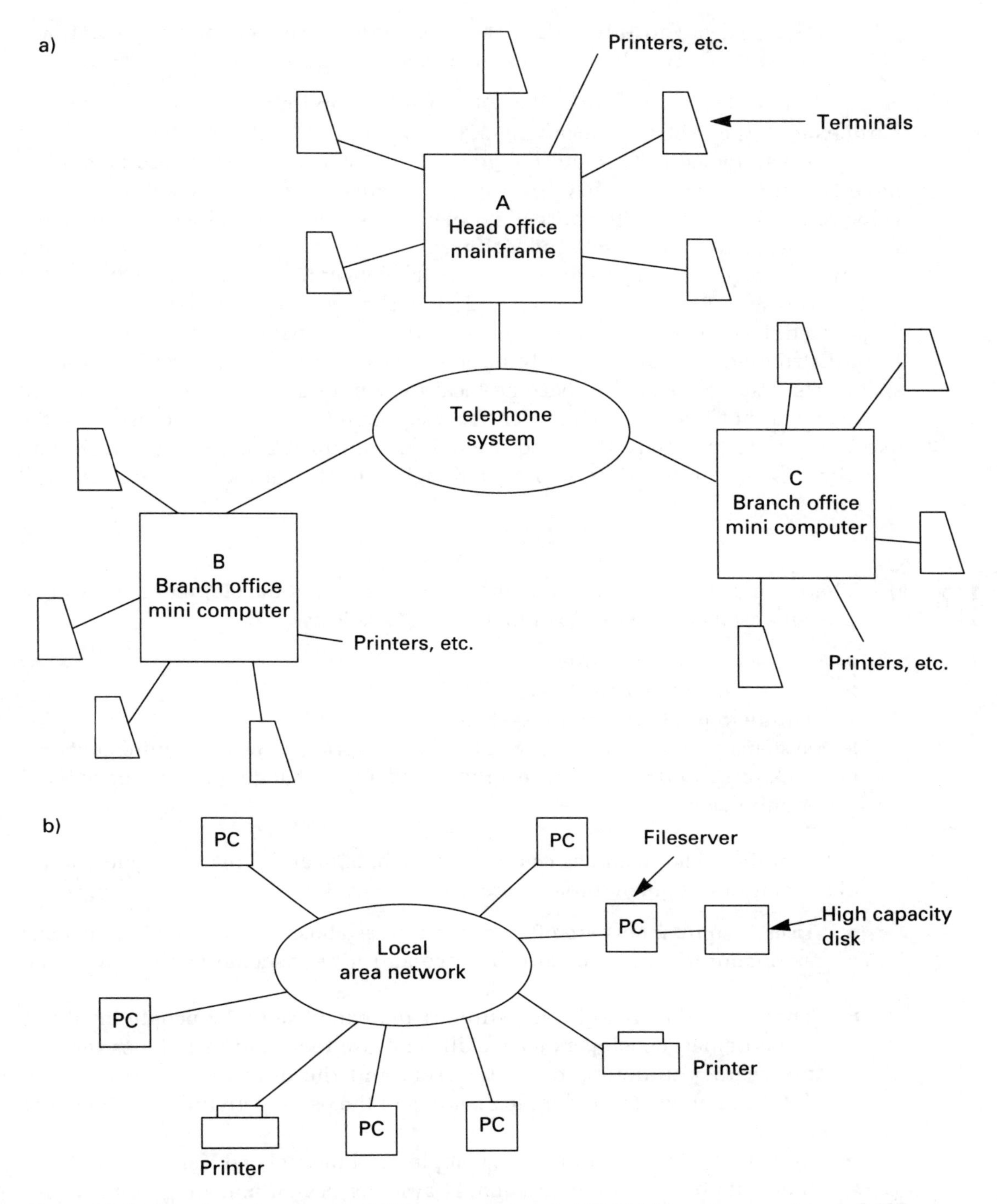

Figure 12.10 Distributed systems: a) Wide area network (WAN) b) Local area network (LAN)

In large organisations, a centralised information system will usually be managed by a specific information systems department or division. This department will usually house the main computer and be staffed by specialist operators, analysts, designers, etc. with a hierarchical structure of managers reporting to an information director. This sort of structure is typical of organisations that use a functional departmental structure. One of the benefits of a centralised system is that it provides good opportunities to exert strict control, since the main components of the system are physically located in one place and the information systems specialists can be given well-defined activities within clear lines and divisions of responsibility. However, the separation of information systems facilities and staff from other departments may lead to conflict with the end users whose requirements the system should be satisfying. The information systems department may lack flexibility and become

12

elitist if its staff fail to fully appreciate the users' needs and the organisation's objectives, particularly as both of these may change as time goes by.

A distributed system is more likely to provide flexibility and allow users to participate in the control and running of the system so that it suits their varied and changing requirements. This and the growing use of small, office-based computers have contributed significantly towards the trend towards end-user computing. However, distributed systems present problems of systems control where equipment is spread over several locations and staff responsible for its use and management are not information systems specialists. There is the danger that work will be duplicated and resources used inefficiently and that the system may become a set of fragmented, incompatible sub-systems. To counter these dangers, organisations with fully distributed systems use an Information Centre run by information systems specialists. Users will tend to become local experts in aspects of systems use and management, but the Information Centre's role includes advising and assisting the users in trying to satisfy their requirements, controlling shared resources and establishing and monitoring overall strategies on things like systems use and security.

13

a) There are a lot of examples of information systems developments that have proven unsatisfactory in one or more of these aspects:

- excessive financial costs
- significant and costly delays
- failure to produce a useful system
- systems proving to be inefficient or inappropriate to users' requirements
- lack of flexibility and an inability to adapt to changing environments and requirements.

Many of these shortcomings can be overcome, but careful planning and control of systems development projects are needed because:

- Users' requirements are often difficult to establish and are likely to change as organisations' procedures change and users become familiar with the system.
- There are differences in the attitudes and expertise of the people involved. In particular, developers have skills and use tools and techniques that are not readily understood by the users and the developers do not have detailed knowledge and understanding of the users' activities and sphere of operation.
- Systems development involves complex and interrelated tasks.
- Elements of development such as systems design and programming are difficult to assess and tangible results which can be accurately assessed may only emerge at later stages of the project .

b) *Network charts and CPA*

Network charts are used to show the relationships between activities and sub-tasks in a project in such a way that calculations can be done on their durations, potential slack, and the effects of changes and delays. They allow project managers to identify the critical activities – those that determine the overall duration of the project. The technique can be extended to take into account the uncertainty associated with estimated timescales.

There are variations on the actual conventions and format of network charts but some basic principles apply:

- A project is analysed and split into smaller sub-tasks, which can be split into progressively smaller tasks until the tasks are considered small and well enough defined to be easily managed and estimated.
- The relationships between tasks are identified in terms of the necessity or desirability of the order that they must occur.
- A chart is constructed to show this information. One format of these charts, called 'activity-on-arrow', uses arrows to represent tasks with circles to represent events – the end of a task and the start of associated tasks which follow it. The arrows and circles are labelled to identify them and the estimated duration written on the arrows. The project manager can then calculate earliest and latest start and finish dates and identify where spare time, called 'slack' or 'float', may be available. The project's network chart is illustrated below:

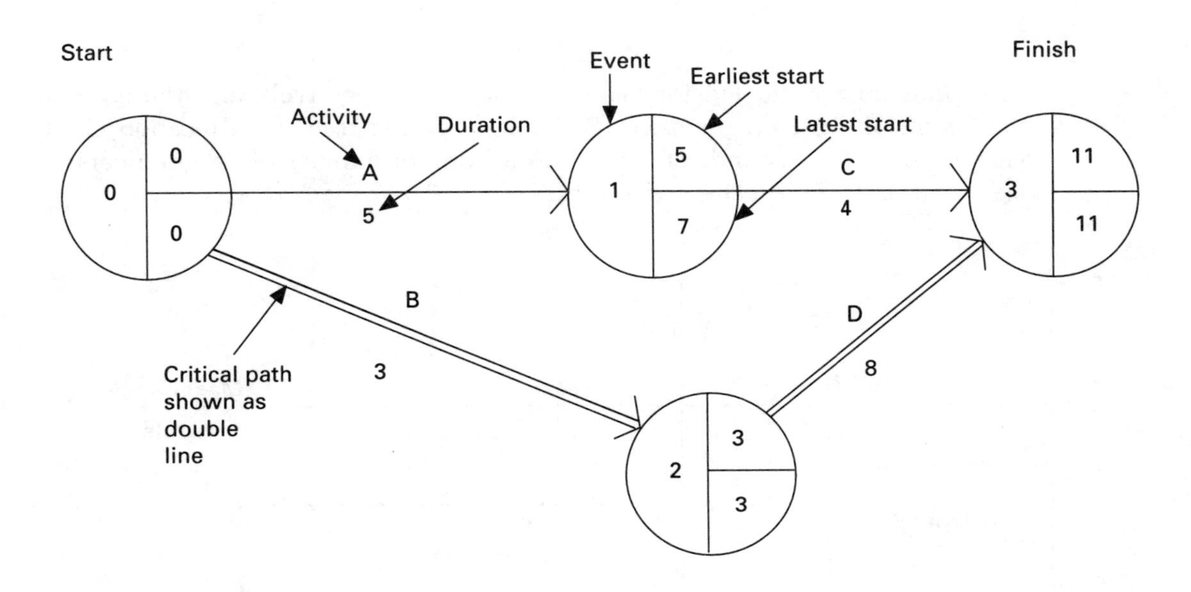

Figure 12.11 A simple network chart

Gantt charts

Network charts are not usually drawn to show time to scale, so it is not easy to see which tasks may be carried out concurrently. This makes it difficult to schedule the necessary resources, since they may be needed in several different activities if their timing overlaps.

Gantt charts do not show the logical relationships between activities but they do show the dates during which they are planned to occur. The activities are listed on the left of a grid which shows dates and appropriate units of time (typically days, weeks or months) along the top. A line or bar is drawn opposite each activity and across the dates that it is planned for, with spare time being shown as a dotted line. The project's Gantt chart is shown in Figure 12.12.

Resource allocation charts

The project manager can estimate the resources required for each activity and draw a block chart for each particular resource over the project's duration. The maximum amount of that resource can be shown as a dotted line and then compared with the levels of the resource required so that periods of over-allocation show up. The project manager can then try to make adjustments to prevent exceeding available resources. For example, if four, three, and six

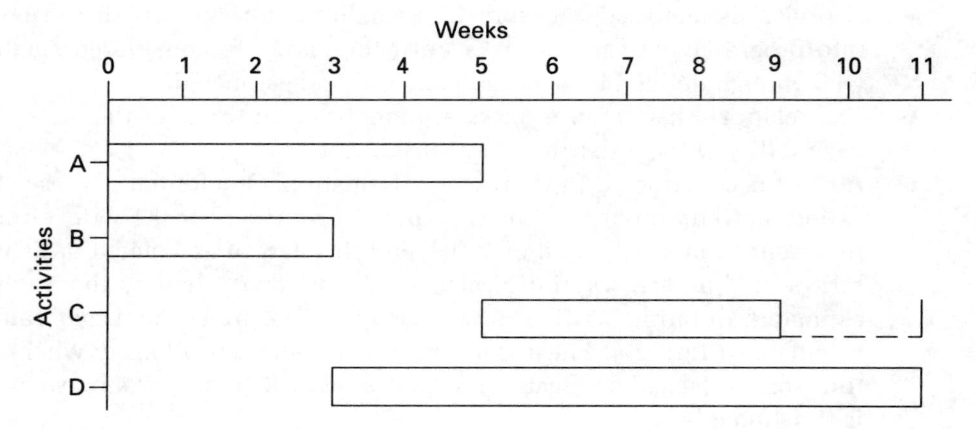

Figure 12.12 A simple Gantt chart

programmers are needed for tasks A, B and D respectively and there are a maximum of eight programmers available, then the resource allocation chart shown below clearly indicates that the maximum number of programmers is exceeded in the fourth and fifth weeks.

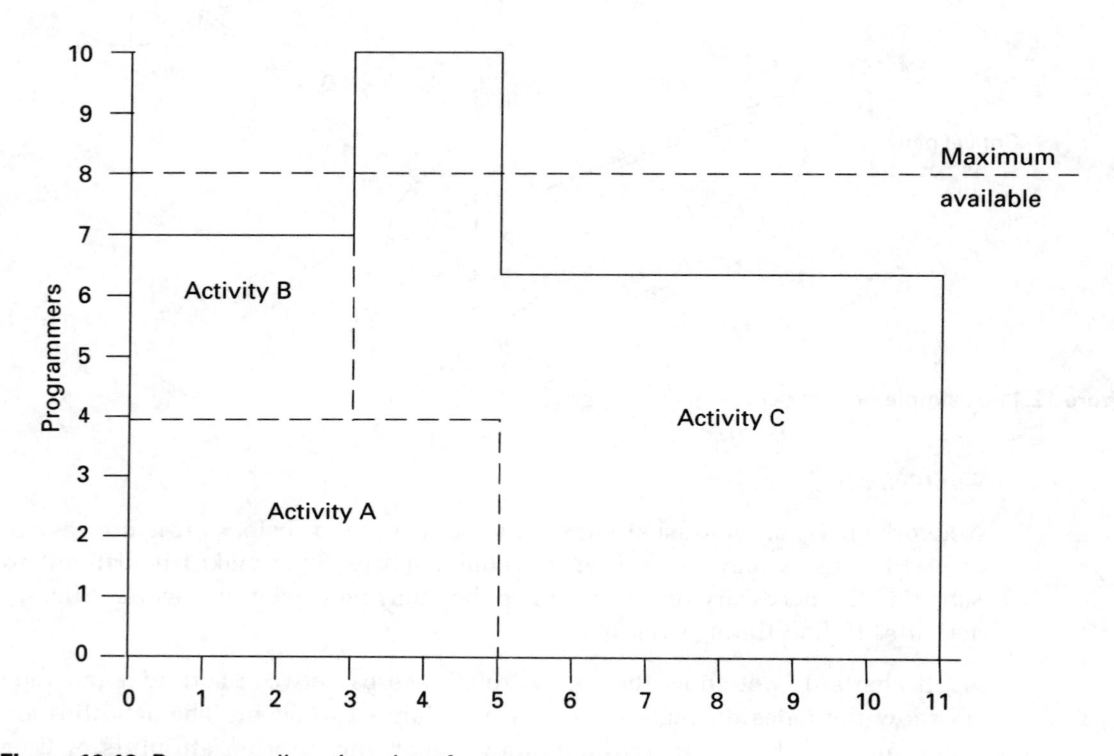

Figure 12.13 Resource allocation chart for programmers

14 a) In general, documentation serves three main purposes:

- to provide a permanent record of information
- to communicate information
- to focus the author on the matters under consideration.

Systems documentation

Systems documentation is produced at various phases of the systems development lifecycle. It is usually provided by, and intended for, the specialist systems development, operations and maintenance staff and, sometimes, the users' management or representatives. It is not usually aimed at the system's end-users. Some of the key documents and their purposes, from which you could have chosen four, include:

- feasibility study reports: to provide decision makers with an outline of various aspects of a proposed system's feasibility such as technical, operational and financial feasibility
- requirements specification: to present the users' information needs in a clear and detailed manner
- systems design documents: the names and format of design documents will vary with the approach that is adopted to the development. Their purpose is to assist the designer with the analysis, preparation and recording of designs for particular aspects of a system. They often use symbols and conventions in a specialised way. Examples include:
  - data flow diagrams, entity-life histories, relational database tables, data dictionaries
  - software design specifications, such as decision trees and structured English text, which outline the logic and processes that the programmer must implement
  - program listings, which contain the instructions that the computer must carry out and are written in a programming language accompanied by comments and commentaries
  - benchmarks and acceptance tests, which provide information about the system's performance under specific operating situations
  - project management plans, which show details of the activities, resources and timescales involved in a development project. Common forms of plans used are network charts, Gantt charts, resource allocation charts
  - system's usage logs and error reports, produced while a system is operating to allow systems managers to monitor usage and errors
  - installation manuals, which include details of how an item of software or hardware can be introduced into a system and are usually aimed at the system's managers.

User documentation

User documentation is supplied to the end-users to enable them to use the system and learn how to get the maximum benefit from it. Typical user documents and their purposes, from which you could choose two, are:

- user guides, which provide comprehensive but non-technical information about all aspects of using the system
- technical reference manuals, which provide technical details of the system which will enable the more experienced users to maximise their use of the system
- quick reference guides, to give users access to basic information in a simple, readily accessible format
- tutorials, which lead the users step by step through sample uses of the system to allow them to familiarise themselves with its principal features
- release notes, details of new features and changes in the current version of the system.

b) On-line help is a term used to describe facilities whereby the user of a software package can summon instructions and information which is quickly presented on the screen of the workstation or terminal. In effect, part or all of a machine-readable user manual is available to be displayed in human readable form without the need to find and then search through a paper document. Many

12

modern software packages include on-line help facilities which are context-dependent – they can automatically identify and display the information most likely to be useful for the user's current command or process. On-line help facilities are claimed to greatly increase user productivity and reduce user frustration.

Software support helplines are a service supplied by the suppliers of systems to provide users of their systems with telephone access to support staff who have a comprehensive working knowledge of the system. These support staff should be technically competent and also able to deal comfortably with non-specialists. A good helpline is a great benefit to users who can gain the reassurance that there is a friendly, knowledgeable person to turn to. These support staff should also collect and log information about users' problems and views which can be useful in enabling the suppliers to update their systems by solving problems and satisfying users' requirements

User groups usually focus on a single type of system or one developer's products. They are usually established and run by users rather than by the developer. although they may get assistance from the developer. User groups provide a forum for users to exchange information and discuss problems and issues relating to the system and to more general issues. They can act as a useful pressure group, allowing users to express dissatisfaction over particular problems and other aspects of the user-developer relationship, such as pricing and upgrade policies.

A concern shared by many users is that they may become locked into a particular developer's systems by virtue of the expense of a system and the time invested by the user in setting up and gaining experience of it. Unless developers produce systems that can work harmoniously with other developers' products, their systems are closed and users become a captive market. There may be products and systems that users wish to use in conjunction with their existing system but cannot take advantage of, due to incompatibilities with their existing system. Many incompatibilities between systems could be removed if developers cooperated and used common protocols and conventions. In the large and increasingly competitive market of supplying information systems, the large and well-established developers have felt pressure from their own users, often via the user groups, who want more open systems. Another factor in the move towards more open systems was the establishment by the International Standards Organisation (ISO) of a model for open systems called OSI (Open Systems Interconnection).

15

a) An interface is the means by which two systems interact and communicate with each other or the common point or boundary between two things. So the 'human-computer interface' (HCI) or 'user interface' is the means by which the user and the computer system interact. The HCI requires two components: physical equipment, which allows input to and output from the system, and a style of interaction.

Equipment

Typical input devices used in the HCI of office-based systems include:

- **keyboards**, which are usually 'QWERTY' style keyboards with additional cursor control keys, special function keys, etc.
- **keypads**, which comprise only the numeric keys or a few special-purpose keys
- **mouse** and pointer-based devices, which control the position of a pointer on a screen

- **scanners**, which convert an image on paper into a digital format
- **microphones** and other devices which convert 'natural language', in either spoken or written form, into digital signals that can be recognised and processed by computer
- **bar code readers**, magnetic ink character recognition devices (MICR), and other devices which recognise data coded as stylised characters, marks or a series of lines
- **magnetic stripe cards**, which contain small amounts of data encoded on a strip of magnetic material.

Typical output equipment includes:

- **visual display units (VDUs)**, monitors and screens which display information in textual or graphical formats
- **printers or plotters** of various kinds, which produce output printed on paper
- **loudspeakers** producing coded bleeps, music or 'natural language'.

Style of interaction

Some of the listed devices have yet to be fully developed, such as natural language devices, or have a fairly limited scope for the style of interaction which they allow, such as MICR and bar code readers. Currently the most widely used and flexible HCI equipment for office applications are a 'QWERTY' style keyboard and VDU, with a mouse and printer. The styles of interaction used in these systems can be categorised as:

- **menus,** which display a limited number of options and allow the user to select one option in a simple manner
- **interactive question and answer** sessions, where the user is asked a series of questions, each answer allowing the system to select the next question appropriately
- **command languages,** where the user types instructions in a particular format – often with the opportunity to vary the instruction by adding further instructions, usually in a short-hand or coded form.
- **input and output forms** displayed on the VDU, where a standard screen layout is displayed, often to reproduce the look of a printed form
- **graphical user interfaces (GUIs)**, which use pictorial symbols, called **icon**s, to represent commands and files. Many modern GUIs are called 'WIMP' systems, which stands for Windows, Icons, Menus, Pointer (or Windows, Icons, Mouse, Pull-down menus)
- **reports**, where information is tabulated and presented on the VDU or in printed form.

b) The main factors which should be used when designing an HCI are:

- The **situation** in which the equipment will be used, such as a clean, secure office or a dusty stockroom.
- **Costs** of the equipment used and of the resources needed to provide the chosen style of interaction. For example, most WIMP interfaces require sufficient processing power to manipulate the images and a VDU capable of displaying detailed images.
- The main **purpose** of the HCI – which may be narrow, such as to read a product code, or much wider, such as to allow the use of a variety of more general applications programs.
- **Ease of use and the users' expertise**. A regular and expert user may prefer the freedom to issue any of a wide range of subtly different instructions where an inexperienced and occasional user needs more guidance and a

limited number of options. An easy-to-use HCI can help to reduce data entry errors and improve the users' attitude towards the system. Advice, instruction and help facilities should be displayed where appropriate.

- **Security and control** which may be necessary to prevent accidental or deliberate damage to the system or unauthorised access to its data. Procedures could include the use of passwords and limitations on the commands that are available to particular users. Controls can also be incorporated into the HCI to trap and check suspect data before it enters the system.

Taking these factors into account, we can design suitable HCIs for the listed activities. A 'QWERTY' style keyboard and VDU, with a mouse and printer would be suitable equipment for all four activities:

- For invoicing and processing sales, purchase and nominal ledger data, a menu to limit the options available and allow the user to quickly select the particular accounting operation they require. Input and output forms displayed on the VDU name the data items and show the expected format of data will help the user to read and enter data and reduce errors. Consistency of layout between the screen display and paper forms will speed up transcription and reduce errors. Lists of transactions and summary information could be generated on printed reports for more permanent recording.
- Development of new applications is likely to be carried out by an expert using some form of programming language, possibly a fourth-generation language (4GL). Initially a question-and-answer style of dialogue could be used to allow users to specify their main requirements and then a command language would allow sufficient flexibility to specify the details.
- Sorting and searching data in a database requires that the user specifies the particular criterion for the operation. A question-and-answer style of dialogue could be used for simple or standard operations. A particular form of command language called a **query language** would allow the more experienced user the flexibility to carry out *ad hoc* and complex operations. The results of operations could be generated on printed reports for more permanent recording.
- Logging the movements of books in and out of the warehouse could be aided by using a bar coding system, with input and output forms on the VDU to display the information in human-understandable form. Again, the results of operations could be generated on printed reports for more permanent recording.

16 *Memorandum to the Managing Director on legal and security issues relating to our new computer system:*

a) The main legal issues and legislation which are likely to relate to our new computerised system are:

The Data Protection Act 1984, which was introduced to safeguard the rights of individuals in relation to the information about them that is stored and processed automatically. It was also needed to bring the UK into line with some of its trading partners. The main definitions in the Act are:

Personal data is information about a living individual which allows that individual to be identified. The person is referred to as the **data subject** and the organisation or person controlling the content and use of the information is the **data user**. **Data equipment** and **data processing** are defined to limit the

Act to data that is electronically processed or stored in a form that will permit electronic processing. The Act does not refer to paper records so we have not previously had to register our manual systems.

The Act is supervised by the Data Protection Registrar and all data users (and organisations such as bureaux who process personal data on behalf of others) are required to register. The Act lays down eight *Data Protection Principles* relating to the acquisition, content, use, disclosure and storage of personal data. Individuals are entitled to see personal data that relates to them, and have it erased or corrected where appropriate. Non-registration or violation of the principles can lead ultimately to criminal prosecution.

The Act has some exemptions where there is either no threat to privacy, or, at the other extreme, where disclosure would not be in the public interest. Use of personal data for payroll, pension and accounting data may be exempt from the Act, so our uses may be exempt.

Along with all businesses using computerised systems, we should study the Act carefully and establish whether registration is required – and consult the Data Protection Registrar for clarification if necessary. Failure to comply with the Act could lead to prosecution, with the risk of punishment and loss of reputation. The Act also addresses the issue of trans-border data flows to try to ensure that data entering and leaving the country complies with the spirit of the Act. This could become an issue if we have dealings with branches or organisations in other countries.

Copyright laws have been updated by the Copyright (Computer Programs) Regulations 1992 to tighten up on unauthorised copying of software. Suppliers of software usually issue a licence to use that software – in effect the purchaser buys the licence to use the software. (Licences can usually be purchased to cover different uses. Alternative licences could be purchased for use by a single user, several users, network use or unlimited use.)

It is important that organisations control the use and copying of software so that licensed use is not exceeded – for example, if we purchase a licence for a single user we must not allow access to the software to all the users on our network. Software suppliers have set up an organisation called FAST (Federation Against Software Theft) to help to police the use of software.

The Computer Misuse Act 1990 has created criminal offences relating to the unauthorised access to computer systems or modification of data held on them. This is an attempt to combat 'hacking', where people try to make unauthorised use of a computer system, either for fraudulent or malicious purposes or simply for the entertainment of breaking security measures. This Act has been difficult to implement so we need to take proper security measures to guard against the risks of hacking and the potential threats to our new system.

Health and safety legislation applies to computer systems and attention has focused on the changes that have occurred in the workplace with the growth of computer terminals and personal computers. There is concern that operators of keyboards and screens should have suitable working conditions including lighting, furniture, rest periods and so on. We should ensure that our new system is installed with these factors in mind and explain the health and safety implications to all our staff.

b) There are several measures we can take to control access to our new system. These include:

Physical access controls

Physical access to the computer equipment, including terminals, storage media and the computers themselves, can be controlled by:

- receptionists or security guards to check people entering and leaving the rooms or building where equipment is sited
- mechanical keys on doors
- keypads, 'swipe-cards' and other systems which use a variety of methods such as infra-red, magnetic or radio signals to sense a user's access code and to restrict access to authorised codes
- keyboard and system locks, which can physically disable either the power to a system or the use of the keyboard.

Logical access controls

The most widely used forms of access control are based on log-in procedures which incorporate the checking of one or more passwords. To be effective, log-in procedures and the use of passwords should be controlled and monitored. Several procedures can be used:

- There should be a minimum length and format of passwords to prevent the use of short or easy-to-guess passwords; users should be forced to change their passwords regularly.
- Further log-in attempts should be refused for a period of time after several failed attempts. Attempted log-ins and log-outs, whether successful or not, should be automatically recorded and scrutinised to look for suspicious circumstances.
- Systems can be set up so that if a user is logged in but not actively using the system then the user is automatically logged out after a period of time.

As well as general access to the system, passwords can be used to allow access only to particular applications programs and to the operations that a user is allowed to carry out.

Control can be refined by varying the permissions that users are granted. A typical set-up is to use:

- three categories of user – all users, a group of users, or systems manager
- three categories of access permission – no access, read-only access, read and write access

and to set the appropriate category of permission to each category of user.

Electronic access controls

A further control measure is to encode or encrypt data so that it is not easily understood by either humans or electronic devices without decoding or decryption. This would help reduce the usefulness of information if it is accessed by an unauthorised user and help reduce the risk of electronic eavesdropping on our network.

Personnel

Personnel should be checked to ensure that they are trustworthy. All staff should be made aware of the need for security, since any system is only effective if it is operated properly and the need for it is understood.

A major criterion when establishing access controls is that they should be appropriate to the organisation's requirements. While making a system more secure, each additional security measure is likely to add to the costs and administration of the system and can increase the inconvenience to users going about their legitimate business. We should evaluate our security policy and take measures which are neither too lax (which will leave us open to unacceptable risks) nor excessive (which will lead to unnecessary costs and reduced user productivity).

17 a) A useful way of considering information in an organisation is to split the activities, and the information required, into three levels: operational, tactical and strategic, with the low-level transaction processing feeding information at the low level. This is illustrated below:

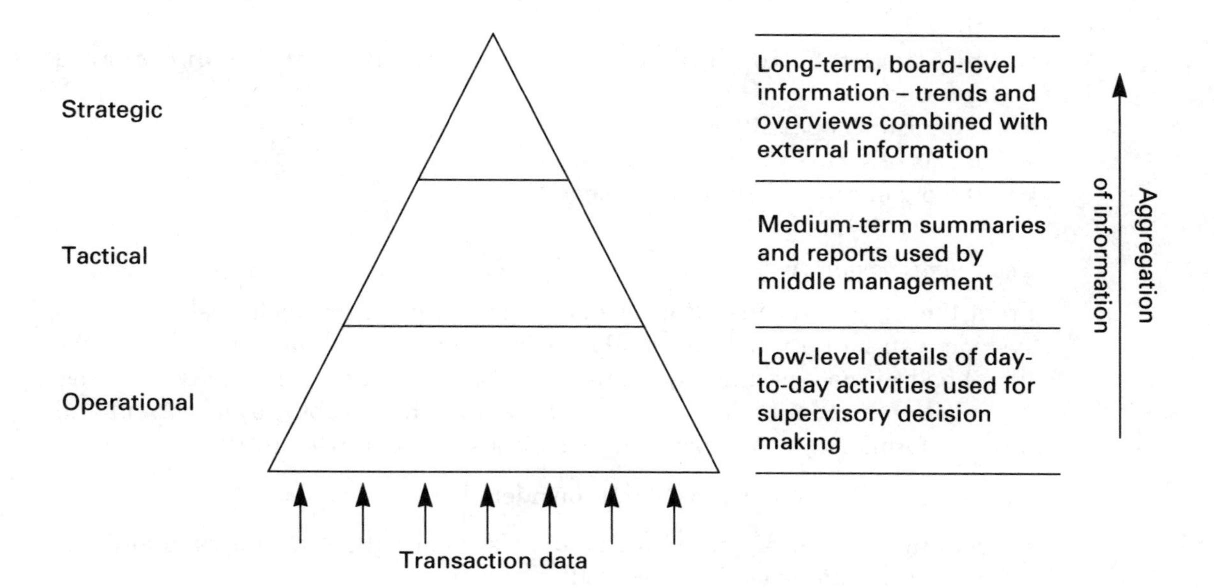

Figure 12.14 Levels of information

Activities and decisions at all levels of the organisation require information that can be provided either directly or indirectly from the transaction processing system.

On a daily basis, detailed transaction information about individual sales and purchases such as names, addresses, product codes, prices, etc. enters at the lowest operational level of the organisation where immediate or short-term decisions are made about availability, delivery, credit, etc. The full, detailed information is processed and stored.

Most transaction processing systems will check the detailed information and consolidate or summarise it to form regular management reports which can be useful at the tactical level. It can be used by middle managers to make medium-term decisions about things like staffing levels, stock requirements, credit-control policies and sales campaigns. Middle managers will generally not need to know details of individual transactions, but there should be reporting-by-exception procedures which will alert them to unusual events such as a massive individual sales order or a substantial increase in suppliers' prices.

The management information can be further summarised or aggregated to provide the board and high-level managers with information about long-term performance and trends. Armed with this information, the board can analyse and compare performance with long-term estimates and with externally gathered information about competitors, market share and economic climates.

This will influence long-term decisions about expansion of the business premises, entering new markets and so on.

b) The main areas which should be included in a feasibility study report are:

Requirements

Before looking at possible options, it is essential that the organisation's current and future requirements in the relevant areas are clarified, at least in outline. These will be specified in terms of factors like:

- the number of users and their expertise
- the response times to execute certain operations under certain conditions
- the number of operations or transactions that must be processed in a certain time
- physical location and the needs for communications and shared information
- expansion capabilities
- levels of security and backup required
- the organisational structures needed.

Technical feasibility

From the initial consideration of requirements, potential technical aspects of systems can be outlined and analysed to establish the main options and the likelihood of meeting the requirements. It is essential that the study team has up-to-date information systems expertise so that the capabilities of current and future information technology and systems are assessed realistically.

Issues that will probably have to be considered are:

- whether a centralised or distributed system suits requirements and the communications facilities needed
- what processing option, or mixture of options, is required, such as batch, demand or real-time, and whether on-line processing is suitable
- whether single-user or multi-user systems are suitable
- the processing power required of the computers
- the storage capacity and format
- security features
- backups and disaster recovery arrangements
- expansion capability
- the user interface and possible training requirements
- the availability of ready-made or easily configured systems, including both hardware and software components, and the possibilities for developing a customised system.

Organisational and operational feasibility

The effects of the the various options on the organisation's structures, policies and personnel need to be examined. These will include factors such as:

- possible reorganisation of departmental structures and responsibilities
- changes to working practices, particularly where these include replacing existing manual procedures with computerised systems
- staffing levels and training
- the effect on personnel of changes to staffing levels, working practices and responsibilities
- the effect on the organisation's image, including the way it is seen by its clients and its staff.

Economic feasibility

In order to compare and evaluate systems, a cost-benefit analysis should be carried out, containing the following items:

- *Direct benefits* such as:
  - reduced operational costs (like staff wages) due to time saved by automation
  - reduced systems costs, such as lower maintenance costs on new equipment
  - reduced rent and rates on storage of manual records.
- *Indirect benefits* like:
  - better information leading to better decision making
  - increased control, leading to lower stockholding and improved credit control
  - reduced routine work, leading to better use of personnel expertise
  - improved image due to better use and presentation of information.
- *Direct costs* like:
  - expert consultancy and advice
  - development costs on analysts, designers, programmers, etc.
  - purchase of hardware and its installation
  - cost of data conversion from the old to new system
  - user training
  - redundancy payments
  - running costs like maintenance, security and backup.
- *Indirect costs* such as:
  - finance costs on loans
  - disruption to normal operation during development and changeover.
- *Other factors* which are not easy to categorise, such as the effect on staff morale and the effect that changes to operations will have on the organisation's clients or customers.

These items are all estimates. Some factors can be assessed and quantified fairly easily, such as the cost of particular items of hardware. Others, such as the cost of software development, are more difficult to assess. Factors which are intangible and very difficult to quantify include the effect of disruption to normal operations. The report should indicate the degree of uncertainty associated with the estimates.

Once the costs and benefits have been itemised, the techniques used in cost benefit analysis include:

- **Volume/cost/profit analysis (VCP)**, a form of breakeven analysis applicable where the costs and benefits are closely related to the volume of transactions handled by the system, which may be the case for systems such as an order processing system. A graph is drawn of the total costs and total benefits against the volume to establish the volume of transactions at which the system becomes profitable.
- **Payback period**, the time it will take for the system's benefits to accumulate to the point where the initial investment is recouped. The payback period does not take account of the longer-term benefits or the time value of money.
- **Net present value (NPV)**, where a discount factor is applied to future cash flows to establish their current value.

12

Comparison of options

The feasibility study report should conclude by comparing the options. Options may be rejected if they do not meet requirements in one or more areas of feasibility. Any remaining options can be ranked and the National Computing Centre (NCC) has developed a weighted ranking system to allow a weighting to be allocated to factors which cannot be easily quantified.

18 a) *Functional organisation structure*

Some organisations can usefully be regarded as a set of functional sub-systems, each carrying out a major function within the organisation. The sub-systems themselves can be decomposed into smaller systems, so that a hierarchy is formed based upon the functions carried out. Typically, the major sub-systems form departments within the organisation, with the departments split into sections. This form of structure is common in large manufacturing and service industries.

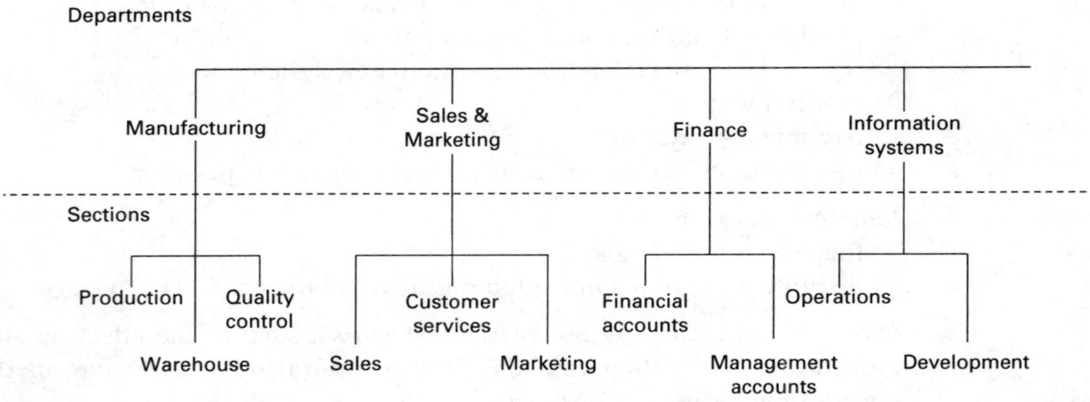

Figure 12.15 Functional organisation structure – a manufacturing organisation

Matrix organisation structure

In a matrix structure activities are divided on a functional basis and a product or service basis.

Clients / *Functions*

	Market research	Design	Finance	---------
Client 1	Members of team 1 --------------------			
Client 2	Members of team 2 --------------------			
Client 3	Members of team 3 --------------------			

Figure 12.16 Matrix organisation structure – marketing consultant

The primary objective of an information system, in common with all support functions, is to provide an effective and efficient support service to its users. This entails that it gathers, processes and provides all the required information in a timely, appropriate and cost-effective manner. In order to achieve this:

- The system should have a a high enough degree of independence from the organisational structure to be able to service the organisation's overall requirements and not just those of one department or function. Information is a valuable resource that should be regarded as belonging to an organisation and not to an individual department or user.
- It should be adaptable and flexible enough to meet new and various requirements.
- It should be properly developed and managed to meet the organisation's information strategy.

Traditionally, information systems have been regarded as a specialist area requiring expensive equipment and skilled staff. Within a functional organisational structure, an Information Systems Department was often formed and grew as new applications of information technology were developed. However, this often led to a situation where the information system was inflexible and failed to fully meet the users' requirements. Information systems staff often tended to regard themselves as an elite group working in isolation from the rest of the organisation and they had insufficient knowledge of the users' requirements and the environment in which the organisation operated. Information systems often failed to meet all three main objectives, because:

- They had too high a degree of independence and placed insufficient emphasis on the fact that the system carried out a support function to other departments.
- There was a lack of flexibility in their design.
- They were developed and controlled by staff who had insufficient knowledge of the organisation and its users.

The traditional computerised information system, consisting of a large and costly computer requiring a special environment with expert staff, does not fit easily into a matrix organisational structure. Consequently, organisations with a matrix structure were slow to take advantage of the benefits of computerised systems or developed fragmented systems without enough control to avoid wasted efforts and duplication of work and information.

b) End-user computing is a term used to describe the situation where the users of an information system have sufficient facilities and expertise to be able to use and control all or parts of a system without total reliance on specialists. There is a growing trend towards end-user computing which has been brought about by:

- the continued technical development of small, office-based systems using micro-computers
- the availability of user-friendly systems and the increasing confidence and ability of non-specialists to use them
- the increasing variety of applications not just for typical data-processing but also for uses like CAD/CAM (computer-aided-design and manufacturing) and DTP (desk top publishing)
- the availability of communications technology and networks
- the use of central but shareable databases which have allowed organisations to adopt a database approach providing users throughout the organisation with a flexible information system
- the use of fourth-generation languages (4GLs) and applications generators which simplify and speed up the development of systems.

12

In an organisation with a functional structure, this trend towards end-user computing may be resisted by information systems departments who see their role being diminished as hardware control and use begin to spread through all areas of the organisation instead of being confined within their department. However, end-user computing requires overall control to avoid duplication of effort and inconsistencies between systems and data, which may occur if users seek to satisfy their own immediate requirements. Many organisations have adopted the database approach to their information systems, giving users shared access to a flexible store of information while allowing central control of the information. In addition, users need more advice on the purchase and use of systems if they are to make effective use of them. A current approach is to adopt end-user computing and change the role of the Information Systems Department to that of an Information Centre. This exercises control over centrally held information and provides expertise to advise users who are more actively involved in satisfying their own information needs. The information centre maintains a level of control over equipment, programs and data which is spread throughout the organisation.

An organisation with a matrix structure is well suited to end-user computing and the flexibility it allows users. There is less likely to be the sort of resistance encountered by an organisation which has a semi-autonomous information systems department, but there is the need for control to avoid the growth of an *ad hoc* and fragmented system and, again, the information centre approach is adopted as a way of providing expertise, control and guidance. Computer systems expertise then becomes another skill which is taken into account when forming teams to handle particular products, services or clients.

19 a) In common with other areas of management, project management is concerned with effectiveness and efficiency – in this case, of the project and the system it produces. Project managers aim at providing a system which is *effective* in that it:

- meets the users' requirements at all levels within the organisation
- is produced according to specified standards
- is properly integrated with existing systems
- has sufficient flexibility to cope with changing requirements.

The objective of *efficiency* means carrying out the project within the constraints set while making the best use of resources.

The key factors involved are the planning, monitoring and control of four elements:

- **Time:** timescales should be carefully and realistically planned and then progress monitored and control action taken where necessary.
- **Resources:** these include equipment, materials and personnel.
- **Quality:** completion of the project and the activities within it is not enough; they must be carried out to the required quality standards to avoid problems later in the system's life.
- **Costs:** the first three factors all involve some sort of cost which can be attributed to the project and, therefore, to the cost of the system itself.

The management of these four items must be integrated since they are all related. For example, extra testing to achieve high quality involves the cost of additional staff time and materials and may also affect the project's duration. Similarly, any attempt to apply additional resources in order to reduce timescales can lead to increased costs and the risk of compromising the system's quality.

The planning will involve structuring the project by splitting it into progressively smaller tasks and activities. The development of the system will involve the sorts of activities described in the systems development lifecycle (SDLC). The project managers will have to be particularly careful about the plans for customising the software, as it is notoriously difficult to reliably estimate the duration of the tasks involved. The duration of tasks will need to be carefully monitored to ensure that costs do not escalate and that the project's timescales are not extended. In addition, the project manager will probably have to deal with changes to the users' requirements during the development, which will necessitate modifying plans.

b)

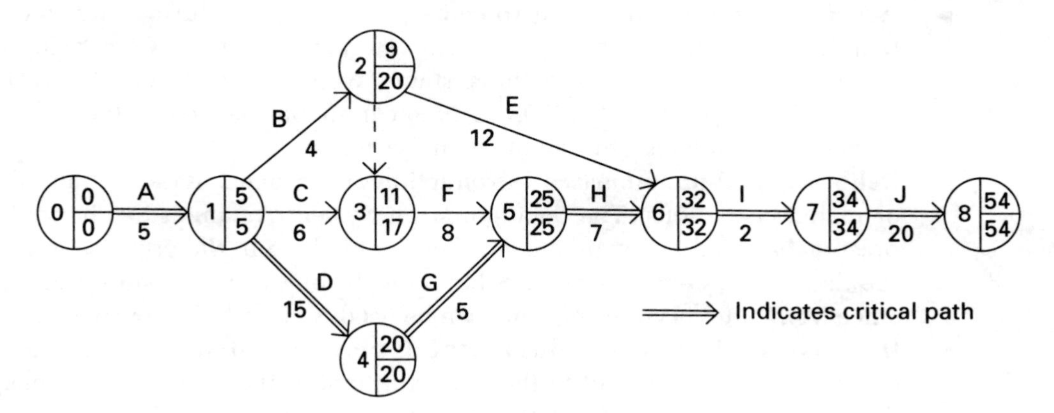

Figure 12.17 Network chart

The critical path, shown as a double line on the network chart, is A–D–G–H–I–J.

The total planned duration is 54 days.

The float associated with each activity (in days):

A	0
B	11
C	6
D	0
E	11
F	6
G	0
H	0
I	0
J	0

20 a) The integrity of a system and its data refers to the level it has of useful properties, such as:

- accuracy
- up-to-dateness
- completeness
- consistency
- security.

The aim should be to keep all these properties at a high level and thus maximise the integrity of the system and its data. The main ways of achieving this are by controlling input data, checking data at various stages and trying to prevent accidental damage or unauthorised access.

Threats to integrity of a system and its data can be categorised as follows:

- **Accidental destruction and damage** caused by natural disasters (such as flood or fire), or by equipment or software malfunction (such as disk heads 'crashing'), or by human error such as failure to carry out basic operating instructions. Both Systems A and B are vulnerable to this threat. But, since System B is a multi-user system, it will involve more people and more equipment, possibly located in more than one office, and will be more vulnerable than the single-user personal computer System A.
- **Deliberate destruction and damage** caused by people intent on industrial sabotage, terrorism or malicious actions. Again, the larger more extensive system, B, is the more vulnerable one.
- **Accidental introduction of erroneous data** occurring during any stage of handling the data – input, processing, storage or output. Comparing the stages of data processing on the systems, we see that System A has data supplied and stored on CD-ROM, which cannot be changed by the user and is therefore much less vulnerable than System B.
- **Deliberate and unauthorised introduction of erroneous data** by fraudulent or malicious actions. The data stored on System A cannot be changed, is presumably publicly available and does not belong to the organisation, but the data on System B is changeable, does belong to the organisation and, since it includes accounting data, can be used for fraudulent purposes.
- **Disclosure of sensitive data**, which may be a disadvantage to the organisation if it is useful to their competitors, or if its disclosure damages the organisation's reputation or contravenes the Data Protection Act.

b) Risk analysis can be carried out to analyse threats in terms of:

- the probability of the threat occurring
- the criticality of the data – the importance of loss of integrity
- the costs of prevention and recovery measures.

Measures to maximise the integrity of data and allow recovery from disasters are often expensive, with associated costs (increasing the administrative overheads) and reduction in ease of use and user-friendliness.

Comparing systems A and B, we see that:

- For System A, the threats are relatively small. The data may be critical to the organisation but the costs of recovery are, at worst, the purchase of a new personal computer and a copy of the CD-ROM holding the data. So recovery would be relatively fast and inexpensive and, in most instances, the costs would be covered by general insurance policies. To minimise the inconvenience and short-term disruption caused by loss of integrity, physical access to the system should be restricted to the staff of the legal department, and logical access can be restricted by implementing a simple password authorisation system.
- For System B, the threats are more serious, since the data is private to the organisation, more widely available within the organisation, and undergoes all the stages of data processing. Accounts data is central to most organisations' operations. Preventive procedures will need to be more comprehensive:
  - Physical access to the system can be controlled by a security system on entry points to the organisation's premises; employing security guards or installing keypads, for example.
  - Logical access to the system can be controlled by using passwords and log-in procedures.

- File access will need to be controlled, since the system is used by all staff and for a variety of purposes. Multi-user operating systems provide facilities for setting file permissions so that users only have the access that is appropriate for their legitimate purposes.
- Staff should be selected carefully to reduce the risk of employing untrustworthy or careless personnel. They should be properly trained to use the system and made aware of the importance of the integrity of the system and its data.
- Checks should be made on data at all stages of processing. These should include verification checks to make sure data is correctly entered onto the system, and a variety of validation checks on data before it is allowed to be processed. Further checks should be made when data is processed and when it is output.
- The system should be regularly audited and audit trails incorporated within the computerised system – not just from paper records.
- Although the system's physical equipment is contained within the building, there may be occasions when users access the system from outside, using modems to connect to the public telephone system. Modems should be taken off-line when not in use and data encryption techniques used to encode data.
- Spurious copies of data should not be kept so as to simplify the administration of the system and avoid the risk of out-of-date and inconsistent copies of data being used.
- Backup copies of all useful data should be regularly and frequently taken and stored securely, with copies kept off-site.

A centralised multi-user system is less flexible than a distributed system and effects of the failure of a single component such as the computer's CPU, RAM or disk drive are more serious. A variety of contingency plans can be adopted:

- ▶ maintaining a duplicate system
- ▶ taking out insurance to allow rapid purchase and establishment of a new system
- ▶ using one of the disaster-recovery services offered by various companies, some of which offer the use of a relocatable computer centre.

21 a) The decision-making process can be broken down into stages and effective decision making relies on suitable information (see Figure 12.18).

At UC Clothing, the trigger is the instruction from the board to the marketing director, which was based on information about falling profits. In order to define the problem, the marketing director will have to get details of sales, expenses and profits over the past few years and also external information about total markets and the economic climate. Structuring the problem will require further information, such as a breakdown of sales and costs by product. Then the marketing director can identify particular areas of interest and possible plans of action. This will require yet more information which can be analysed to try to predict the outcomes. If the information is adequate then a decision about a course of action can be taken; otherwise, the marketing director will have to identify where information is insufficient and re-analyse the situation again when further information has been gained.

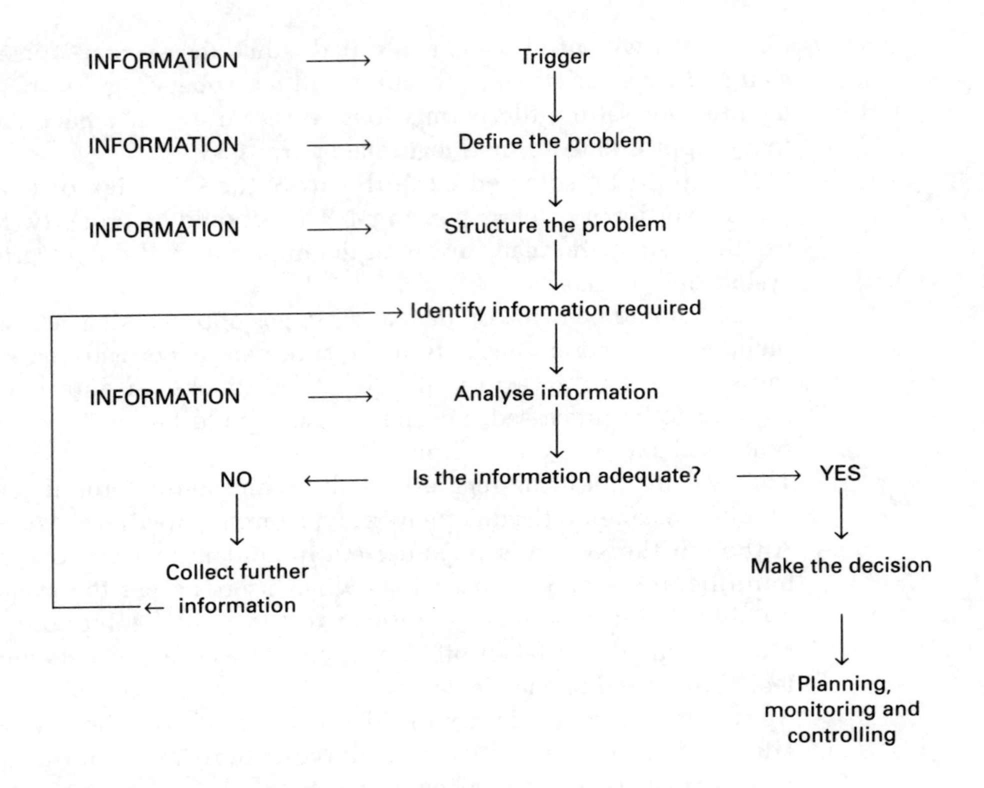

Figure 12.18 Stages of the decision-making process

b) Better-quality information can be the basis for making better decisions. Computerised information systems can help UC Clothing in the decision-making process in several ways:

- **A transaction processing system** can provide the low-level information which can be analysed and summarised by a **management information system** to provide figures for current overall performance in terms of total sales, expenses and profits and also by breaking down the information to show the performance of particular products or range of products, the performance of particular sales outlets or salespersons, and so on. Computerised transaction processing and management information systems can help to provide accurate, up-to-date information. However, this information relates to UC's current and past performance.
- **Decision support systems** can help UC to make better decisions by providing the tools for modelling parts of the organisation and allowing 'what if' analysis to predict the outcomes of different courses of action. For example, a spreadsheet can be used to set up a financial model of the business, showing profits based on UC's profit margin, which can then be set to different levels and the results compared. In this way information about the future, in the form of estimates, can be gathered.
- **An executive information system** could be used to help UC's decision making, as it combines information which is internal to the organisation, possibly fed from its management information system, with external information from its environment, such as indicators of general economic climate and details of competitors in UC's markets. The information is usually displayed graphically and the user can 'drill down' to get more detailed information about lower levels within the organisation. This may allow the marketing director to quickly identify problem areas or less profitable products and compare UC's performance with that of its competitors.

The transaction processing and management information system provide current information. The decision support system allows modelling of future performance. The executive information combines information from the other systems with external information and displays it clearly at an appropriate level of detail.

22 a) The main elements of a system, in general systems theory terms, as they relate to UC Designwear are:

- the system itself – UC Designware
- its environment, which includes the general economic climate, current fashion and trends, the labour market, etc.
- the boundary between the system and the environment, such as retail outlets
- the interfaces in the boundary through which information passes to and fro
- inputs and outputs, such as fabrics and finished goods, etc.
- processes such as design and manufacturing
- sub-systems, often in the form of departments or sections, which usually handle processes such as the design or manufacture of products.

The system has objectives. Probably UC Designware's objectives include making a profit from the sale of fashion clothing. Some of the sub-systems perform processes which are primary to this objective, such as manufacturing; others carry out support processes, such as administration. The sub-systems also have objectives; so, for example, the design department aims to design good-looking, fashionable clothes, the manufacturing department aims to cost-effectively produce high-quality clothes. The sub-systems' objectives may to some degree conflict; this can lead to entropy, in the form of wasted effort and materials, and to sub-optimal performance of the overall system. For example, a feature of a design which is currently fashionable and therefore considered desirable by the design department may require an expensive manufacturing operation which will increase costs significantly and is considered undesirable by the manufacturing department.

b) A **closed system** is shut off and independent from its environment – it can neither affect nor be affected by its environment. An **open system** is one which interacts with its environment and receives a variety of inputs, some of which are predictable and controllable but some of which are not. Similarly, an open system can influence its environment in both predictable and unpredictable ways. Systems can be considered as being more or less open depending on the character of their interaction with their environment – but the complex and unpredictable nature of human activity means that systems involving humans tend to be more open rather than closed.

The management of UC Designware may try to operate the manufacturing department as a more closed system than the design department. The manufacturing function aims to supply goods for mass markets so will probably be operated as a production line, with processes being automated or carried out in a prescribed manner in order to produce goods of a consistent pattern and quality. Its inputs will be strictly regulated according to rules about expected demand and the materials and personnel needed to satisfy demand. The design department will produce output in the form of design ideas which will need to be considered by other departments, such as marketing, and then processed to produce the patterns required by manufacturing. The design department needs to be able to collect and react to changing fashions and will welcome the creative, but unpredictable, input of designers.

12

c) Feedback plays a vital role in the control cycle that is applied to a system, since it provides the information about the effects of the system's output on the environment. Feedback into UC Designware will be in the form of information about levels of sales and returned goods and also in the form of opinions about the products' style and quality.

The manufacturing department will be more interested in *quantitative* information about the popularity of particular styles, sizes and colours and also levels of complaints about poor materials or workmanship. The reaction to this feedback should be fairly predictable – positive feedback in the form of higher than expected sales figures will lead to the corrective action of increasing planned production levels, and negative feedback will lead to reductions in planned production levels.

The design department will be influenced by this quantitative information but will be more concerned to get *qualitative* information in the form of people's views on the attractiveness of particular colours and designs. The design department's reaction to feedback will be less predictable, since negative feedback, indicating that progress is less than satisfactory, may lead to design changes which will tend to be subjective rather than laid down in objective rules.

23

a) There are several factors to be considered when looking at the three options for acquiring software.

Suitability for requirements

An off-the-shelf software package may not have all the facilities that Department X requires – particularly as it will be expected to support a wide range of activities, all levels of which will probably be fairly specific to Department X's particular objectives and methods of operating.

A properly resourced and managed software development should result in a system which satisfies Department X's requirements. However, it is recognised that user involvement, particularly during the requirements specification, increases the chances of developing a satisfactory system. The off-the-shelf package will have been developed without any reference to Department X's staff. It may be more difficult to include members of Department X's staff if the development is carried on by a specialist software house rather than their own specialists.

Problem solving and maintenance

Problems in an off-the-shelf package may be identified early in the system's life, since there are likely to be several organisations using it and fixes may be applied even before Department X experiences the problem for itself. Although problems may be identified and fixed, Department X will have much less control over the maintenance of the package and will have to rely on the suppliers for updates and enhancements.

If Department X uses its own staff to develop the system, they should have more control over maintenance but will have to retain the experts. If the system is developed externally for Department X then a maintenance contract should be included – but it may be difficult to take effective action if the developers fail to provide satisfactory maintenance.

Costs

Initial costs for an off-the shelf package should be less than for a specially developed one, since the developer can spread the costs across its customer base. Salaries for information systems development specialists tend to be expensive and Department X will have to cover all those costs, whether directly to its own staff or to the software house contracted to do a special development.

Availability and risk

Developing software takes time and there is always the risk of unforeseen problems which may delay delivery of the completed system and possibly increase the costs. An off-the-shelf package to run on the existing system may well be available immediately and if there is an existing user base then its performance can be checked with other users prior to purchase.

b) A computer bureau usually has its own computer systems and may offer a range of computer-related services. Organisations usually use a bureau if they cannot justify the costs of keeping full-time staff or acquiring permanent computer systems to do a specific task. Typical services are to run regular jobs such as a monthly payroll, or carry out one-off processes such as a major data-conversion. Bureaux may also offer consultancy and some software development services. It is unlikely that Department X would find a bureau useful, since it wants a permanent and comprehensive system and will want more direct control over the system's operation. If it opts for specially developed software then Department X is more likely to opt for a specialist developer rather than a bureau.

Computer facilities management organisations have prospered in recent years as organisations experience the difficulties and costs of managing their own computer departments. Where a computer bureau operates externally for its customers, a facilities management organisation will usually operate within the customer's premises. The customer retains more control than if it used a bureau but costs can be ascertained in advance and there may be economies if the facilities management organisation can spread the cost of expert staff between several clients. Some organisations have changed their internal information systems departments into separate facilities management companies.

A facilities management company could be of use to Department X by taking over some or all of the development of the software package within Department X. On a longer-term basis, Department X may find the use of a facilities management company a cheaper option than continuing to run its own department. However, it would involve a loss of control over the computerised information system and may lead to Department X's management failing to make proper use of the systems.

24

a) The term **systems documentation** is used to refer to the various documents that are produced and used during systems development and which may be referred to by systems maintainers once the system is in operation. It may be quite technical and make use of specialist terminology, symbols and diagrams. Systems documentation includes things like:

- feasibility study reports
- requirements specifications
- analysis and design documents, including data flow diagrams, entity relationship diagrams, etc.
- program specifications
- specifications of tests and reports on the results of testing
- program source code
- maintenance logs.

12

Systems documentation provides:

- a focus for the developer's ideas which can be recorded in a clear and consistent format
- communications links between the activities in systems development. For example, the design of a program module in the form of structured English links the designer's ideas to the programmer's code
- reference material for people who need to examine and maintain the system later in its life.

Systems documentation is not intended for the ordinary end-user of the completed system although, during the development process, end-users may be included in development activities and may need to understand the technical terms and conventions used. Some documents, such as a feasibility study report, will be aimed at the users' management, who will not usually be information systems specialists.

User documentation

User documentation accompanies a system when it is released for normal operation. It is intended for users who may be non-specialists. The complexity of the system will determine the form of the user documentation but it will usually be composed of the following:

- tutorial material to familiarise the new users with the system's basic facilities and operation and guide them through it with simple examples
- a users' guide giving full details of the system's facilities and operation.

In addition, modern applications software for personal computers will often also include some material which would be considered as systems documentation for a larger system. For example:

- installation and configuration instructions
- a technical reference manual giving details of things like the system's internal structures and file formats.

b) i) Systems maintenance is work on the system once it has been released to the users and is required to keep the system operating in line with users' requirements. Different types of maintenance and their purposes are:

- *Corrective*

  To cure problems or 'bugs' which have been identified in the way the system operates. Computerised information systems are usually a complex mixture of hardware and software components and testing during development, however rigorous, may still fail to uncover all such problems.

- *Perfective*

  As new techniques, components and methods of operation become available they may be incorporated into the system to make it more effective and efficient in the way it satisfies users' requirements.

- *Adaptive*

  It is reasonable to expect users' requirements to change, particularly as they become more familiar with the system, and if the system is to have a long, useful life it will need to be adapted to suit them. In addition, external factors may require the system to be adapted: for example, an accounting system may need to be kept in line with changes in government legislation.

- *Preventive*

  Some larger computer systems need routine maintenance in the form of servicing, such as changing of air filters and the cleaning and alignment of magnetic tape drive heads. This form of maintenance is becoming less necessary as hardware which is more tolerant of an ordinary office environment is produced.

ii) The systems maintenance phase represents a system's useful operational life and is the period where the users capitalise on the cost and effort of the earlier phases of development. It is therefore important that the maintenance is carried out properly to prolong the system's use.

An effective way of controlling system maintenance activities is to approach them as a form of mini-systems development. When the need for a maintenance activity occurs, the system's maintenance staff should investigate and document the need. Maintenance can be disruptive to the users as it often involves upgrading the system, which requires a period of downtime and some change in operation. Unless there is a need for urgent action, maintenance activities should not be carried out in isolation immediately they are identified. Changes should be prioritised and where possible carried out together in one period of maintenance activity to minimise disruption.

Whenever possible, changes should not be implemented initially on the live system but on an identical system, so that each change can be checked and tested, firstly in isolation and then together with any other changes that are being carried out at the same time. All changes should be carefully recorded, showing what was changed, why it was changed, when it was changed and by whom. The systems maintainers should try to avoid making quick problem-solving changes without considering either their effects on other parts of the system or the difficulty with which future changes can be made.

Only when the developers and users are satisfied that the changes are suitable should the live system be updated; the previous version should be kept in case it needs to be resurrected. Many organisations use computerised source code control systems which include change control mechanisms to help maintainers manage changes to software.

25 a) In order to do work at home which is currently done in an organisation's office, workers will need some basic equipment and facilities such as:

- a personal computer with sufficient processing power and storage capacity for the applications they use or a terminal (visual display unit and keyboard)
- a communications link to the employer's central database or system to allow data to be transferred to and from the office system – this can probably be provided by a modem which will allow the workers to connect their equipment to the telephone system
- suitable applications software to carry out their work and communications software to communicate with the office system. An electronic mail package could be very useful
- a printer, although maybe not one of high quality if it is only needed for draft documents

- sufficient working space and furniture to provide a proper work area
- a means of centrally storing data provided by the organisation, so that any workers who are telecommuting can share data and communicate with each other electronically
- a backup system, either using disk or tape drives at the worker's home or a facility for backing up data over the communications link.

b) Obviously the most suitable jobs are those which require little face-to-face communication between staff and no access to central physical resources or machinery. The staff will need to be reasonably expert at using the applications and familiar with the equipment that they use at home in order to be reasonably self-sufficient. The increasing sophistication of telecommunications systems, such as e-mail software and digital telephone systems which allow voice, textual or graphical data transfers, will make telecommuting a feasible option for an increasing range of jobs.

The sorts of jobs suited to telecommuting include:

- jobs which include a lot of travelling, such as sales representatives, where communication with the central office is limited to daily or weekly reports and the collection of schedules
- those involved in document production – authors, proof-readers, etc.
- administrative jobs where the necessary data is held centrally on computer
- designers who can use computer aided design software
- computer programmers.

c) For the employee, the benefits and disadvantages of telecommuting include:

Benefits

- saving on travelling time
- flexibility of working hours
- reduced interruptions from colleagues and customers
- freedom to determine the working environment
- time saved in the formalities of business contact.

Disadvantages

- need for more self-discipline
- the difficulty within the domestic environment of creating a suitable working environment that is free from the distractions of domestic life
- lack of social contact and feeling of isolation from colleagues.

For the employer:

Benefits

- increased worker productivity because of the benefits the worker gains
- reduced rent and upkeep of office space
- reduced travelling expenses.

Disadvantages

- costs of setting up the worker with suitable equipment and software
- ongoing costs of telephone communication
- lack of direct control and the ability to closely monitor workers' progress
- unavailability of staff when urgent contact is necessary.

26 a) Many organisations which established large information systems formed information systems departments which fitted into the existing functional hierarchy of departments separated physically and logically from each other. The staff in the department tended to be specialists – such as systems analysts, designers and programmers, or people with a narrow area of expertise, such as keyboard operators or computer operators.

A large mainframe-based computer system such as MultiShop's will require special environmental conditions and the computer will be housed in a purpose-built room with additional physical security precautions. This will increase the perceived isolation of the ISD from the other departments.

A typical structure is:

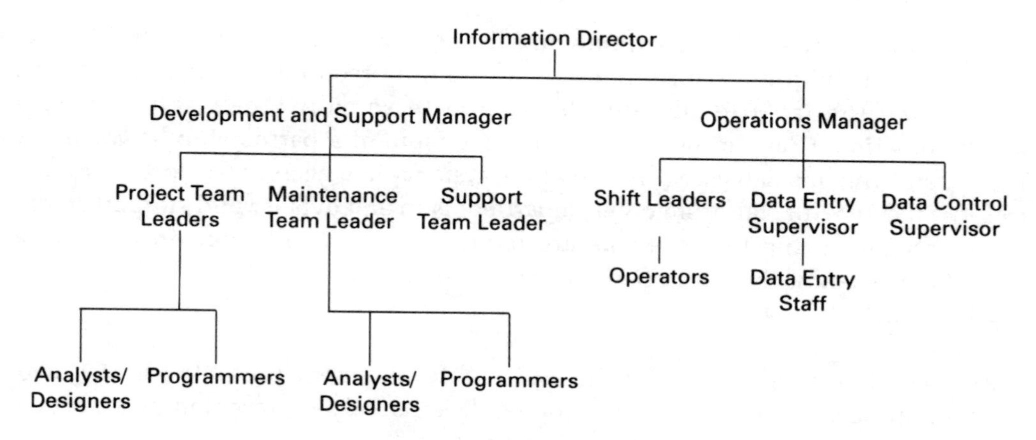

Figure 12.19 Structure of an information systems department

b) 'End-user computing' refers to a current trend where the end users who are not information systems specialists are taking a more active role in the purchase, development and control of the systems they use. The main reasons for this trend are:

- the availability of relatively cheap but powerful personal computer systems capable of operating in a general office environment
- the growth of user-friendly software and sophisticated applications generators which allow users to develop their own small applications
- the growth of distributed computing, based on personal computers and local area networks, allowing organisation-wide databases and communication systems to be accessible from the users' desk-top computers
- a backlog in the development of applications and user dissatisfaction with existing applications which have led to the recognition that users can and should be more involved with the development of their systems.

c) The main areas where personnel problems could be expected are:

The information system specialists whose domain is eroded as users take on more of their computing activities. A related trend is that of down-sizing, or right-sizing, where organisations replace their large central computer systems by small but more powerful modern computers or opt for a distributed system of small computers. Information systems specialists are likely to lose their traditional expert role within a large specialist department. Their options are to seek employment elsewhere in a diminishing marketplace, or adapt to the role of supporting the end-users in their computing activities. Organisations need to be aware of the effects on the information systems specialists and encourage them to use their skills within the new role, whilst being aware that disenchanted employees are likely to be unproductive or even disruptive.

Managers may wholeheartedly adopt the additional responsibility and changing working practices that accompany end-user computing. However, they may feel anxious about new technology if they are unfamiliar with it and may feel threatened by less experienced colleagues who show an aptitude for computing.

The users, who will need to be trained to make effective use of the facilities available to them. Some will be resistant to change and reluctant to learn new skills; others will be enthusiastic but will need to learn to harness their energy towards the organisation's objectives and not spend time on interesting computing activities which are not actually cost-effective.

The information systems managers, who have seen their role and responsibilities change. End-user computing requires different sorts of control than the traditional centralised, and to some extent isolated, computing function. Computing activities become more of a partnership between the user and the specialists, so information systems managers need to be able to work closely with staff from other departments in an advisory and support role, while still ensuring that systems are monitored and controlled in the interest of consistency of use and maximised productivity.

27 a) The traditional model of the systems development lifecycle (SDLC), which is appropriate to software development, is usually represented as a sequence of distinct phases in a diagram like this:

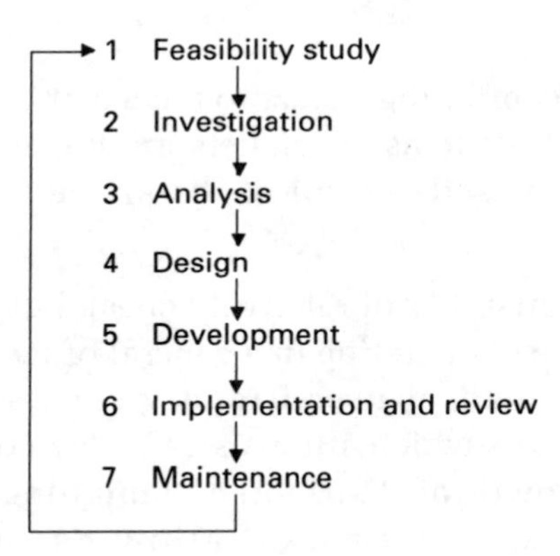

Figure 12.20 The traditional model of the systems development lifecycle

For a software development project, the activities involved will include:

Feasibility study: An initial examination of the current system takes place and alternative solutions are examined. From outline cost-benefit analyses, an option is recommended for further development.

Investigation: Detailed information is collected about the current system, its problems and the users' needs. Tools used at this phase and in subsequent ones include:

- data flow diagrams (DFD) to look at processes that transform data
- entity relationship diagrams (ERD) to model the data's structure
- entity life histories (ELH) to show the events within the system.

Analysis: From the investigation of users' needs, a detailed requirements specification of the current and future needs is produced.

Design: The detailed description of the proposed system is produced, possibly including decision trees, decision tables and structured English to design processes, program structure charts to show the program modules, and normalisation techniques to design data structures.

Development: The software is coded and module-tested before full testing.

Implementation: The full system is tested with live data; data files are converted and changeover to the new system is carried out. The new system and its development are evaluated.

Maintenance: In response to problems and to changes in the users' needs and in the environment, potential modifications to the code are analysed, designed and implemented.

b) SureBond may have some information systems specialists but will probably be unable to carry out a major software development without taking on temporary staff. This can cause friction with permanent staff, who may regard contract staff as highly paid but having little insight into SureBond's activities and requirements.

Data conversion may involve considerable additional keyboard data entry – which may fall as an extra burden on in-house staff or be carried out by temporary staff, who may not have the same commitment to maintaining the data's integrity.

If users are to become involved in the development then suitable staff will have to be made available – which may mean extra work for other staff and lead to jealousies.

All levels of staff will be affected by the new system, so suitable training and awareness sessions will have to be organised. It will be counter-productive to try to reduce costs by not investing the time and money to train staff to use the system effectively. There may be staff who feel threatened by the change, possibly justifiably if redundancies are planned. Managers may feel that the introduction of new systems threatens their authority and expertise; operational level staff may feel that their working practices will change for the worse with the reduction in opportunities for human contact. These problems must be addressed since users' commitment to the new system will be important for its success. It will be important that SureBond keep the staff informed of plans and progress to avoid the spread of exaggerated rumours.

c) Many computerised information systems are criticised for being overdue, over-budget and failing to satisfy user requirements. Increased user involvement is seen as one way of avoiding these criticisms. The main benefits of user participation are:

- Users are able to state their initial requirements rather than have the system developed on the basis of other people's assumptions about their requirements.
- Users who are involved in the development will become familiar with it and may suggest changes to requirements, which can be implemented early in the development rather than later (when changes become more difficult and expensive to implement).
- Users can learn about the system before it goes live and therefore reduce the subsequent training requirement.
- Users feel more committed to the success of the system if they feel a sense of ownership and will be less likely to worry unnecessarily about the

effects of changing to the new system.

- Changes to the original plans, whether costs or timings, may be better understood and more likely to be seen as necessary or unavoidable rather than as caused by the developer's inefficiency.

28 a) The human-computer interface (HCI) consists of physical equipment and a style of interaction. The main principles of HCI design are:

i) take account of the **users' physical working environment**, for example:

- an office where general conditions are likely to be reasonably friendly to standard computer keyboards and visual display units
- a factory or warehouse where dusty and dirty conditions call for a simple interface using robust components and simple operation
- a travelling representative who needs a portable interface with robust components
- a publicly available interface, like a bank automated teller machine (ATM), which may need to be weatherproof and may be protected from malicious or fraudulent physical actions.

ii) consider the **users' level of expertise**:

- A novice user who is unfamiliar with computer systems will need a simple interface, such as a menu, with clear, concise instructions at every stage of operation.
- An experienced user who is skilled at using keyboard and mouse may be most productive and comfortable using, for example, a graphical user interface (GUI) with on-line help facilities available on request.
- an expert user who is not only skilled at using the physical interface but knows the intricacies of the system may prefer to use a more direct interface (such as a command language) where commands can be issued in shorthand form directly to the system.

iii) analyse the **users' applications**, which will help the designer to achieve an HCI which is:

- clear, complete and concise. For example, an application which involves routine transaction details could use a screen laid out as a form, with related information grouped together and with data entry routines which allow data to be entered in a logical order
- consistent so that, where possible, different operations which use similar data display the data in a consistent format so that users are faced with a familiar layout. This principle can be extended so that different applications use a consistent interface where common commands are handled identically on each application
- efficient, so that the user is helped rather than hampered by the interface. The use of GUIs is claimed to increase user productivity but there may be applications which require keyboard input and where the use of a mouse or tracker-ball device will hamper the user who would prefer not to have to move between different input devices.

b) The warehouse administration system will be used by two sorts of people – the warehouse staff who handle the electrical components and their supervisors and managers. There may be more than one terminal or personal computer attached to the system – for example, one in the warehouse storage area and one in the office area. Different types of HCI will be appropriate for them.

A terminal is perhaps all that is needed in the actual storage areas of the warehouse, where it is likely to be exposed to dust, dirt and maybe accidental physical knocks – so a physically robust system will be needed. A simple menu system with screens designed as consistently laid-out input and output forms will allow staff to quickly become familiar with the system, and a clear and logical layout with built-in verification and validation checks will help reduce errors. The system should be capable of basic operations with a few keystrokes, as the users may not always wish to sit down each time an operation is required. To read details of components, a bar-code system could be helpful, with a hand-held bar-code reader attached to the system. Alternatively, a hand-held data logger could be used into which data can be read from a large number of components and which is then attached to the main system to download the data. A printer may not be required in this area.

If the managers use the system from an office then a standard personal computer could be used, as it will also provide other applications such as word-processing, access to a central database, and electronic mail. For consistency, the HCI giving access to the warehouse administration system should have at least the same facilities as the system in the warehouse store. The system could have a password access control and the top-level menu can have a variety of options, some of which are only available to certain users. If management wish to interrogate the system for various *ad hoc* purposes then a query language-based style of HCI could provide the necessary power and flexibility, assuming the users are expert enough to cope with it. A printer will be required for reports and possibly letters to suppliers and other correspondence.

c) Electronic data interchange (EDI) is currently being used or considered, particularly by large organisations. EDI is a form of electronic mail which allows for computer-to-computer communication but the actual data exchanged is often in a fixed format that is understood by both the sending and receiving systems. By the use of a consistent format much of the process of preparing and interpreting the data can be done automatically by the system.

EDI is likely to grow, along with improved telecommunications facilities including those offered by digital telephone networks using systems such as ISDN (Integrated system digital networks) and fibre-optic links. The lack of standards for EDI is currently proving to be an obstacle, but pressure from commercial organisations should see standards introduced and adopted in the near future.

Select Components could use EDI to automate its communications with suppliers, so that when goods reach reorder levels the system will automatically transmit purchase orders to the appropriate suppliers, with little human intervention required other than possibly an authorisation code. This could also apply to goods received where bar-coded items are checked into the system and also transmitted to the supplier's system for verification.

29

a) **Centralised systems** refers primarily to the use of a single computer system which handles all, or almost all, of the users' processing requirements and usually all data storage requirements as well. Systems may be multi-user with access available from terminals physically separated from the central computer.

Distributed systems refers to systems which have two or more computer processing systems which are linked together and which are used to share the users' processing requirements. Some or all of the data may still be centrally stored (for example, if corporate databases are used) but it can be accessed and processed by the other systems.

When computers were first used for commercial data processing they were large, expensive mainframe systems requiring special machine rooms and were, by today's standards, not very powerful. As the technology developed computers became smaller, cheaper and more powerful. (Today's personal computers and computer notebooks are particularly compact and significantly more powerful than the mainframe systems of the 1960s.) Instead of only being able to acquire a single computer, it became feasible for organisations to acquire two or more smaller systems which could be situated at different sites. Alternatively, a centralised system could become distributed by acquiring additional computers to link up with the initial one. The trend towards distributed systems of smaller, more powerful computers has been a major factor in the growth of end-user computing and has led to changes in organisation structures where the functions of the traditional centralised information systems department have been spread through the organisation.

Organisations have realised the advantages to be gained from not being limited to a single large computer system and so there are many system variations. For example, an organisation operating in several countries may have a large central system at its head office, handling corporate database operations, with smaller mini-computers at national offices and each office also having a network of personal computers. All the computers may be linked using both local and wide area networks (LANs and WANs).

b) *Flexibility*

Distributed systems generally offer more flexibility than centralised systems. With a distributed system, an organisation may decide to allocate particular functions to each processor or the processing may be organised according to the most appropriate geographical area. If one processing system becomes overloaded, it may be possible to balance the processing load. It is also generally easier to expand a distributed system by adding further processing systems, whereas a centralised system will require the upgrading or replacement of the main vital component. A failed component in a centralised system will lead to disruption of its functions while it is being repaired or replaced, whereas it may be possible to reorganise the functions on the remaining parts of a distributed system.

Compatibility

A problem with a centralised system is that an organisation may become tied to one particular manufacturer, whose equipment is the only route for expansion and upgrading – unless the whole system is scrapped and replaced with a new one. Distributed systems can allow equipment from several manufacturers to be linked, but compatibility has to be considered. Similarly, data files formats used by different applications may not be compatible and therefore may prevent exchange of data. The International Standards Organisations (ISO) introduced a model for 'open system' called 'Open Systems Interconnection' but it was rather too general to be used as a basis for a common set of compatible hardware and software protocols and industry standard protocols are only really starting to emerge now.

Security and control

Generally, an organisation will be more reliant on the main components and data of a centralised system than on any one part of a distributed system. However, although security and control of a centralised system may be more critical it is often also easier to implement them centrally.

The physical equipment of a centralised system can be in one place, where its environment and physical access to it can be carefully controlled. A distributed system is less easy to secure physically, especially if it includes personal computers situated in ordinary offices. The logical access to, and use of, a centralised system can be monitored and controlled by suitable administrative controls on the main system. Although there is systems software to monitor networks and distributed systems, it tends to be less effective and monitoring and control are required at each site of a distributed system.

The flexibility of a distributed system allows essential functions to be transferred to other parts of the system if a part of it fails, but in a centralised system backup systems are required which may never be used. Integrity of data is more straightforward to control if it is stored in one central system, but several inconsistent versions of the same data may possibly be used on different parts of a distributed system. Similarly, data held centrally can be backed up by a single operation controlled by a single operator, but distributed data will need to be backed up at each location.

30 a) For many organisations the computerised information system has become an essential part of their operations and constant attention and modification to their systems is vital if they are to gain competitive advantage from them. This is particularly true of organisations such as banks and other financial organisations, chains of retail outlets and multinational organisations. It becomes a more important factor as an organisation grows and its communication and information needs increase. However, there are still areas of activity where the human factor is the most important (such as consultancy and counselling services) and where the use of computers has had less impact. So it is not true that *all* organisations need computers to remain competitive.

It is certainly true that the components of computerised information systems are becoming smaller, cheaper and more powerful; this has enabled organisations to adopt distributed systems and end-user computing, which has made them more productive and effective. In addition, powerful commercially useful computers and telecommunication systems have also allowed people to use computers and access systems when it was not previously possible.

It should be remembered that most computers are used for support activities. There is a danger that organisations may try unnecessarily to keep pace with the technological advances and thus divert attention, funds and resources away from their primary activities. There are risks associated with both the development and the use of computerised systems and organisations should implement proper control and backup procedures as they become more reliant on their computers.

If an organisational objective is to provide employment and income for people, then the increasing use of computers which reduce the need for human activity may conflict with that objective. But it may be possible to find alternative activities for the people concerned or to maintain their incomes in some other way.

The statement that organisations must take advantage of smaller, cheaper and more powerful computers is true for many but not all organisations and there are risks and problems which grow in proportion to the use of computers.

b) During the past few decades the use of computerised systems has increased dramatically. It was generally felt that skilled information systems specialists such as systems analysts, programmers, computer operators, computer engineers and keyboard operators were in short supply and that a training for these roles would guarantee well-paid employment. The use of computer equipment in all walks of life has become more widespread but a major factor behind this has been the improved reliability of the equipment and the reduction in the need for human intervention in its operation. This has reduced the need for some specialists such as operators and engineers.

Similarly, automated and computer-assisted software development techniques have improved and the development of sophisticated application generation tools has reduced the human activities and skills required in the development and maintenance of new applications. The trend towards end-user computing means that many people who are not primarily information systems specialists are now able to satisfy more of their own information systems needs. This has reduced the need for programmers and other specialist software developers.

More non-specialists have acquired typing skills and the development of new styles of human-computer interfaces, such as graphical user interfaces and natural language interfaces, has reduced the need for keyboard operators such as specialist data entry staff.

These factors have led to a decline in the need for the traditional skills associated with computerised systems. To a certain extent, information systems specialists regarded themselves as an elite profession but the myth that non-specialists could not enter the specialists' world has been undermined as more of the workforce have become computer-literate. However, many skills that had been expected to become redundant, such as programming in the early programming languages like COBOL, are still required to maintain systems and this will continue for many years.

In general, the roles and skills associated with the information systems specialist have changed. Users, many of whom have grown dissatisfied with the systems designed by information systems specialists, now have the skills and desire to become far more involved in the development and operation of the system. The specialist is still required but operates more in partnership with the users and in support of them. The most useful information systems specialists will be those who also have an understanding of an organisation's sphere of activity and business operations.

c) Electronic communications systems should reduce, but not eliminate, the need for the traditional use of paper communications in business. Computer networks, both wide and local area, have facilitated the use of electronic mail (e-mail) which has advantages over telephone and paper communications in combining the following:

- speed, since electronic messages are delivered almost instantaneously
- the possibility of a permanent machine-readable record which can be printed if necessary
- delivery to more than one person by a single operation
- messages able to be read immediately or stored for later attention
- automatic forward and reply facilities
- preparation, sending, receiving and processing from the usual work area.

However, it will take some time before the majority of users have access to e-mail and have sufficient confidence in it to discard keeping paper records. There is also a tendency to generate and distribute more information, some of not which is not required, and this may increase the amount of paper record-keeping.

Electronic data interchange (EDI) will definitely reduce the time and paper used in business communications. An example of the use of EDI is where a customer and supplier have computer systems which use compatible data formats for their accounts functions. Conventional ordering procedures involve the customer printing off a paper purchase order and mailing or faxing it to the supplier, who then enters the details onto its computer system. With EDI, instead of printing off a copy, the data is transferred over a network where it is automatically received into the suppliers' systems without the need for manual input. However, until standard data formats are introduced, only organisations who have worked closely together will have compatible system.

Paper documents have some advantages:

- They can be read by anyone without the need for any electronic equipment.
- Some documents, such as legal documents and documents used to identify a person, require the uniqueness of a single paper document.

31

a) *Separate application-specific systems*

The way that many organisations initially developed computerised data processing systems led to separate application-specific systems. Typically the accounts functions and payroll functions were computerised first. Then stock control, for example, was computerised but using a separate application, even though the various applications may have run on the same central computer. Often, the data formats of the various systems were different and the users in each department controlled the data, which was regarded as their own, without consideration for other departments. In this way each application had its own separate and independent system.

Data exchange between separate systems is time-consuming, as data cannot be exchanged automatically but has to be output on paper from one system and then input manually into the other. The integrity of data across systems is difficult to maintain, as each additional manual stage in processing may introduce errors and there will be multiple copies of the same data which have to be kept up-to-date and consistent. For example, some or all of the information about a customer's order may be processed and stored separately by a sales order processing system, an accounts system, and a stock control system.

Advantages that can claimed for using totally separate applications that each have their own copies of the data are:

- Data formats can be kept simple and suitable for the application.
- Confidentiality is easier to maintain.
- The organisation is less vulnerable to loss or damage of data than if a single copy of data is used by all applications.

Integrated systems

Integrated systems enable each application to operate on its own independent data but they use compatible data formats and include facilities for data transfers between applications. This means that the advantages of reducing vulnerability to loss of data and confidentiality are retained – but the manual effort involved in keeping data up-to-date and consistent between systems is reduced, as are the opportunities for errors to creep in. Systems development and maintenance may be more difficult than with totally separate applications, since the data format has to be kept compatible for all applications.

A comprehensive database system

With a comprehensive database system there is only one copy of the working data which is shared by all applications. This eliminates the need for data transfers between applications and avoids the problems of multiple copies of the data having to be kept in line with each other. However, it does require an organisation to consider all its information needs and to develop a system which stores data in a flexible manner suitable for all current and expected future requirements. Since every application accesses the same data, it is essential that backup, security and control systems are adequate to avoid the loss or damage to the data.

b) A database management system (DBMS) provides the facilities that the database administrator and the database users require to make effective use of the system without necessarily needing to be systems development specialists.

Typical database operations that users require are:

- data entry routines, preferably with verification and validation procedures included
- data editing or amending
- deletion of unwanted data
- sorting of data in various ways
- searching or querying the data in various ways
- reporting facilities to generate output to screen or printer
- security procedures to control access to the data
- record-locking and file-locking to prevent simultaneous operations from interfering with each other's data
- backup procedures.

A DBMS will allow the database administrator to set up the facilities that users require. The most important aspect will be the development of the database structure and this should be managed as a form of systems development in order to ensure that users' requirements are fully investigated and specified before the structure is designed and then implemented. The DBMS will have facilities for:

- specifying the data record structure in terms of field lengths and formats and setting limits on considerations like the range of values that can be inserted in a field
- linking data from separate files so that data can be combined without the need for users to be aware of the underlying structure
- setting up of the tables that form the relations, if the database uses a relational structure
- setting up and maintaining a data dictionary which holds definitions and descriptions of all items in the system
- setting up security procedures
- automating backup procedures.

32 a) Risk analysis of a computerised information system should:

- methodically assess the threats to the system
- establish the effects of the damage if the threat becomes reality
- identify the available counter-measures to protect the system
- select suitable counter-measures by weighing the costs of the measures against the potential damage of the threat.

Counter-measures can also be considered as either:

- preventive, if they are designed to reduce the threat
- curative, if they are designed to allow recovery after a threatened event has occurred.

The areas of risk can be categorised firstly by their effects on the data, and then according to whether the threat is posed by accidents and natural disaster or deliberate human actions. The categories and some examples of threats are:

Effect on data	*Risk*
▶ Major damage or destruction	
– accident/natural disaster	Fire, flood, power failure, incorrect operation of system, faulty equipment
– deliberate action	Vandalism/terrorism leading to physical damage, viruses, deliberate deletion
▶ Alteration/inconsistency of data	
– accident/natural disaster	Incorrect operation of system, poor verification and validation procedures, software bugs, hardware faults
– deliberate action	Fraud, viruses
▶ Unauthorised access or disclosure	
– accident/natural disaster	Data left on display on screen, discarded printouts
– deliberate action	Industrial/commercial espionage, hackers

b) i) A policy should be formulated which includes:

- a clear statement of areas of responsibility
- access controls which limit authorised access to appropriate people only
- instant dismissal of anyone caught tampering with the system.

This will deter permanent staff from attempting unauthorised access but is less of a deterrent to temporary staff. A programmer will often have or can obtain the knowledge of the system necessary to bypass security procedures. However, contract programmers should not really be working on a live system, since much of their work is in development or modification of software, which should be done on a test and development system separate from the live system. If the programmer's work increases the risk of access to confidential data then proper supervision should be applied.

ii) If a system is vital to an organisation's operations then preventive measures can include using well-established, fault-tolerant hardware which may incorporate techniques like disk-shadowing, where a second disk is kept constantly updated in line with a working disk. The system should be regularly checked and serviced to detect and prevent deterioration of its components.

In addition, curative measures can be taken, such as the maintenance of a hot stand-by system, so that in the event of failure of the working system, the backup system can be used with a minimum of disruption. Disaster recovery procedures should be tested regularly to ensure that staff are aware of them.

iii) If incorrect payments have been made over several years because of faults in the system then this indicates that both preventive and curative measures have failed to identify the mistake. Computerised information systems should be thoroughly tested at all stages of development before they are released for use, but fully exhaustive testing is often very difficult or impossible in practice. However, priorities should be established so that the more critical parts of a system receive most testing.

In any case, an error of this sort should be identified when the system is audited. The fact that it has not may mean that the system itself has no built-in procedures for assisting the auditors or that the procedures are also faulty, possibly due to the same design fault. It is important that audit procedures are considered during development and that work on the operational areas is carried out separately from work on audit assistance procedures.

SECTION

13

ANSWERS TO MOCK EXAMINATION 1

This section enables you to judge how well you fared in the first mock examination given in Section 10. You will find advice on how each question should be approached, which topics which should be included and how the marks are allocated. Don't forget, to gain maximum benefit from this section, you should attempt the mock examination under exam conditions first.

Section A – Case Study

Better Blocks Limited

1 The term 'end-user computing' refers to the use and control of computerised information systems by the system's users rather than by information systems specialists. More organisations are able to adopt a policy of end-user computing because:

- Computer hardware is becoming smaller, cheaper, more powerful and more suitable for operation in the physical environment of an ordinary office.
- More powerful hardware, particularly in the form of personal computer systems, enables the software developers to incorporate sophisticated techniques into the human-computer interface and into mass-produced applications which allow them to be more easily used and more readily adapted by non-computer specialists.
- Users are becoming more aware of the use of computer systems and more adept at using them.
- There has been a backlog in the development of applications software and many users have been dissatisfied with the applications developed for them by information systems specialists.
- Computer communications systems, in the form of both local and wide area networks (LAN and WAN), allow users to share some data whilst still being able to work independently without necessarily affecting other users of the system.

The main benefits claimed for end-user computing include:

- increased productivity
- better response times (since users can access data directly)
- better information, since users can access and adapt data to suit their requirements.

These benefits come about because:

- Users are able to access and work on data directly without the need for the intervention of information systems specialists and other personnel such as data entry staff. This is particularly the case with modern user-friendly software packages.
- End-user computing allows users to develop their own small-scale applications and also to become more actively involved in the development of larger-scale applications. Thus, the end result of a development is more likely to satisfy the

13

users' actual requirements.

- Users feel more sense of ownership of, and commitment to, a system or application which leads to more positive attitudes to the system and a better understanding of its purpose and operation.

If Better Blocks introduce end-user computing in their local sales offices then the staff at these offices could:

- use word-processors and desk-top publishing packages for letters and marketing materials
- analyse sales forecasts and budgets using spreadsheets
- analyse data about customers and products using databases
- prepare presentations to customers using presentation graphics packages
- use other packages for work planning and diary systems.

However, there will still be a need for centralisation of some data (such as customer accounts) so, as well as computer facilities in the local offices, there are benefits in connecting all the local offices to the central mainframe so that up-to-date customer account information is accessible from the local offices.

Bill Keane has noticed that the managers of the local sales offices are purchasing computer equipment but trying to hide the nature of the equipment from the central purchasing system. This would indicate that at least some of the staff are keen to use computerised systems but also highlights the problem that end-user computing requires careful planning and control. If it is not carefully controlled then there are dangers, such as:

- duplication of effort
- neglected opportunities for sharing data
- lack of standards in hardware and software standards leading to incompatibilities
- under-utilisation of resources and uncontrolled expenses which do not prove cost-effective
- risks of unauthorised access to data
- risks of loss of data and ineffective backup procedures.

In addition to these dangers, Janet Carlton will need to consider the general problems associated with changing staff working practices, particularly if the policy involves the sales offices compulsorily adopting end-user computing in a wide range of their activities.

Janet Carson should initiate a feasibility study to look in detail at the options and carry out a cost-benefit analysis, although estimating and quantifying the costs and benefits may be difficult.

2

The justification for the current policy, advocated by George Carlton, is that centralisation allows tighter control of the organisation's data and cost-effective use of staff's specialist skills. However, the continuing efforts of many computer hardware and software developers are towards more compact but easier-to-use systems which reduce the need for specialist skills. So the justification that data entry is best carried out centrally by trained, full-time data entry staff carries less weight.

The main benefit to Better Blocks of decentralisation of the data entry of delivery notes and other basic transaction data is that it will allow data to enter the system much more quickly, which should in turn speed up customer invoicing. This should then improve the cash flow and credit control, and provide much better information about customers for the sales staff to act upon.

Currently all computerised data processing is carried out using the mainframe as a batch processing system. This allows for:

- careful control over the data entry with the opportunity for data verification and validation
- control of access to the system during critical update and backup procedures
- spreading of the loading on the system by carrying out some processing outside of office hours
- ideal opportunities for backup at the beginning and end of a batch run.

Janet Carlton's idea of decentralisation of data entry entails the costs of providing the builders' merchants, quarries and local sales offices with computer equipment such as terminals, and communications equipment such as modems to allow them access to the central system. Staff will have to be trained and new procedures devised.

However, the logical extension of Janet's idea is that these same facilities will provide for other activities such as enquiries and reporting from the data held centrally, as well as other possibilities such as electronic mail. This goes beyond Janet's original ideas but highlights the need to take a high-level view of information systems and not concentrate on single applications in isolation.

A major consideration will be whether the existing batch processing is still appropriate or whether on-line processing should be used to allow Better Blocks to capitalise on having up-to-date information more readily available in most areas of the organisation. If on-line processing is chosen then the factors to be considered include the following:

- Can the existing software be adapted for on-line use or will new software be required?
- If new software is required, can it be purchased off-the-shelf or will Better Blocks need to become involved in a software development project?
- Will the increased workload on the system mean that new hardware is required; to be effective, on-line processing facilities will need to be available during normal office hours?
- What sorts of security features will be required to guard against unauthorised access – and will additional backup procedures be required if the computer systems become a more essential part of the information system?

Compared with batch processing, on-line processing makes some operations more difficult, such as:

- checking that data entry and processing are carried out properly
- controlling access to the system and data
- taking backups
- spreading the loading on the system.

However, there are advantages to on-line processing, such as:

- reduced staffing costs as specialist data-entry staff are not required
- cash flow and credit control can be improved
- there may be other, less tangible benefits, such as improved image and better customer relations.

3 Better Blocks currently have a functional, hierarchical organisation structure: each department is responsible for carrying out a particular set or related functions. This allows staff who are doing similar activities to be grouped together within levels in each department as is felt necessary to identify sub-functions. The further down the hierarchy a staff member is, the narrower their responsibilities are and the lower their status is. The organisation's primary activities relate to producing the raw materials (the Quarries function) and selling, either through the builders' merchants or direct to construction companies (the Sales function). The other three departments provide support functions to enable Better Blocks to carry out its primary functions.

This is a traditional structure found in many organisations but, in systems theory terms, it may be prone to entropy if the various sub-systems (the departments) are not appropriately linked or if the goals of the sub-systems become incompatible with the overall system's goals. Feedback may be delayed, resulting in poor monitoring and control of activities. For example, the Sales sub-system may be aware of large orders being placed – but there may be no simple mechanism for alerting the Quarries sub-system in order that appropriate changes to output schedules can be made in time to satisfy the increased demand.

In order to reduce the entropy, thereby making Better Blocks more likely to achieve its overall objectives, some changes to the organisation structure will be required. Instead of grouping staff according to the actual activities they normally carry out, it may be more effective to group some of them in line with the organisation's primary activities, irrespective of the actual tasks each staff member carries out. This would result in a structure which more resembles a matrix.

Matrix structures are typified by organisations that group staff according to a particular organisational objective – so, in a manufacturing organisation, the objectives are the making and selling of products. Therefore staff groups may be regarded as teams rather than departments: a team has responsibility for a particular product line, carrying out manufacturing, selling, accounting, and providing information relating to that product line.

If Better Blocks adopt Janet Carlton's ideas for end-user computing at the sales offices and for decentralisation of much of the data entry work, then some of the work on support activities will be best handled by staff at the sales offices, and also at the quarries and builders' merchants if they are included in the decentralisation. There will be less work for the Finance and Administration staff, since tasks such as typing, data entry and producing reports can be carried out away from the central building in Leeds. Similarly, end-user computing at the local sales offices will entail support and development work being taken away from the central building, which will reduce the need for information systems specialists in the Information Systems department. This should mean that Better Blocks can reduce their staff at their central office but that more staff will be needed to work at the sales offices, builders' merchants and quarries. For example, instead of grouping primarily sales staff at the sales offices, the staff will form a team with more diverse activities that will include data entry, word processing and the other tasks that have been decentralised. In effect, Better Blocks should develop a hybrid structure combining elements of both hierarchy and matrix. This may lead to an overall reduction in staffing levels throughout Better Blocks.

There will still be the need for central staff to operate and manage the central mainframe system but many organisations that have adopted end-user computing have also set up an information centre to help users and to control and coordinate users' computing activities. Some of these staff may be allocated to support one or more sites and may spend only a little time at the central building.

4 The information technology and systems to assist retail operations like Better Blocks builders' merchants have been available since the 1970s and are still evolving. Many organisations are now dependent on information technology. The three main applications are:

Electronic Point Of Sale (EPOS)

These systems involve having data about each product encoded in some way on the product – typically using a bar code. The codes are read with a scanner which may be fixed in the sales checkout or hand-held. The scanner, or bar code reader, transmits the code to a computerised till that checks the details of the product and can display them in human-readable form, either on a visual display unit (VDU) or on a printout. The till automatically adds up the price of goods and generates a till receipt for the customer.

The EPOS system could be linked to a stock control system so that quantities of goods in and out are automatically fed into the stock control system, which provides up-to-date information about stock levels and can be processed to give useful information about sales trends. Better Blocks could consider setting up a central warehouse for some goods with electronic links to the builders' merchants so that information about sales and stock requirements can be processed centrally. This should allow Better Blocks to take advantage of bulk buying and fewer but larger deliveries from suppliers to the central warehouse. This would bring under Better Blocks' control the distribution of products from the central warehouse and allow reduction of stock holding at the builders' merchants. Better Blocks would have better information about current stock levels and requirements, thereby reducing problems with stock-outs and unnecessarily high stock levels. It may enable them to hold a wider range of stock and lead to an improvement in customers' perceptions of the organisation.

Electronic Funds Transfer (EFT)

An electronic funds transfer system is fed with the details of a customer's purchases. It reads the customer's bank details (usually from a swipe card) and, using electronic communication links, passes details of the transaction to both the customer's and the retailer's bank accounts. This speeds up the transfer, reduces the retailer's paperwork and gives customers an easier payment method than traditional cheques or credit cards.

EFT and EPOS systems can be combined so that the amount of manual work involved in making a sale is considerably reduced and, if properly managed, they reduce the risk of data entry errors.

Electronic Data Interchange (EDI)

EDI is a general term used to describe the many ways that organisations can exchange information electronically – so EFT, EPOS and electronic mail systems are all forms of EDI. However, it is often used to describe the use of electronic systems to ease communication between, for example, a supplier and its customers. If Better Blocks have regular customers and/or suppliers then there is the possibility of using EDI to transmit purchase orders, invoices, etc. To use EDI both the sending and receiving organisations must have compatible data processing systems; this has slowed down the adoption of EDI. Better Blocks should investigate the possibilities of using EDI before settling on a system, since it may be very difficult to incorporate EDI once a system is in place.

At its builders' merchants, Better Blocks could use an integrated system combining EPOS, EFT and stock control to maximise the amount of useful and up-to-date information that is available and to allow data to pass automatically between the systems. In addition, EDI could be established as Better Blocks' preferred method of carrying out transactions with external organisations.

5 Better Blocks currently uses traditional methods and structures with its centralised support departments and extensive use of manual methods. It seems that the organisation could greatly benefit from better use of modern computerised information systems and may actually be dependent on their introduction for its survival. The ideas that Janet Carlton and Bill Keane are interested in would involve a major systems development.

Many major developments cause dissatisfaction when the completed system is actually delivered and put into use. The main criticisms are that systems are over-budget and overdue and do not satisfy users' requirements. It has been acknowledged that increased user involvement can help to reduce these problems by ensuring that the developers and users have a clearer picture of each other's requirements, so that the system more closely matches user expectations and the reasons for delays and additional expense are better understood. In Better Blocks' case the dangers are particularly relevant, as the majority of staff do not use computer systems in the normal course of their duties, or they use them in a very traditional setting.

The benefits of user involvement are:

- The final system is more likely to satisfy the users' actual requirements, since users have the opportunity to explore their requirements and the ways that the system can be built to suit them.
- Users are more committed to the success and effective use of the system if they have been part of the development and feel a sense of ownership.
- Users have the opportunity to gain knowledge and insight into the system and can make better use of it when it is operational.

The traditional systems development methodologies can be considered 'hard' systems methodologies, based upon tools and techniques used in development projects where the end result can be clearly stated and defined and agreed; an example is the introduction of a new production line in a manufacturing plant. However, computerised information systems are often introduced into 'fuzzy', people-based situations where different users have different requirements and views of what should be achieved and how to achieve it. This has led to the adoption of some of the ideas of 'soft systems methodologies' (SSMs) such as Checkland's SSM. These acknowledge that in many situations it may be difficult to specify actual requirements and that the best approach is for developers and users to work together to look at the complete situation from all points of view and reach agreement on requirements through a series of consultations and suggested solutions. This will be particularly important in Better Blocks' situation if a comprehensive information system is introduced, since it will affect almost all the staff's working practices.

Tools and techniques which can be used by Better Blocks to encourage user involvement include:

- Fourth-generation languages (4GL) and development tools, which are designed to enable systems to be developed without the need for highly specialised programming techniques and languages. 4GLs enable users and systems analysts to develop systems designs together.
- Prototyping – a technique where a working model of some or all of a system is produced quickly and early in the development. Users gain a better understanding of what the system will be like, so they can suggest changes early in the development which can be implemented much more easily than after the full system is delivered. Prototyping often takes the form of using screen generation facilities to rapidly produce data entry and output screens whose suitability can be discussed by users without their having to acquire expert knowledge of the system's inner workings. This would be very useful, since much

of Better Blocks' system will be based on data entry and output screens for a variety of purposes.
- ▶ Query languages enable users to satisfy their own small-scale requirements or use a system in a more flexible way.

The increasing power and sophistication of modern computer systems allow the use of computerised development tools to carry out many of the low-level tasks of systems development and enable users and developers to concentrate on the higher-level or more overt features of the system. Better Blocks' management need to be aware that there are large benefits to be gained from a suitable computerised system. They should be prepared to set up a steering committee and allocate some of their own staff to work closely with the developers.

Section B

6 a) A system's boundary and its means of interaction with the environment are referred to as its interfaces.

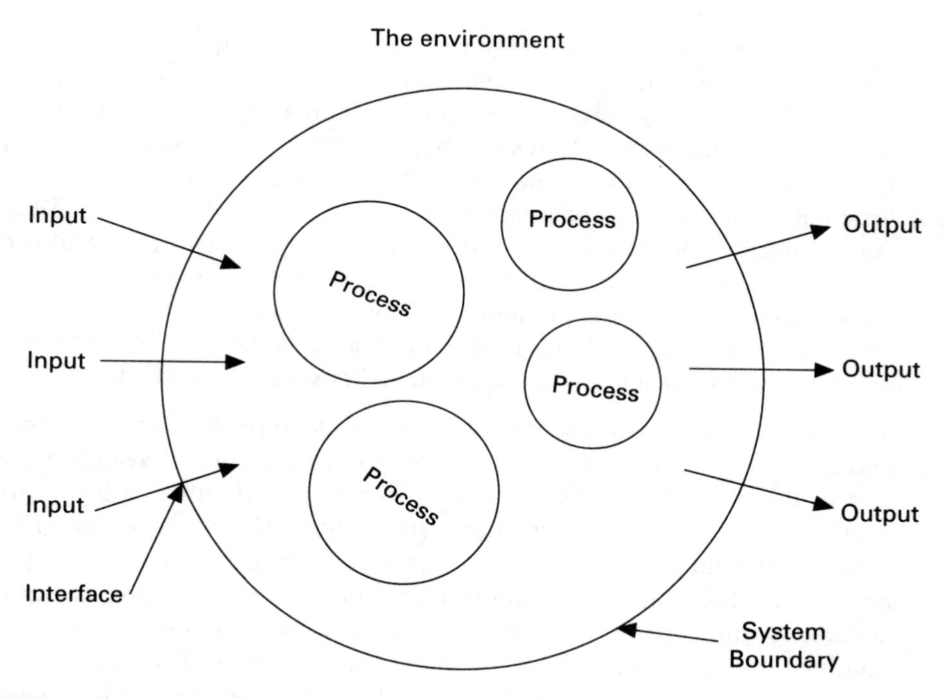

Figure 13.1 Elements of a system

A **closed system** is shut off from its environment; it is totally self-contained with no inputs or outputs. In reality, few systems could be described as closed, although in some scientific experiments we may try to establish conditions where there is no interaction between the system and its environment, so that the activity within the system can be established without external interference. It will probably have fairly narrow objectives.

An **open system** has various inputs and outputs and there are complex and unpredictable interactions between it and its environment. Social systems such as families and businesses are all open systems. Because of their complexity and unpredictability, it is difficult to exert rigid control over open systems. There may be many varied (and sometimes conflicting) objectives for an open system. A business may have objectives such as survival, profit and employment of its workforce.

13

Between these two extremes, we can consider a **semi-closed system** as one that has predictable and controllable inputs and outputs. A central heating system can be considered semi-closed, since we can use a thermostat to control its outputs and predict the seasonal range of temperatures, fuel inputs, etc. There may be benefits to be gained by operating business systems, such as a transaction processing system, as semi-closed by establishing the allowable inputs and applying rigid rules.

b) By analysing the main functions that are carried out by an organisation, it can be regarded as a collection of interacting sub-systems – one sub-system for each main function. Many organisations formalise this into a functional structure with each department carrying out a particular function such as accounting, manufacturing, sales and warehousing. These operate as systems within the environment of the organisation, which is itself a system within the wider environment.

By structuring the people and activities into smaller sub-systems, the organisation is able to exert better control and management by stating narrow objectives for each sub-system, defining the interfaces between the sub-systems and monitoring and controlling their performance. People involved in the sub-systems can be given clear objectives and so develop a sense of purpose.

There is a danger that the organisation may not operate to its maximum potential, its performance may be sub-optimal, because the sub-systems come to regard their objectives as primary when they should be regarded as secondary to the organisation's overall or primary objectives. For example, the manufacturing sub-system may regard maximum output as its objective and establish procedures to generate maximum output, while the quality control sub-system's objective is to limit production to items of a certain quality. Similarly, there may be conflict between the sales and accounts sub-systems caused by credit-control procedures. The benefits of focusing people within their functional sub-systems may lead to a 'them-and-us' attitude within the organisation as a whole and to antagonism between departments.

c) The main reason why accounts and payroll were the first functions to be computerised was that accountancy and payroll functions have clear objectives and well-defined interfaces. They are primarily made up of a large number of routine financial calculations and transactions, which can be described by a series of simple steps and rules. Large amounts of data need to be processed and stored. Computers are able to carry out the required processing rapidly, accurately and reliably according to the rules, because many of the decisions involved are programmable. Computers can also be used to efficiently process and store large amounts of routine data. In systems theory terms, accounts and payroll sub-systems are relatively closed compared with other sub-systems (such as marketing and personnel) where the inputs are less predictable and the interfaces with other sub-systems and with the external environment are less well defined. Computers were regarded as primarily useful for automating existing processes and procedures, and this attitude often led to missed opportunities for change and innovation.

7

a) The traditional model of the systems development lifecycle (SDLC) is usually represented as a sequence of distinct phases in a diagram like this:

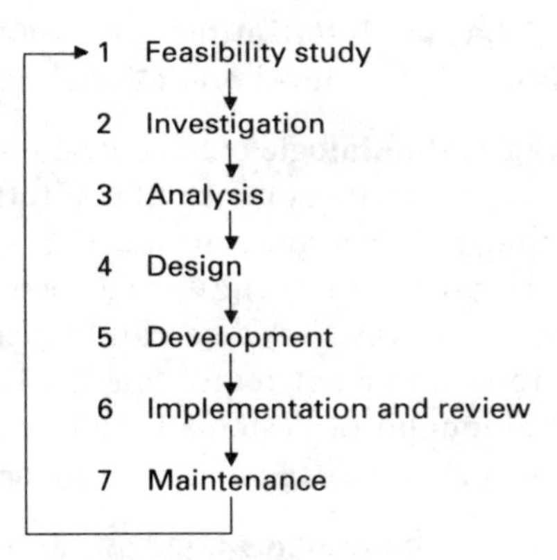

Figure 13.2 Phases of the systems development lifecycle

Phase	*Description*
1 Feasibility study	An initial examination of the current system takes place and alternative solutions are examined. From outline cost-benefit analyses, an option may be recommended for further development
2 Investigation	Detailed information is collected about the current system, its problems and the users' needs
3 Analysis	From the investigation of users' needs, a detailed requirements specification of current and future needs is produced
4 Design	The detailed description of the proposed system is produced
5 Development	The hardware and software are purchased or written and tested
6 Implementation and review	The full system is tested and put into operation and changeover takes place. The new system and its development are evaluated
7 Maintenance	In response to problems or to changes in the users' needs and in the environment, potential modifications are analysed, designed and implemented.

The SDLC is only a model and, in reality, the development of a system may not follow this neat sequence of discrete phases, because:

- The SDLC assumes that it is possible to clearly identify systems options and complete each phase in turn.
- The discovery of errors and the identification of changes to requirements may necessitate a return to an earlier phase.
- The production of a prototype system as part of the development will proceed more quickly, and possibly superficially, through the phases while the main systems development proceeds more slowly and thoroughly.
- The system may be split into sub-systems, such as software and hardware, whose development proceeds at different rates.

b) **Process-driven methodologies** are based on the principle of functional decomposition, where the designer concentrates on the processes that a system must perform and breaks them down into smaller and smaller sub-processes, each with a well defined interface consisting of the data that flows in and out of it. They tend to concentrate on how the system should operate and are most suitable to the computerisation of transaction processing systems which handle an organisation's low-level operational data in routine, mechanistic ways.

Data-driven methodologies concentrate on designing a system's data structures and the ways that data is manipulated rather than how it is to be processed. It is claimed that many organisations will want to modify the way that data is processed and identify new processes. It is more important to provide flexibility in the way that data can be used and stored than to fix and limit its structure to suit current requirements. Data-driven methodologies are suitable to the development of systems based upon an underlying large-scale database, where all levels of management require access to it in non-routine ways.

User-driven methodologies concentrate on the behavioural aspects of systems development and highlight the importance of the users' role, on the basis that users understand their own requirements and should be fully involved in the development of a system if they are to make effective use of it. It is claimed that this approach leads to more flexible systems and reduces users' reliance on technical expertise. It is most appropriate where the objectives of a system are not easy to define and vary according to each user's particular problems, viewpoint and priorities.

8

a) The ELH for the 'customer' entity is shown below:

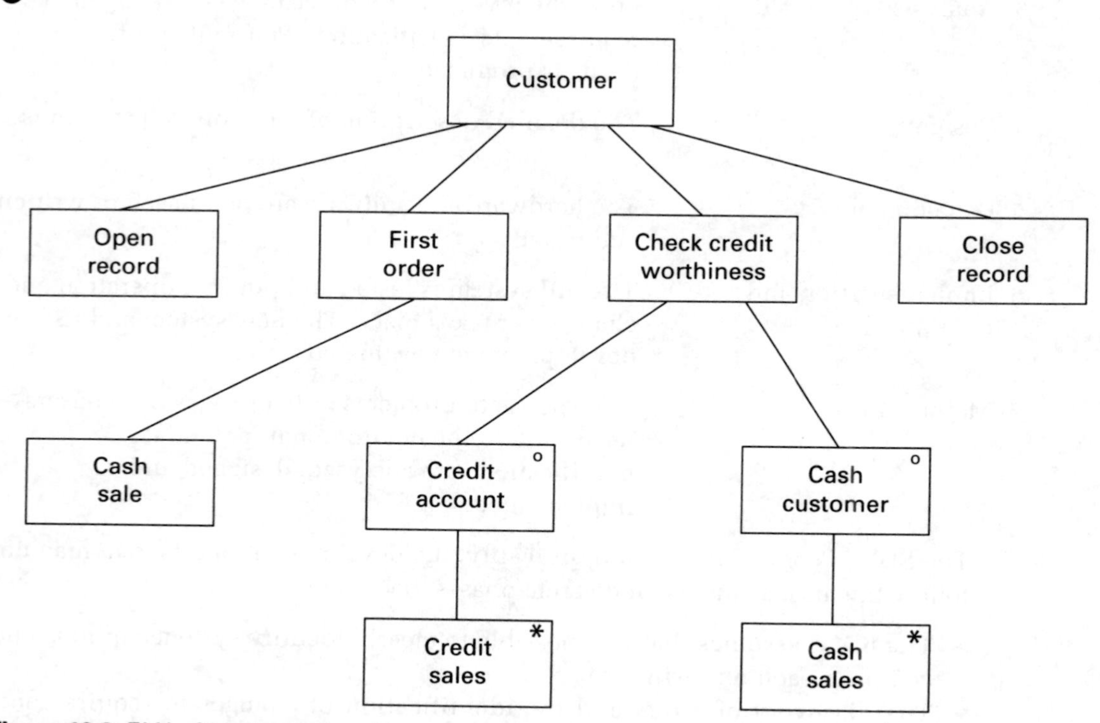

Figure 13.3 ELH of 'customer' entity

The sequence of events is shown by reading the diagram from left to right, moving down a level when a link is shown. The asterisk (*) in the top right-hand corner of a box indicates that the event may be repeated (iteration), and selection between events is shown by a circle (°) in the top right-hand corner of the boxes.

b) The term 'software engineering' is used to emphasise that software can be developed in a disciplined way, using a set of formalised principles, tools and techniques. The aim is to cost-effectively produce high-quality software for complex applications. Computer-aided systems (or software) engineering

(CASE) tools are computerised tools used in software engineering.

CASE tools can be used to provide or assist with functions such as:

Diagram construction: many of the techniques used in systems development use diagrams (for example, DFDs and ELHs). Using a computerised tool can ensure:

- correct and consistent use of symbols and conventions
- clear, well presented work
- reusable and easily modified diagrams.

Construction and update of the data dictionary: using a computerised tool helps with

- the creation and maintenance of a data dictionary
- automatic cross-referencing between dictionary items
- checks for errors, duplications and inconsistencies in dictionary items.

Querying existing documents to search for key words and definitions. This may be carried out using a form of query language to specify where and what to search for.

Help facilities, which provide guidance with the way that the tools and techniques of a particular methodology should be used.

Production of structured English and program code: the basic conventions of structured English such as the use of indentation, the capitalisation of keywords and the underlining of items defined in the data dictionary can be automated to some extent. Similarly, programming languages use very precise conventions – something as simple as a missing comma or semi-colon can cause an error or change the meaning of the instructions. An automated tool can help to avoid such errors as well as ensuring consistency of indentation, use of comments, and so on.

Document production: some methodologies use standardised documents which are required at specific stages of development; CASE tools can produce those and fill in some or all of the relevant details.

4GLs: applications generators and screen generators can be considered a form of CASE tool, since they automate processes in the development of a system which would otherwise have to be done by hand.

Project management: tools and techniques such as network analysis, Gantt charts, and resource allocation charts can also be automated.

CASE tools can provide substantial benefits when compared with manual methods, and many of them are common to other application areas. Benefits include:

- improved accuracy
- faster processing and production of systems designs and documents
- improved presentation
- consistency of methods and presentation
- ability to readily adapt plans and try 'what-if' analyses
- producing initial plans from a minimum amount of basic data.

A package of tools is said to be **integrated** if they work in a consistent manner and information can flow between them automatically. This integration brings further benefits, such as:

- Tools work in a consistent manner which cuts down the users' learning curve.
- Information used for one tool can be used automatically by other tools. For example, initial construction of a DFD may automatically lead to the setting up of data dictionary items for entities, processes, data stores and data flows.
- Ease of use and automatic flow of information not only cuts down the time and effort required but also reduces the risk of data entry errors and inconsistencies.
- Users can concentrate on their real objective without being distracted by having to draw a neat diagram or a properly structured document. For example, a systems analyst would want to aim to produce a DFD which accurately represents requirements without having to worry too much about the DFD's layout and construction.

9 a) A review of disaster prevention and recovery procedures should consider these factors:

The threats

Disasters such as systems breakdowns, power failures, fires, floods and explosions can occur for various reasons such as equipment failure, human error or negligence, sabotage, vandalism and terrorism. A mainframe system is vulnerable to all these threats, as it involves the use of complex electronic equipment that requires skilled operation and is a clearly identifiable target area for for anyone contemplating sabotage or terrorism.

The value of an information system

The equipment that comprises a large mainframe computer system is itself expensive, running into millions of pounds, but it can be insured for its replacement value. More importantly, the information it stores and provides will be essential to the bank's operations. The value of the system can be assessed in terms of the effect of its loss – this will include lost business and opportunities while it is unavailable, and perhaps more importantly, the longer-term effects on the bank's reputation.

The bank should remember that the law of diminishing returns may apply to measures aimed at safeguarding and recovering its system; there comes a point where the cost of additional measures does not provide sufficient additional security.

Preventive measures

Having established that the information system is critical to the bank's operations, and that the central mainframe is the key element in that system, preventive measures can be considered in terms of their costs and effectiveness. In the bank's case, preventing disaster should be given a high priority and they should not simply rely on having effective recovery procedures. Prevention can be considered by looking at each threat:

Hardware failure

Modern computer equipment can be manufactured to provide a high degree of reliability and fault-tolerance. The bank should ensure that its equipment is supplied from reputable manufacturers and that the specification is sufficient to handle expected operational demands, with a high level of fault tolerance. In addition, hardware should be regularly serviced by reputable maintenance staff or organisations.

Power failure

Computer equipment can be particularly vulnerable to power failure and even minor power fluctuations can cause systems to 'crash'. The mainframe, and any other critical equipment, should be powered by a UPS (uninterruptible power supply) which monitors the mains power supply, smooths out fluctuations and has its own power source in the form of batteries or generators.

Fire, flood, explosions

Large computers need special operating environments where the air-conditioning and temperature can be controlled. They should be physically isolated from the rest of the organisation, with appropriate air-conditioning. Physical isolation also provides the opportunity to fit security systems to restrict physical access to authorised personnel only. Water and smoke detectors, fire alarms and extinguishing systems should be fitted and checked regularly. Emergency procedures and drills should be practised regularly and a list or rota should be kept of staff who should be alerted in the event of emergencies.

Human error or negligence

The risk of human error and negligence can be reduced by ensuring that all staff who operate or use the system are properly trained for their tasks and made aware of their responsibilities. Competent, well-motivated staff who take a pride in their work are much less likely to make errors. The system itself should incorporate suitable access permissions to restrict the availability of potentially destructive operations such as disk formatting and master-file updates.

Sabotage, vandalism and terrorism

Deliberate destructive acts may be attempted by people from inside or outside the organisation. The bank should ensure that recruiting procedures include checks on applicants' trustworthiness and that references are verified. Passwords and security locks should be changed regularly and disaffected staff prevented from having access. Vulnerability to external forces can be reduced by siting the equipment well away from the public eye and using specialist security staff who are aware of the threats.

Initial recovery

The three main elements in recovering from a disaster are having suitable hardware and software and an up-to-date copy of the data. A centralised processing configuration, like the bank's mainframe system, is dependent on the central computer. A duplicate computer system could be maintained as a backup to the front-line system. This is an expensive option, particularly as the backup should be readily available, preferably situated away from the front-line system. It may be possible to offset some of the costs, for example by using it for a limited number of functions or at periods of peak demand to take some of the load off the front-line system. Alternatively, an external organisation such as a computer manufacturer, computer bureau or another bank with a similar system can be contracted to provide an appropriate system or handle the bank's processing in the short term.

Whatever arrangements are made for providing a backup system, the bank will still need to ensure that a backup copy of up-to-date data is available. Backup copies should be taken at frequent and regular intervals, stored off-site and restoration procedures tested regularly.

Long-term recovery

Having established a minimal system after an emergency, the bank will need to restore a full system so that it can operate normally again. It may be possible to repair or replace their original system, financed by insurance cover.

Conclusions

Having considered its current position with regard to all these factors, the bank should look at the need for additional measures and assess their cost-effectiveness.

b) The bank seems to have two main alternatives to its current centralised system:

External organisations

The responsibility for providing the bank's information system, and ensuring its security, can be shifted to an external organisation such as a computer bureau. A bureau may have sufficient expertise and equipment to be able to provide cost-effective backup systems by offering them to several organisations. However, the bank is unlikely to relinquish direct control of such a critical aspect of its business. An alternative is to use a facilities management organisation which is contracted to provide the information system from within the bank – but, for similar reasons, this is unlikely to be acceptable.

Downsizing and distributed computing

The trend in information technology is to produce physically smaller but more powerful systems which are easier to use and manage, and require less demanding operating environments. As a result, many organisations are 'downsizing' their information systems by using smaller hardware systems and reducing their information systems specialists. In addition, organisations are making use of modern communications equipment to operate distributed information systems, where computing resources such as processors and storage are spread through the organisation using LANs and WANs (Local and Wide Area Networks). In terms of disaster recovery, this would seem to be an attractive alternative for the bank. For example, several linked mini-computers in different locations could be used to provide processing power, with one acting as a central file store, called a file-server. The other systems can be provided with the necessary equipment to enable them to take over the role of file-server in the event of emergency.

10 a) The cost-benefit analysis of the proposed system or systems is a key section in a feasibility study report, since it should attempt to quantify all the factors involved in the proposal. It should be prepared after the other aspects of feasibility, such as technical and social feasibility, have been considered. The costs and benefits that emerge from the feasibility study can be viewed in several ways:

- according to when they occur during the system's life
- as direct or indirect
- as one-off or ongoing
- as tangible or intangible
- as capital or revenue items.

One way of categorising the cost-benefit items, with examples in each category, is:

Direct benefits – reduced staffing costs, reduced storage costs, reduced error rates, income from sale of old equipment

Indirect benefits – improved presentation of information, better decision-making

Development costs – consultancy fees, analysts' and designers' time, staff time spent in investigation and analysis

Implementation costs – purchase of hardware and software, programmers' time, installation costs, staff training

Running costs – maintenance contracts and activities, power supply, consumables such as stationery and printer supplies, security and backup

Other direct costs – redundancy payments, upgrade and expansion of equipment

Intangible items – some things may be difficult to categorise as a potential cost or benefit: for example, the effect on staff morale, staff turnover and the organisation's image, or the comparative return from investing in an alternative area of the organisation such as advertising or new products.

The economic feasibility of proposals of this sort can be very difficult to assess because of the uncertainty associated with many items in the cost-benefit analysis. Even simple items like the cost of hardware can be difficult to ascertain, particularly if they have to be estimated months or years in advance of actual purchase. Estimates of the time saved on operations, such as data entry of customers' purchase order details, may be based on observations which do not supply realistic estimates for the average time per operation.

The processes involved in the development of systems, particularly where new software is to be produced, are particularly difficult to assess in terms of their costs and timescales. Progress during development can be difficult to monitor because the outputs, like design specifications and program code, are difficult to test. Errors may only be identified when the complete system is being integrated in the later phases of development when corrective action can be difficult and expensive. So development costs are subject to variation and the effect of delays may have additional costs that have not been covered in the cost-benefit analysis, such as additional fees to specialists to solve problems and added disruption to the organisation's operations.

Similarly, problems created by inadequate requirements specifications, poor designs and software 'bugs' can lead to additional and unacceptable running costs of maintenance. The estimated benefits may not be realised because of poor systems performance and inflexibility in meeting the users' evolving requirements. For example, the response time of the file-server may be inadequate at periods of peak demand, due either to lower-than-specified performance or to underestimated levels of traffic. Actual operation of the system may not realise the anticipated benefits if, for example, users do not achieve the expected reduction in the time and costs of handling paperwork.

b) Most of the techniques which can be used to assist economic evaluation of the proposal rely on having costs and benefits quantified as cash inflows and outflows.

13

Payback period

The payback period is the time that it will take for the system to pay for itself in terms of recouping the initial investment; the shorter the payback period, the more favourably the proposal is regarded. Payback does does not take either the time value of money or the pattern of the cash flows into account. It emphasises short-term returns and ignores long-term benefits.

Net present value (NPV) and internal rate of return (IRR)

These methods use discounted cash flows (DCF) which take the time value of money into account by using a discount factor, often called the cost of capital, to put a present value on future cash flows. The NPV is the current net value of the system when all future cash flows are taken into account. The IRR method involves comparing the percentage rate of return expected from the system, which can also be compared with the figure that would be expected from other forms of investment.

The accounting rate of return (ARR)

This method uses an accounting formula, such as the estimated average profits as a percentage of the average estimated investment, to arrive at an ARR which can be compared with a predetermined target figure. The method is widely used and understood but it emphasises accounting profits rather than cash flows.

Since the estimation of costs and benefits involves uncertainty, the cost-benefit analysis can be carried out using more than one set of figures – for example, by using best-case and worst-case scenarios.

ANSWERS TO MOCK EXAMINATION 2

This section enables you to judge how well you fared in the second mock examination given in Section 11. You will find advice on how each question should be approached, which topics which should be included and how the marks are allocated. Don't forget, to gain maximum benefit from this section, you should attempt the mock examination under exam conditions first.

Section A – Case Study

Johnsons Specialist Books Ltd

1 Probably the two most obvious techniques used for assessing the economic feasibility of computer based projects are initial costs, payback period and net present value (NPV) using discounted cash flows (DCF). These measures can be calculated but Johnsons will have to also consider some overall objectives. Is the aim to minimise investment or maximise profit? How cautious should Johnsons be? Is the system necessary for the organisation's survival regardless of its cost?

We have been told that this system (Option A) was selected because of its lower initial costs compared with the other options. This may be an overwhelming consideration if the initial cost of the other options exceeds Johnsons' capability for expenditure. However, it may mean that potentially more profitable options are rejected.

To calculate payback and net present value further calculations are required, as shown in the following table. The top section of the table shows the five years' data given in the feasibility study report. For each year the quantified costs and benefits are shown and the net cash flow calculated. From this the cumulative cash flow is calculated.

The lower section shows the discounted cash flows (DCF) which are used to calculate the net present value (NPV) of the system. These take the time value of a cash flow into account. The NPV of a future cash flow is calculated by discounting it, using a suitable discount factor. In this case the figure is 12%, which Johnsons take to be the cost of capital. Note that cash flows are assumed to occur at the end of the year in which they are listed.

Johnsons Specialist Books Ltd
Discounted cash flow analysis for proposed new computer system – Option A.

End of year	*1*	*2*	*3*	*4*	*5*
Costs	93	37	37	37	37
Benefits	23	89	64	52	42
Net cash flow	– 70	52	27	15	5
Cumulative net cash flow	– 70	– 18	9	24	29
*Discount factor	0.89	0.80	0.71	0.64	0.57
Discounted cash flow	– 63	41	19	10	3
Cumulative discounted cash flow	– 63	– 21	– 2	8	11

Cost of capital = 12.00%. All figures in £'000.

*The discount factor shown is $\left(\frac{1}{1 + 0.12}\right)^n$ where n is the year.

From this table we can calculate the payback period. This is the time it will take for the system to pay for itself in terms of recouping the initial investment. The shorter the payback period, the more favourably the system is regarded. The Cumulative Net Cash Flow figures show that the system starts to generate a profit in Year 3. A reasonable estimate would be that the payback period is 2 years and 8 months. However, this does not take into account the time value of future cash flows. If we look at the Cumulative Discounted Cash Flow figures we see that it is not until Year 4 that the system shows a profit. A reasonable estimate would be that the payback period is 3 years and 3 months.

It is usually sensible to use a discounted cash flow figure, since this calculation will take some account of the time value of money. However, the method assumes that the discount factor remains constant for the span of the analysis, which is unlikely to actually be the case. For a system of this sort a two- or three-year payback may be considered reasonable and it is relatively easy to compare the payback period of several options. A major drawback of using the payback period as a measure in isolation is that it ignores the pattern of cash flows – a system may be slow to recoup the initial investment but show large potential profits in the long run.

The same table can be used to show the **net present value (NPV)** of the system. In this case the NPV of the system over five years is £11,000, which would probably not be considered very favourable. However, it should be remembered that the figures are only estimates – the costs and, particularly, the benefits of these sorts of comprehensive computer system can be difficult to predict.

A further consideration is whether a five-year analysis is appropriate for a system of this sort. Whilst it may be reasonable to plan to replace the system in five years' time, the future costs and benefits become increasingly difficult to estimate with any confidence. For example, requirements can change and lead to high maintenance costs if the system is modified to keep it in line with requirements. Taking more than a five-year timescale is probably not reasonable and, even within the five-year analysis, it may be better to look not just at the final figures but also at the pattern of cash flows. For example, it may be possible to determine when the the anticipated annual profit, or positive cash flow, starts to diminish, which could indicate when the system is nearing the end of its useful life.

2

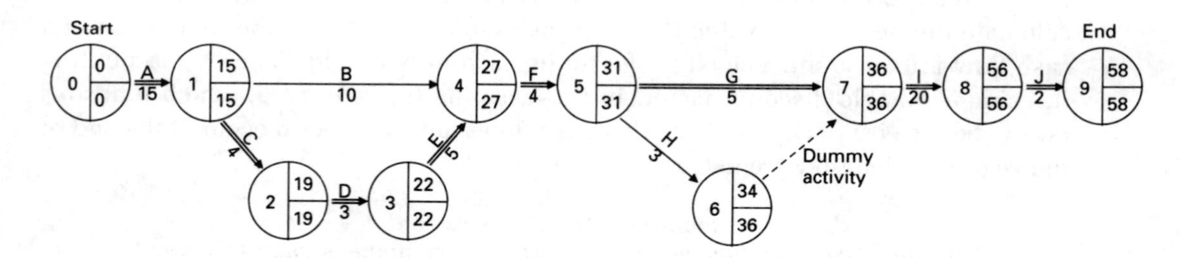

Figure 14.1 Network chart for Johnsons Specialist Books Ltd new computer system – Option A

The network of the activities listed shows the overall project duration is 58 days, and that activities A, C, D, E, F, G, I, and J form the critical path, shown as a double line – any delay in their completion is likely to extend the overall duration of the project unless measures can be taken to reduce the duration of other activities on the critical path.

Alan Baker is probably right to feel concerned about the probability of getting the project completed smoothly and on time, for several reasons:

- There is already pressure because Alan was late starting his employment. This can easily lead to hasty decisions and increases the temptation to skimp on activities like testing.
- Activity B, 'modify software', is not on the critical path – there is two days' slack compared with the other path through the network that must be completed before installation and testing of the software. However, software development or modification needs to be carefully planned and controlled and it is often difficult to monitor its real progress until some actual results are generated by it. If problems show up at this late stage then it will be difficult to correct them without significantly extending the activity and disrupting the overall project.
- In addition, it is not clear whether or not the four days' allocation to Activity F, 'installing and testing the software', includes any provision for fixing any problems that are shown up by the testing – and this activity is on the critical path.
- Since the software modification is not under Alan's direct control, he may not be able to allocate extra resources to the activity in order to speed it up.
- The critical path actually involves all but two of the activities, and one of them, 'modify software', is liable to delays. So delay in almost any activity is likely to extend the project's duration.

3

The UK Data Protection Act 1984 relates to the storage and use of personal data by electronic equipment – principally computers. It was introduced in response to pressures from the civil liberties lobby and to bring the UK into line with some of its trading partners that already had similar legislation. The increasing use of electronic data communications is regarded as increasing the need for such legislation.

The Act defines:

- **personal data** as data about a living individual from which the individual can be identified
- **data subjects** as the individuals to whom the personal data relates
- **data users** as the people or organisations who electronically store personal data with the intention of processing it
- **computer bureau** as a place which stores and processes data on behalf of data users.

Data users must register with the data protection registrar, giving details of the kind of data they hold and the purposes it is used for. The Act lays down eight data protection principles which data users should apply to personal data. These include, for example, that personal data must be:

- held for one or more specified and lawful purposes
- adequate, relevant and and not excessive for these purposes
- accurate and, where necessary, kept up to date.

The Act provides data subjects with some rights which allow them, upon request, to be informed of personal data held by data users and to be supplied with a copy of it. It also provides the right to have inaccurate data corrected and for compensation for harm caused by loss of data or inaccurate data.

There some exemptions from the Act. Some of the most important exemptions are:

- Data held for some government functions is excluded from the Act where this is felt to be in the public interest – for example, where disclosure of data would impede investigations of crimes.
- Basic information held by clubs about members, such as name and address

lists, is excluded, provided it is used only for purposes such as collecting subscriptions and circulating information to members.

- Data held solely for statistical and research purposes.
- Data in the form of basic records held for ordinary business activity such as payroll, pension and accounts. This is an important exemption which data users must interpret carefully, as it applies only to basic transaction data. Registration with the data protection registrar can be a complex procedure and the exemptions may relieve a small business from having this additional administrative task.

The last exemption mentioned here could allow Johnsons to use a computerised accounting and/or payroll system without having to register under the Act. However, organisations claiming the exemption should realise that any change of use or purpose may mean that their data is no longer exempt. For example, if Johnsons use their accounting data to check on customers' creditworthiness then this goes beyond the limited scope of the exemption and Johnsons would have to register for this use of the data.

While data held simply for payroll purposes may be exempt under the Act, it is likely that Johnsons will use other data about their staff, such as an individual's performance review information. If this data is processed or stored on computer then Johnsons will have to register it under the Act.

If Johnsons use computerised systems to maintain records of customers' requirements they will have to register under the Act if it includes personal data such as the research work the customer has requested or their particular areas of interest.

4 The main areas which Alan Baker should consider when assessing the risk of unauthorised access to the new system are:

- access to the mini-computer from within Johnsons' offices
- access to the data held on the researchers' portable computers
- the communications links allowing the researchers to access the mini-computer over the telephone lines
- problems associated with staff being made redundant, who may be disgruntled and tempted to take malicious action on the computer system.

The steps that can be taken to combat these risks include the following:

Physical security

Modern mini-computer systems require less stringent environmental conditions than their earlier counterparts and they can be used in general office environments. However, since the mini-computer will be central to Johnsons' operations, it is important that direct physical access is strictly controlled by keeping the system isolated from the general office areas, with entry to the area controlled by keypads or swipe card readers. Only operations staff should be allowed into the area. Most organisations employ general security measures to prevent public access to their work areas, but these should be reviewed because of the ease of access to large amounts of data on the new computerised system.

Johnsons should adopt a policy on the use of portable computers which includes keeping the power on/off mechanism locked and storing them under lock and key when not in use.

There should be a firm policy on the use of storage media such as floppy disks. Staff should not be allowed to use their own media unless it has been virus-checked and the use of the data has been properly authorised.

Division of responsibilities

Johnsons should allocate duties in a way that ensures that no one person operates a complete process where there is a risk of fraud or of sensitive information being tampered with. For example, computer operations or development staff should not have access to original accounts documents.

Logical access

Johnsons should operate a strict password system on their mini-computer, with procedures which require that passwords should be non-obvious, of a minimum length and regularly changed. Most modern computer systems allow for passwords to be applied at three stages: general access to the system, access to particular applications programs and access to particular data files. Access permissions can be used to prevent access or to provide read-only access. Users can be allocated various access permissions, depending on their work and level of responsibility, so that they can only legitimately access those parts of the system that are needed for their work.

Similar facilities may be available on the personal computers but the researchers should be made aware of the need to operate strict security arrangements and not to hold data on their systems unless strictly necessary. The personal computers should be subject to regular audits of the data and programs held on them.

Communication procedures

The researchers will need to use modems to access the telephone system and link up with the mini-computer. These links should be carefully controlled and not left open. Data encryption techniques can be applied on the data passed over the links.

Guarding against disgruntled staff

Alan Baker will have to carefully consider the effect that the possibility of redundancy may have on staff. The issue should be discussed by Johnsons' management, since if disgruntled staff work on the changeover to the new system or have access to the new system then they may have the opportunity to corrupt or destroy data, either directly or by leaving computer viruses or 'time bombs' in the system. Such precautions may be difficult to achieve, since it may not be possible to dispense with staff until the new system is fully operational.

Management support

It is important that Alan Baker explains the risks and the need for security arrangements to Johnsons' management and gets full management support so that awareness of the need for security permeates the whole organisation.

Section B

5

a) Important factors in choosing which investigation method to use are:

- the volume and completeness of the information
- the accuracy and validity of the information
- the effect that the method will have on the people involved.

The main fact-finding techniques that can be used during the investigation into the council's information requirements are:

14

Reading and analysing documentation

There are different types of document that can provide useful information, such as:

- organisation plans and policy statements which provide an overview of the council's high-level aims, objectives and structures
- procedure manuals and the forms used to record and communicate data which provide lower-level details of how the current system operates.

As documents such as policy statements indicate what the objectives of the council were at the time they were compiled, there is the danger that they are out-of-date or were written idealistically without due regard to the practicalities of the situation. Similarly, procedures manuals and forms for record keeping indicate what *should* happen and, in reality, procedures may be different and forms not filled in in the intended way. Analysts can examine documents without disruption to other people and can obtain useful information about what should happen.

Interviews and group discussions

Key personnel can be interviewed, either individually or in groups, to gain information about their work and their views and attitudes. The people who could be selected for interview include the councillors and representatives of all levels of the council's staff. Similarly, the council's clients – the people of the town – can be interviewed to establish their requirements and views.

Interviews and group discussions allow the analysts to pose different types of question:

- **open questions** where the responses are not limited in advance by the analyst and the interviewees can answer in their own words. However, the analyst may find it time-consuming to analyse the information and produce quantifiable results.
- **closed questions** where the responses are limited and the interviewer imposes a tight structure on the interview. Closed questions can provide information that is easy to analyse and quantify, but there is always the danger that the allowed responses do not include all the appropriate replies, so the information gathered is incomplete or misleading.

Interviews and group discussions are time-consuming and best suited to gathering information from a relatively small number of people using mainly relatively open questions.

Questionnaires

Questionnaires can provide opportunities for gathering information from a large number of people about a range of topics. They are most suitable for asking closed questions of a relatively large number of people. The questions must be carefully formulated and tested before the full survey is carried out. It can be very difficult to get further information from respondents once the forms have been returned.

Observation

The way that procedures are actually carried out can be observed. Observation can provide information about variations in the way different people carry out similar operations and also about fluctuations in the workloads – for example, by studying the behaviour of queues at a public information desk.

The analyst has a problem, which is common to interviews, questionnaires and observation, in that the information gathered may not be accurate. People may, subconsciously perhaps, provide invalid information for a variety of reasons:

- They may feel anxious about the situation and wary of the purpose of the investigation.
- They may want to please the analyst by giving the answers or behaviour they think the analyst wants.
- Their responses or behaviour may be distorted by feelings of antagonism.

The council's staff will be the users of a new system if it is developed and the analyst should remember that they may first become aware that a new system is being considered when they are asked to cooperate during the investigation. The analyst should try to encourage users' involvement and commitment to the system and reduce the natural anxieties and resentments that new technology and changes to working practices often create.

The production of a prototype may be a useful additional way of gaining information, although it will not be considered until one option has been selected.

b) The main contents of the statement of requirements will be:

- *Volumes of data*
  This will cover the amounts of data in terms of:
  - permanently stored data
  - data entered monthly.
- *Processes*
  The frequency of, and facilities required, for:
  - routine input of monthly details
  - changes and modification to individual's payroll details
  - *ad hoc* access to data to answer individual enquiries
  - routine output of monthly salary cheques, bank standing orders, payslips, etc.
  - *ad hoc* output of specific data about individual members of staff
  - management reports.
- *Response and processing times*
  Since the system has to service *ad hoc* enquiries, the loading on it will vary, so there should be average and maximum times for things like:
  - routine input of monthly details
  - monthly batch payroll run
  - routine output of monthly details
  - retrieving and displaying details of an individual's payroll details
  - production of management reports
  - taking backups.

The order of priority of processes should also be stated.

- *Input and output formats and requirements*
  Specific requirements about the details and layout of screens and documents should be stated.
- *Security and access*
  - general security arrangements to prevent unauthorised access to the system
  - specific security arrangements to allow different access permissions for different levels of user
  - backup and disaster recovery requirements.
- *Communications, interfaces and integration* with other systems, such as:
  - the payroll system and its data may have to be compatible with data from other systems
  - the computer equipment, such as terminals, may be required for other uses as well as the payroll system.

- *Expansion and future requirements* should be estimated and stated.

6 a) There are two main alternative methods of changing over from a manual information system to a computerised one:

- *Direct changeover*
  The new system is put into live operation simultaneously with the cessation of the old system. This is a simple approach where a target date is set for the changeover which provides developers and users with a clear target. However, it is a risky method compared with parallel running.

- *Parallel running*
  For a period of time the new system is run alongside the old system. This method minimises the risks involved, since the actual operation of the new system can be checked with the old one, and the old system is still available if the new one needs to be taken out of operation for modifications. Users can be given the opportunity to learn and be trained on the new system before the company becomes dependent on it. However, there are high costs involved in operating both systems together for a period of time and there may not be the manpower or resources available. There is also the temptation to defer discarding the old system and the changeover period then becomes excessive.

There are several other methods which combine aspects of both the above methods in order to reduce the costs associated with parallel running without running the risks associated with direct changeover. These are given various names but they all involve partial use of the new system so that it can be checked thoroughly before the old system is completely discarded. Some of the variations are:

- *Phased modular changeover*
  Functional areas of the information are each changed over separately; perhaps the new system's stock control module is used and (if it proves satisfactory) then the new customer records module is used, and so on.

- *Pilot running*
  Where an organisation has several branches, the new system can be used and tested in one of them before being introduced into the rest of them.

- *Gradual changeover*
  The new system is brought into operation but the volume of data and transactions is built up gradually. For example, new customers' accounts could be handled by the new system while information about existing customers is still handled by the old system. Unless customer records only have a short lifetime, there will have to be a cut-off point where old records are transferred to the new system.

Choosing a suitable changeover method

The main factors to be considered when choosing a changeover method are:

- *Risks:* How critical is the application? A bank which is dependent on the efficiency and constant availability of its information system would be unlikely to use a direct changeover if it could be avoided.

- *Costs:* The cost of parallel running of complete or partial systems in terms of staff and systems can be very high and the organisation may have to accept some element of risk.

- *Practicality:* Operating both old and new systems together may be impractical; for example, there may not be enough space for both systems.

There may be insufficient staff with the required skills to operate both systems but temporary staff could be considered – although they are costly and there may be problems of training and motivation.

b) The main issues involved in transferring the data from the manual to the computerised system are:

- *Data integrity:* it is important to try to make sure that the data is as clean and consistent as possible when it is transferred and that errors are not introduced during changeover.
- *Timing:* the timing of the changeover may be important, for various reasons. For example, there may be external reasons: the new system may be required to cope with legislation or procedures that come into force at specific dates and are difficult to handle with the old system. Alternatively, there may be internal reasons why the organisation chooses a particular date by which the changeover must be complete, such as its financial year-end.
- *Staff:* there will be additional work involved in transferring the data to the new system and much of it will be keyboard data entry. There are benefits to be obtained from using existing staff, since they are familiar with the data and may spot errors and anomalies. In addition they are likely to be the eventual users of the operational system, so it can allow them to become familiar with it in advance. The managers of the business should be aware of the extra work and inconvenience that staff may be involved in and, importantly, the anxiety and resistance to change that may be encountered. It is important that users are encouraged to take a positive attitude towards the new system and use it effectively; training and staff awareness should be considered for the staff affected. Automation of some or all of the data transfer may be possible for converting from an existing computerised system but not in this case, although modern techniques such as OCR (optical character recognition) may be of some use.

Whichever changeover method is chosen, the data of accounts, stock and customer records is suitable for transfer in stages over a period of time which will allow better control over the process. An important feature of most data is that a large proportion of it may be relatively fixed or static, for example, name and address, product codes and descriptions. Other data, including account balances and stock levels, is more volatile and variable. Fixed data can be transferred over a period of time in advance of the variable data which must then be transferred quickly at a particular date. A suitable plan would be:

1 Prepare the original data – check that it is complete, consistent, accurate and up to date before the transfer starts. Take a reference copy or 'snapshot' and store it securely.

2 Transfer the static data over a period of time and check it. This can be started weeks or months in advance of the changeover date.

3 Transfer the variable data rapidly to prevent it becoming out of date. This may require hiring extra temporary staff and working overtime. A weekend may be a suitable period so as to avoid the distractions of normal business activities.

4) Verify the data on the new system – check that it has been entered correctly by comparing it with the paper records and, if possible, check the system's operation and compare outputs with the old system's. The system

may involve internal validation checks on the format, range and consistency of the data but these will themselves need checking before they can be relied upon.

5) If some or all of the new system is to be run in parallel with the old system, a series of checks should be made to compare the data on the old and new systems.

7 a) i) Information has many qualities, each to a greater or lesser degree. The specific degree that is required to make information useful for its purpose often depends on the purpose and situation in which it arises.

You could choose six qualities and examples from:

- *Level of detail* – fully detailed or summarised
  A complete report of every overdue debtor's account details; or a total of the value of overdue accounts
- *Accuracy* – exactly right or approximate
  Exact figure for last year's sales; or projected sales figures for next year to the nearest £10,000
- *Accessibility* – whether it is readily available or difficult to collect
  Publicly available salary scales; or sensitive details of an individual's income tax code
- *Timeliness* – provided at the time it is required or else overdue and out of date
  A telephone message delivered as soon as it is taken; or held back for two days
- *Completeness* – fully comprehensive or incomplete
  A quotation which itemises all costs; or one that omits essential items such as delivery and insurance
- *Relevance* – appropriate or inappropriate
  Summary of worldwide sales figures when details of UK sales figures have been requested
- *Openness to bias* – objective or subjective
  A projected estimate based on observed trends; or an intuitive estimate
- *Verifiability* – self-evident, checkable or uncheckable
  Delivery dates contained in a written quotation or communicated verbally
- *Quantifiability* – quantitative or qualitative
  Cost of an item of hardware in a cost-benefit analysis; or the opinion that morale is low
- *Degree of uncertainty*
  A long-term loan on a fixed interest rate; or one on a variable interest rate
- *Degree of clarity* – clear or 'noisy' and ambiguous
  A quotation where the currency could be in pounds sterling or French francs
- *Credibility* – believable or open to question
  A statement from the Bank of England that base rates have been changed; or a rumour that they are about to change.

ii) There are many situations where the practicalities of providing the information mean that it cannot have all the qualities which would make it ideal for its purpose and a compromise will have to be made. For example:

- Ideally, complete and accurate end-of-year accounts would be audited and available immediately at the end of the year or within days of it. In practice, timeliness and accessibility have to be sacrificed, sometimes at great inconvenience, as accuracy and completeness are of prime importance. Eventually there comes a point where, due to inaccuracies or lack of detail in the accounting information, auditors have to accept that they will not be able to say that the end-of-year accounts are completely accurate in every detail and must express their opinion about the degree of certainty and accuracy.

- Ideally, sales organisations would have immediate access to accurate information about a customer's creditworthiness upon which to make judgments about the prudence of a sale with a high degree of certainty. In practice, checking creditworthiness takes time – which may reduce the possibility of a sale. This situation can occur where there is conflict between the sales function and the accounting function within an organisation over what the compromise should be between certainty and timeliness of information used for checking customers' creditworthiness.

b) All organisations have a combination of formal and information information systems. Formal information systems use meetings, written reports, and fixed and hierarchical communication links. Informal information systems use less well-defined communication lines that may more closely follow the organisation's social structure.

Formal systems use more clear and rigid communication lines and often have permanent records of the information and its source. This encourages people to be accountable and to provide accurate and detailed information and allows the system to be audited and verified. The accessibility of the information can be more easily controlled, either making it publicly available or limited to particular personnel. (This is much more difficult with an informal system.) Communication through formal procedures takes more time and is often less direct than using an informal system. Informal systems are more likely to encourage rapid communication, particularly of opinions, feelings, approximations and estimates. It is therefore likely to be less clear or verifiable and more susceptible to bias.

Organisations should try to get the benefits of combining both formal and informal systems. Some information needs to be formally, accurately and completely recorded – low-level accountancy information, for example. It is often these sorts of systems that are most readily computerised. However, a system that is too formal may become too bureaucratic and will stifle the ability to respond to information by delaying its communication and discourage staff from being innovative and using their initiative. So, informal systems may be needed to maximise the benefit of getting timely opinions and judgments. They also allow information to be quickly and cheaply communicated, which is appropriate to many day-to-day situations. There is a danger that relying too heavily on informal communications may lead to fragmented, uncoordinated communications that are rife with rumour and speculation.

8 a) The traditional model of the systems development lifecycle (SDLC), based on the one suggested by the National Computing Centre in the 1960s, is shown below.

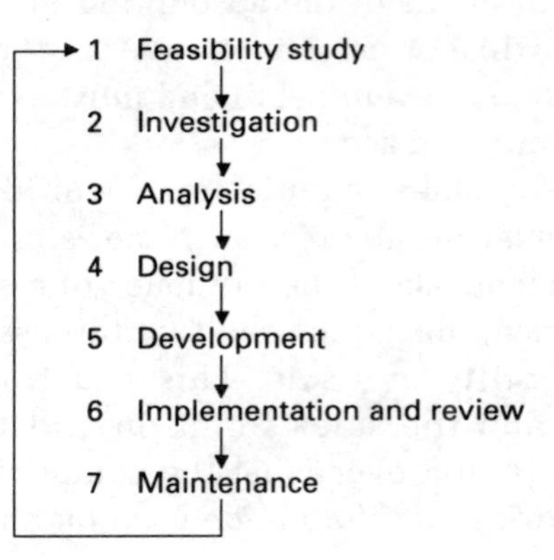

Figure 14.2

The length of the maintenance phase of the SDLC represents the length of the system's useful operational life. Most systems are planned to have a useful life that will be considerable longer than the time taken to develop the system. The total costs incurred by routine and non-routine activities during the maintenance phase often exceed the initial development costs. These costs may be difficult to estimate during the early stages of development and are often underestimated. However, the system should be capable of evolving and of being adapted in line with users' requirements. Maintenance activities are not limited to curing problems but often involve making modifications to meet changes in the users' requirements. It is important that users and developers appreciate the factors involved in maintaining a system so that it continues to satisfy users' requirements, and that they cooperate during the early stages of development and keep maintenance factors in mind when designing the system.

Cutting costs on the maintenance of a system is a false economy because, in the long term, the organisation will find that it is not maximising the benefits from the system and that its useful life is reduced, which will necessitate the development of a replacement system.

b) Maintenance activity can be considered in four categories:

- *Corrective maintenance* to correct errors in the way the system operates. Modern systems are a complex mixture of hardware and software. It is difficult, often impossible, to test for, identify and then eliminate all mistakes or 'bugs' in the design and implementation of a system. An example of a trigger of corrective maintenance in an accountancy and stock-control system would be the discovery of erroneous calculations or rounding errors which come to light when reconciliation procedures are carried out.

- *Adaptive maintenance* to keep the system in line with users' requirements – which can change as their operational procedures change, or when external factors such as legislation are introduced. Examples of triggers would be a change to VAT or auditing requirements, or the introduction of new types of stock which require that additional information. For example, perishable items may have to be stored and a 'use by' date added to the information system.

- *Perfective maintenance* to take advantage of new hardware or more efficient data processing procedures, such as optimising program code, to increase its execution speed. Users may suggest enhancements, particularly as they become experienced and familiar with the system and the way it operates. Examples of changes to hardware are the introduction of scanners and other input devices such as bar-code readers and character-recognition systems. A user may suggest an option so that reports on stock movements can be easily changed to show the items in order of the volume of items, or the number of movements, or simply in part-code order.

- *Preventive maintenance*, or servicing, is required on some hardware devices, although modern office-based computer systems require less routine servicing than larger or older systems. Examples of things that need preventive maintenance are the read/write heads on tape and disk drives which may need regular cleaning.

9 a) A review of the types of controls within the computer department should cover:

- *Administration controls*, for example:
  - clear division of duties between data entry staff, computer operators, development staff, and control staff so that, for example, only control and data preparation staff have access to source documents
  - use of operating standards manuals and computer-maintained logs of all computer processing and operator interventions
  - regular backups of data and programs taken and secured off-site
  - rules for physical security of the installation
  - standby and recovery procedures
  - proper control of systems access by the use of passwords and file permissions.
- *Systems development controls*, which should be supported and monitored by organisational structures such as steering committees and project teams. Controls will include:
  - new or modified programs or systems to be fully tested before going live, with similar procedures and controls on maintenance procedures
  - strict control of master file creation
  - systems specifications to include details of error conditions, valid and invalid data and procedures for handling errors
  - standards for documentation.
- *Processing controls*
  - input controls for verification, such as double-keying data and keeping proof listings and/or audit trails
  - input screens designed to assist accurate data entry with transactions checked by online programs
  - checking of file identification prior to processing with file-locking and record-locking during processing
  - checks such as check digits, range tests, reasonableness checks, completeness checks, sequence and format checks
  - output controls to ensure reports are complete, accurate and properly distributed
  - controls on access to communications links and encryption of data transferred over communications links.

b) Computer-assisted audit techniques (CAATs) can be considered in three categories:

i) Techniques used to test processed data or extract data for subsequent testing. These include:
  - data retrieval software allowing the auditor to extract data in a format suitable for audit purposes

- parallel simulation, where the auditor re-performs critical procedures and compares results with those achieved by the system
- embedded or resident audit routines, which are built into the system's program code to check data and program activity at key stages of processing and may generate output data for further testing.

ii) Techniques used for testing the actual procedures and controls in a system. For example:
- test data that is specially prepared and run through the system to test some or all of the system's procedures. The actual output can then be compared with expected results
- program review and code analysis, where the system's source code is examined and methodically worked through to ensure that it works accurately and incorporates the specified controls
- program comparison, where programs which include changes made for maintenance purposes are checked against the original program.

iii) Other CAAT software, which may not be specifically designed for audit purposes but can be used during auditing, includes:
- random number generators
- statistical analysis packages
- operating systems utilities.

Evaluation form – Revision texts 1995 edition

We are interested in knowing what you think of our products and would appreciate it if you could spend a few minutes completing the following questionnaire.

Please tick the appropriate box where necessary

Paper No. ____________ **Paper title** ____

Are you a

Student ☐ **Lecturer** ☐

Have you purchased other CAEP products

Textbooks ☐ **Revision Texts** ☐ **Open Learning Packages** ☐

Did you obtain this book through: your college ☐ your lecturer ☐
an order form in *Students' Newsletter* ☐
a bookshop ☐ other ____________________

What do you think are the best features of this revision text?

____

____

____

____

What improvements need to be made?

____

____

____

____

How does the revision text compare with other material you have used on your course?

____

____

____

Did you find any errors? If so, we apologise and would greatly appreciate it if you could list them below with the relevant page number or attach a photocopy.

____

____

____

____

If you would like to receive more information on CAEP's products please supply your name and address below.

____

____

____

Please return your completed questionnaire to the address overleaf.

Thank you for your help

✂ Please detach here

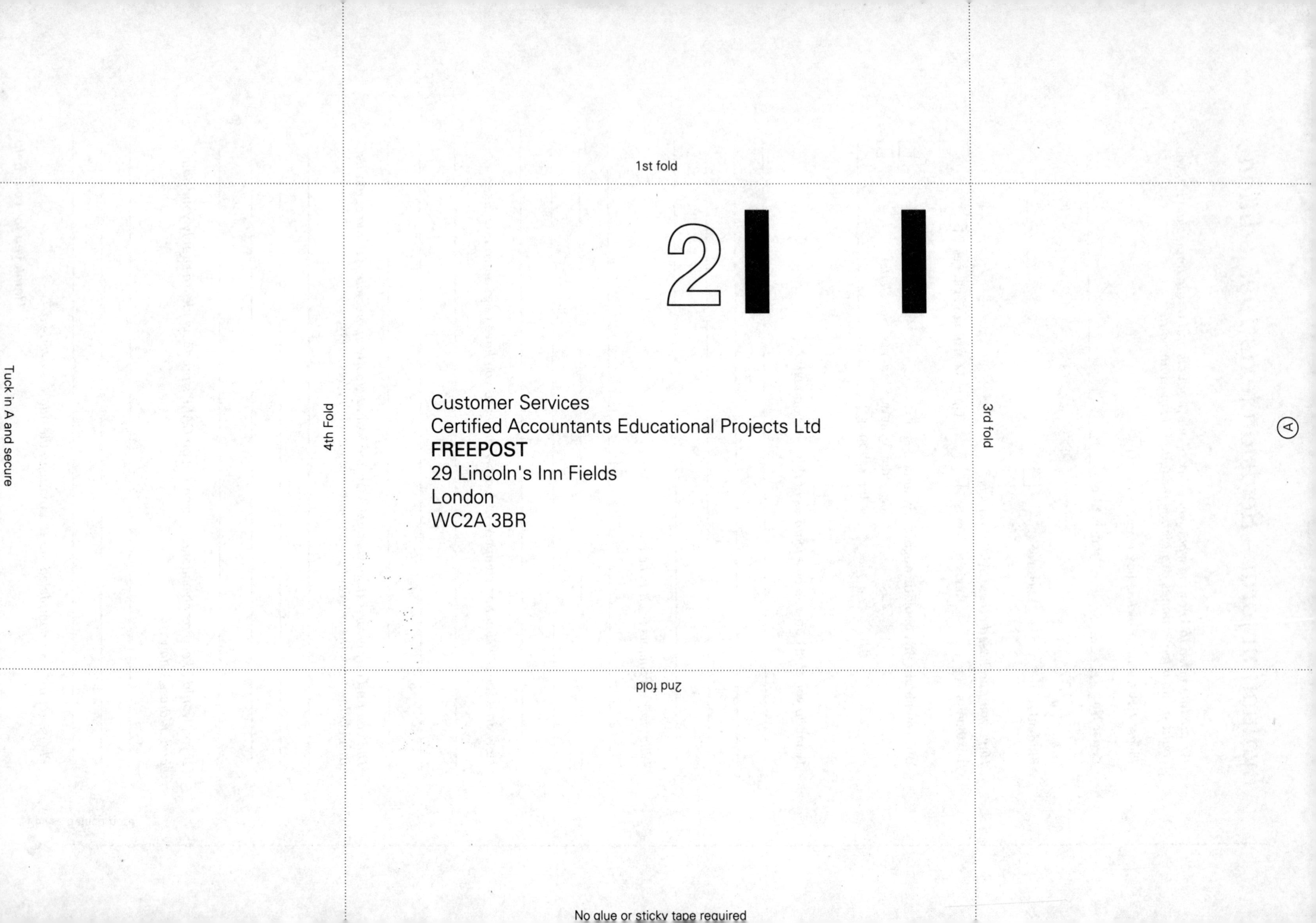

1st fold
2
Customer Services
Certified Accountants Educational Projects Ltd
FREEPOST
29 Lincoln's Inn Fields
London
WC2A 3BR
4th Fold
3rd fold
A
2nd fold
Tuck in A and secure
No glue or sticky tape required